Computing and ICT in the Primary School

D1610357

Now fully updated to reflect recent changes in the curriculum, *Computing and ICT in the Primary School* encourages teachers, and pupils, to realise the potential of a full range of ICT and computing resources.

Tackling computing head on, this book enables trainee and experienced teachers to better understand what computing is and how to use ICT effectively in teaching and learning. It is not a 'how to' guide or a collection of lesson plans, but instead balances research-based theory with everyday experiences, challenging readers to understand teaching methods and how they translate into a range of suitable teaching and learning strategies using ICT.

This book offers primary teachers the knowledge, skills and confidence to plan, teach and assess creatively to enhance learning across the whole curriculum. This second edition includes updates of all chapters and completely new chapters on:

- mobile technologies
- social media, and
- modern foreign languages.

Gary Beauchamp places theory and practice hand in hand, providing a uniquely relatable resource based on his own teaching practice, classroom experience and research. This text is crucial reading for both serving teachers and those in training on undergraduate and PGCE courses, Education Studies courses and MA (Ed) programmes.

Gary Beauchamp is currently Professor of Education and Associate Dean (Research) in the Cardiff School of Education at Cardiff Metropolitan University. He worked for many years as a primary school teacher before moving into higher education. His research interests focus on ICT in education, particularly the use of interactive technologies in learning and teaching. He is an Additional Inspector for Estyn and a Governor in two primary schools, and has served as external examiner for many universities.

Computing and ICT in the Primary School

From pedagogy to practice

Second edition

Gary Beauchamp

Routledge
Taylor & Francis Group

LONDON AND NEW YORK

Second edition published 2017
by Routledge
2 Park Square, Milton Park, Abingdon, Oxon OX14 4RN

and by Routledge
711 Third Avenue, New York, NY 10017

Routledge is an imprint of the Taylor & Francis Group, an informa business

First edition published by Pearson 2011

British Library Cataloguing in Publication Data
A catalogue record for this book is available from the British Library

Library of Congress Cataloging in Publication Data
Names: Beauchamp, Gary, author.
Title: Computing and ICT in the primary school : from pedagogy to practice /
    Gary Beauchamp. Other titles: ICT in the primary school
Description: 2nd Edition. | New York : Routledge, 2017. | Revised edition
    of: ICT in the primary school. Harlow : Pearson, 2012.
Identifiers: LCCN 2016011968 (print) | LCCN 2016023988 (ebook) |
    ISBN 9781138190603 (hbk : alk. paper) | ISBN 9781138190610 (pbk :
    alk. paper) | ISBN 9781315628042 (ebk)
Subjects: LCSH: Computer-assisted instruction—Great Britain. | Educational
    technology—Great Britain. | Information technology—Study and
    teaching (Elementary) | Education, Elementary—Great Britain.
Classification: LCC LB1028.5 .B396 2017 (print) | LCC LB1028.5 (ebook) |
    DDC 372.133/4—dc23
LC record available at https://lccn.loc.gov/2016011968

ISBN: 978-1-138-19060-3 (hbk)
ISBN: 978-1-138-19061-0 (pbk)
ISBN: 978-1-315-62804-2 (ebk)

Typeset in ITC Giovanni Std
by Swales & Willis Ltd, Exeter, Devon, UK

This book is dedicated to Janet, Owen, Elin, Bob, Minnie, Jean and Bill who, in different ways, have provided encouragement, ideas, support and belief.

Contents

Acknowledgments

Author's acknowledgments

I have been fortunate to work with many people who have developed my thinking on the use of ICT in education. As a result, many of the ideas in this book are the product of debate, experiment and argument from a team, rather than any individual. In addition, I would also like to acknowledge the helpful suggestions of reviewers at various stages in the production of the book. Having said all this, any mistakes or omissions in this book remain my responsibility.

Publisher's acknowledgments

We are grateful to the following for permission to reproduce copyright material:

Figures

Figure 6.1 from *Progression in Primary ICT*, David Fulton (Bennett, R., Hamill, A. and Pickford, T., 2007, Routledge), Copyright © 2007, David Fulton. Reproduced by permission of Taylor & Francis Books UK; Figure 8.2 from 'Graphicacy for life', *Primary Geographer*, June, pp6–8 (Mackintosh, M., 2011), The Geographical Association, www.geography.org.uk.

Tables

Table 3.2 adapted from Dabbagh, N., The Instructional Design Knowledge Base, http://cehdclass.gmu.edu/ndabbagh/Resources/IDKB/models_theories.htm; Table 8.2 from Dialogue table, http://dialogueiwb.educ.cam.ac.uk/resources/, Sara Hennessy.

Text

Extract on p173 from Ofsted (2009) *Mathematics: Understanding the Score: Improving Practice in Mathematics Teaching at Primary Level*, London: Ofsted, © Crown Copyright; Extract on p174 from Ofsted (2009) *Mathematics: Understanding the Score: Improving*

Practice in Mathematics Teaching at Primary Level, London: Ofsted © Crown Copyright. Crown Copyright material is reproduced with permission under the terms of the Click-Use Licence.

Photos

The publisher would like to thank the following for their kind permission to reproduce their photographs: p141 Talking Products Ltd.

All other images © Pearson Education

In some instances we have been unable to trace the owners of copyright material, and we would appreciate any information that would enable us to do so.

Introduction

In the previous edition of this book, when I was looking at what might come in the future, I suggested that:

> Perhaps the only thing we know for certain about the future of ICT is that we do not know what will happen! . . . it is probable that the technological needs of industry will continue to drive the development of technology, but this does not mean that it is preferable. Indeed, this is one of a series of such dilemmas that could affect the future of ICT in education . . . Perhaps in the medium term, ICT as a 'label' will be replaced to reflect changing priorities?

It is always reassuring when your predictions come true, but, for instance, the advent of computing in new curricula (in England completely at the expense of ICT), and the refocusing of ICT to reflect digital competence (for example in Wales), means that this new edition needs to reflect such changes. What is also reassuring, however, is that the fundamental principles of using technology (whatever it is called) – that is, the underlying pedagogy – remain just as relevant in any new incarnation of ICT.

The difficulty with any new label, such as 'computing' or 'digital competence', is that the rationale for its use can be driven by a range of factors, from the perceived needs of industry to political dogma. In addition, each new term needs to be clearly and consistently understood by both policy makers and practitioners. An added complication in the United Kingdom (UK) is the growing divergence in education policy and practice caused by devolved powers, including education, in Northern Ireland, Scotland and Wales. Beauchamp et al. (2015, p164) assert that 'In Scotland, Northern Ireland and Wales education is clearly important in the construction of developing and/or re-affirming national identities', but a consequence is that England is 'emerging as the outlier'.

Thus, although the needs of students and teachers based in England are a major consideration, we also need to examine and reflect the diversity of practice throughout the UK and, indeed, the rest of the world. This book is therefore aimed at an international audience and research and practice from around the world will be an important influence in what follows, as the principles of effective pedagogy transcend national boundaries.

All changes in curricula, however, have to be set in the context of the ever-increasing confidence and competence of primary-age children in a wide range of technologies, whether they are supposed to use them or not! In this environment, the idea of a traditional classroom and even a fixed 'class' are becoming increasingly irrelevant. As the Digital Education Advisory Group (2013, p4) in Australia stated:

The walls of the classroom and the home have been expanded by social media, the cloud, wikis, podcasts, video-conferencing etc. These are new learning environments and they are local, national and global and populated by whole communities in addition to family, teachers and friends . . . The challenge for us is to embrace, and respond to, not just the technology, but the extraordinary pace of change. We can't underestimate how rapidly things are changing and we need to make sure no opportunity passes us by to improve learning outcomes.

If you are ready to make sure no opportunities pass *you* by, I hope the rest of this book will help you achieve this aim at whatever stage of your career you are. To help contextualise your own work, we will now briefly examine how we have got to where we are and provide a rationale for the introduction of computing into this second edition.

The rise of computing in the primary school: where are we now?

In 2012, the Royal Society produced a publication entitled *Shut Down or Restart? The Way Forward for Computing in UK Schools*. This concluded that:

The current delivery of Computing education in many UK schools is highly unsatisfactory. Although existing curricula for Information and Communication Technology (ICT) are broad and allow scope for teachers to inspire pupils and help them develop interests in Computing, many pupils are not inspired by what they are taught and gain nothing beyond basic digital literacy skills such as how to use a word-processor or a database.
This is mainly because:
1.1 The current national curriculum in ICT can be very broadly interpreted and may be reduced to the lowest level where non-specialist teachers have to deliver it;
1.2 there is a shortage of teachers who are able to teach beyond basic digital literacy.

This report, however, was at odds with Ofsted (2011, p4) judgements about ICT in the primary school from the time, which concluded that:

The teaching of ICT was good or outstanding in nearly two thirds of the primary schools visited, with many teachers and teaching assistants increasingly confident and able to support pupils effectively. There were weaknesses in the teaching of more demanding topics such as data handling or control, but in many of the schools this gap had been identified and was being addressed.

Unfortunately, instead of seeking to further improve this situation, the government in England chose to make more radical changes justified by their prevailing rhetoric regarding the need for greater 'rigour'. For example, in January 2014 the then Secretary of State for Education (England), Michael Gove, asserted that the existing 'unambitious, demotivating and dull' ICT curriculum 'had to go' (https://www.gov.uk/government/speeches/

michael-gove-speaks-about-computing-and-education-technology) – although he did not produce any evidence to support his claims. In this speech, he was not only introducing a completely new computing curriculum, he was also expecting it to come into effect nine months later. It is notable that this was drawn up largely by 'industry experts', rather than by education experts!

Unsurprisingly, this change was welcomed by some organisations, such as Computing at School (CAS), and they pointed out that: 'The focus of the new programme of study undeniably moves towards programming and other aspects of computer science' (CAS, 2013, p4). We will return to what computer science and programming are later in this book, but it is worth noting here that the narrow focus on computing in the primary school in England was not being reflected by developments elsewhere in the UK. In fact, the whole notions of subjects, programmes of study and key stages have been challenged by developments in Northern Ireland, Wales and Scotland. Table I.1 below shows a summary of the current and proposed content of the curricula of each country and the role of technology within them.

It is apparent that the English curriculum's focus on individual subjects is in sharp contrast to the rest of the UK, which has already changed, or is in the process of changing, to curricula with broader 'areas of learning' or 'curriculum areas', all of which are required to integrate with each other to 'to make relevant connections for children' (CCEA, 2007). Donaldson (2015) reports that this reflects an international trend and, as well as Scotland and Northern Ireland, gives examples in Australia, New Zealand (eight areas of learning) and the Netherlands (six broad areas).

Table I.1 Primary curricula in the UK			
England	**Scotland**[1]	**Wales**	**Northern Ireland**[3]
National Curriculum	*Curriculum for Excellence*	*Successful Futures*[2]	*The Northern Ireland Curriculum Primary*
Revised 2014	Introduced 2010	Proposed and accepted 2015 – timetable for implementation not yet confirmed	Introduced 2007
Early Years Foundation Stage: pre-school, nursery and reception Key Stage 1: 5–7 years Key Stage 2: 7–11 years	Curriculum 3–18	Curriculum 3–16	The Foundation Stage: Years 1 and 2 Key Stage 1: Years 3 and 4 Key Stage 2: Years 5, 6 and 7

(continued)

Table I.1	(continued)		
England *National Curriculum*	**Scotland[1]** *Curriculum for Excellence*	**Wales** *Successful Futures[2]*	**Northern Ireland[3]** *The Northern Ireland Curriculum Primary*
The statutory national curriculum has 11 subjects that should be taught to all pupils.	The curriculum 3–18 is organised into eight curriculum areas.	The curriculum 3–16 should be organised into six Areas of Learning and Experience with three cross-curricular responsibilities which should underpin all subjects.	The curriculum applies to all 12 years of compulsory education. In primary school, it is made up of six Areas of Learning.
		In addition, literacy, numeracy and *digital competence* should be cross-curriculum responsibilities for all teachers.	Through opportunities to engage in active learning contexts across all areas of the curriculum, children should progressively develop the following cross-curricular skills: • Communication • Using Mathematics • Using *Information and Communications Technology* (across the curriculum).
1. English 2. Mathematics 3. Science 4. History 5. Geography 6. Foreign Language (KS2 only) 7. Art and Design 8. Physical Education 9. Design and Technology 10. Music 11. *Computing*	1. Mathematics 2. Sciences 3. Religious and Moral Education 4. Expressive Arts 5. Health and Well-being 6. Languages 7. Social Sciences 8. *Technologies*	1. Languages, Literacy and Communication 2. Mathematics and Numeracy 3. Science and *Technology* 4. Expressive Arts 5. Health and Well-being 6. Humanities	1. Language and Literacy (including Talking and Listening, and Reading and Writing; schools are also encouraged to teach additional languages) 2. Mathematics and Numeracy (focusing on the development of mathematical concepts and numeracy across the curriculum) 3. The Arts (including Art and Design, Drama and Music)

4. The World Around Us (focusing on the development of knowledge, skills and understanding in Geography, History and Science and *Technology*)

5. Personal Development and Mutual Understanding (focusing on emotional development, social skills, learning to learn, health, relationships and sexuality education and mutual understanding in the local and global community)

6. Physical Education (focusing on the development of knowledge, skills and understanding through play and a range of physical activities)

1. For more details, see http://www.educationscotland.gov.uk/learningandteaching/thecurriculum/whatiscurriculumforexcellence/understandingthecurriculumasawhole/index.asp.

2. Currently Foundation Phase (3–7 years) with seven Areas of Learning and Key Stage 2 with 11 subjects (English, Welsh, mathematics, science, design and technology, information and communication technology, history, geography, art and design, music, and physical education).

3. See http://www.nicurriculum.org.uk/docs/key_stages_1_and_2/northern_ireland_curriculum_primary.pdf.

It is also important to note that the term 'ICT' still retains a place in Scotland, where it is situated in the 'Technologies' curriculum area, and *computing* science is only one of six 'organisers':

- technological developments in society
- ICT to enhance learning
- business
- computing science
- food and textiles
- craft, design, engineering and graphics.

In Northern Ireland primary schools, there is also an expectation that ICT remains a cross-curricular skill. However, in the new curriculum being introduced by 2021 in Welsh primary schools, 'literacy, numeracy and digital competence should be Cross-curriculum Responsibilities for all teachers and people who work with children and young people' (Donaldson, 2015, p40). There is, however, no explicit mention of ICT in the new curriculum.

We are thus faced with the use of a range of terms, including the ongoing use of ICT, but with new concepts, including digital competence and computer science, all of which are to be used creatively by teachers and learners across the curriculum – whatever form it takes. Before examining how this might happen, we will further explore and define each of these terms in the next chapter.

References

Beauchamp, G., Clarke, L., Hulme, M. and Murray, J. (2015) 'Teacher education in the United Kingdom post devolution: convergences and divergences', *Oxford Review of Education*, 41(2), pp154–70.

CAS (2013) *Computing in the National Curriculum: A Guide for Primary Teachers*, Swindon: Computing At School (CAS), http://www.computingatschool.org.uk/data/uploads/CASPrimaryComputing.pdf (accessed 7 January 2016).

CCEA (2007) *The Northern Ireland Curriculum: Primary*, Belfast: Council for the Curriculum, Examinations and Assessment (CCEA), http://www.nicurriculum.org.uk/docs/key_stages_1_and_2/northern_ireland_curriculum_primary.pdf (accessed 16 June 2016).

Digital Education Advisory Group (2013) *Beyond the Classroom: A New Digital Education for Young Australians in the 21st Century*, https://docs.education.gov.au/system/files/doc/other/deag_final_report.pdf (accessed 15 October 2015).

Donaldson, G. (2015) *The Donaldson Review of Curriculum and Assessment*, Cardiff: The Welsh Government.

Ofsted (2011) *ICT in Schools 2008–11: An Evaluation of Information and Communication Technology Education in Schools in England 2008–11*, Manchester: Ofsted.

Royal Society (2012) *Shut Down or Restart? The Way Forward for Computing in UK Schools*, London: The Royal Society.

1 ICT and computing in the primary school

In this chapter we will define ICT and computing and the key components of each. We will then consider the unique features and capabilities of ICT and begin to examine how pupils and teachers could use them in the primary school to replace or enhance current learning experiences.

Introduction

It was a relatively short time ago that Information and Communications Technology (ICT) took its place in the curriculum of the primary school in the United Kingdom (UK). More recently, as we have just seen, computing has to a greater or lesser extent taken its place, but, as Turvey et al. (2014, p4) remind us, 'it can be argued that the focused and specific construction of the new programme of study for computing as a subject . . . Now leaves more room for innovation in ICT', defined as 'the broader application of digital technologies to enhance learning throughout the curriculum'. This can be achieved as ICT is a 'complex tool which can be used by teachers and by pupils in teaching and learning' (Higgins, 2001, p164). To enable this complex tool to be used effectively, however, teachers have to develop practical ICT and computing skills both during their training and throughout their career. This is not only to use ICT in the classroom, but also to teach pupils new skills.

As hardware and software develop, the skills required also change, and any book that deals with specific hardware resources or software packages is out of date very quickly. What changes less quickly, and is arguably more important, is the pedagogic thinking that underpins the use of both hardware and software by both pupils and teachers. This book is primarily concerned with the latter and is not intended to equip you with practical ICT or computing skills. It should, however, allow you to critically explore the fundamental principles behind the ways in which ICT and computing can help in developing effective teaching and learning in early years settings and primary schools. This exploration will be based on evidence from international research and practical experience gained in a wide range of learning settings. Although part of this exploration will help address some Qualified Teacher Status (QTS) standards, the main intention is to examine how ICT (including computing) can be used as an effective pedagogic tool at *any* point in your career. It should also help you if you are studying the use of educational technology in any context, as many of the principles outlined will be equally applicable to all ages.

The introduction of new technology, such as tablet devices into the classroom, as well as technological advances allowing personal computers (PCs) and other mobile devices to become faster, smaller and easier to use, has been rapid. As John and Sutherland (2005, p406) point out, 'in recent years the emergence of new digital technologies has offered up the possibility of extending and deepening classroom learning in ways hitherto unimagined'. These possibilities have ensured that opportunities and challenges have presented themselves to teachers and pupils in equal measure. One of the most important advances has been in the increased availability and speed of access to the internet, which, together with other advances in mobile and other technologies, has enabled the development of e-learning opportunities. Definitions of e-learning vary, and Mayes and de Freitas (2007, p13) go so far as to suggest that 'there are really no models of e-learning *per se* – only e-enhancements of existing models of learning'. In this book we will examine a range of such enhancements but, given the pervasive (and contested) nature of e-learning, we will adopt Holmes and Gardner's (2006, p14) simple definition as 'online access to learning resources, anywhere and anytime'.

Alongside technical developments, there have also been changes in thinking about education in general terms, specifically in the early years and more generally in the role pupils play in their own learning. In 2009, the 'Rose Review' in England (DCSF, 2009, p9) concluded that 'primary children relish learning independently and co-operatively'. Although the report itself was ultimately rejected, research evidence examined below will show that such an approach remains beneficial. In this context, the roles of teachers and learners have evolved to reflect greater autonomy for pupils and a more facilitating role for teachers. In other words, education is not something that is done *to* children, but is something that is done *with* them as active partners who are able to influence the course of their learning.

Many advocates of ICT in education would share this view and adopt a socio-cultural perspective in which learning is situated and socially constructed (Vygotsky, 1978). Beauchamp and Kennewell (2010) suggest that the classroom is an ecology of resources, defined by Luckin (2008, p451) as 'a set of inter-related resource elements, including people and objects, the interactions between which provide a particular context'. This perspective will be considered in more detail in Chapter 2, but at this stage it is important to note that a key part of a socio-cultural perspective is the assertion that 'tools', both 'technical' and 'cognitive', play a central role in mediating human action. Although language remains the most important cultural tool, other tools can include paper, books, pens and, of course, ICT resources. It is the ability of ICT to provide a range of tools in one place (such as the interactive whiteboard (IWB), mobile handheld or tablet device) that makes it such an important means of mediating learning. However, as Wertsch (1991, p119) points out, 'only by being part of action do mediational means come into being and play their role. They have no magical power in and of themselves.' In other words, ICT tool(s) need to be actively involved in achieving both activity and outcomes in lessons; just using them is not enough. It is also important that all people are involved in their use. If we return to the idea that learning is socially constructed, we see the importance of everyone in the classroom using ICT to construct (and even deconstruct) knowledge and understanding. A belief that pupils should assume some responsibility for, and control over, their learning would also apply to the use of the relevant 'tools'. As part of this process, ICT has evolved from being a subject that was taught by teachers to learners, or a resource or tool 'owned' by the teacher, to become a shared resource or tool for learning and teaching by both. Such a change requires teachers to examine both their pedagogic beliefs and classroom practice, especially how they plan and use ICT in learning.

This change in 'ownership' of ICT and its implications will be discussed in more detail in Chapter 2, but before this I want you to imagine arriving at school (early, of course!) and finding that the classroom projector bulb has blown and the internet connection is not working. Worse still, you have forgotten your memory device with all your resources for lessons. Could you still teach effective lessons? The answer, of course, is yes, which poses the question: do we really need ICT in the primary school and early years settings? It may seem somewhat strange to start a book about ICT by asking this fundamental question, but in addressing it we begin to identify *why* we should use ICT, *how* and *when* it should be used, and *who* should use it to best improve learning and teaching. In answering these questions we also need to examine the relationship between ICT and computing. Unfortunately, this is not straightforward as, although ICT is already a familiar term as an established part of the curriculum in the primary school, 'terms like computing, computer programming, and computational thinking are often used interchangeably, [which] may cause definitional confusion . . . [and] . . . these terms are sometimes used to describe other educational technology applications and general use of software such as word processing' (Israel et al., 2015, p263).

As with much specialist vocabulary employed in the curriculum, however, it is necessary to understand both what it means and how terms relate to each other in a way that can be translated into classroom activities. It is necessary, therefore, to briefly explore different definitions of key terms used in primary curricula (specifically computational thinking, computer programming, digital literacy/competence computing and computer science) before moving on to examine ICT more generally.

Computational thinking

We will begin with computational thinking, as although '[c]omputational thinking lies at the heart of the computing curriculum . . . it also supports learning and thinking in other areas of the curriculum' (CAS, 2015, p5) and 'is in line with many aspects of 21st century competencies such as creativity, critical thinking, and problem-solving' (Lye and Koh, 2014, p52). Reassuringly, primary teachers already use computational thinking in the way they approach teaching and learning, but perhaps do not realise they are doing so. For instance, it is not unusual to ask pupils to think carefully about a problem and to break it down into smaller parts, focusing on the important things and ignoring unnecessary details. They then use new ideas, together with patterns or sequences they know from previous work, to create new ideas in a given format – such as solving a maths problem, planning a story or composing a piece of music. They will often do this by using approaches such as experimenting or playing with ideas, trying out these ideas (debugging) to see if they work, and persevering and collaborating before evaluating the finished product. In essence, computational thinking (CT) is applying these same skills and approaches, but they have specific 'labels' in the context of CT.

Unfortunately, the way these labels are used is not straightforward, and Grover and Pea (2013, p38) highlight the 'definitional confusion that has plagued CT as a phrase'. They continue to provide their own definition and suggest that, in essence, CT 'is thinking like a computer scientist when confronted with a problem' (ibid., p39). However, if you do not know how a computer scientist thinks, this does not help us much! Voogt et al. (2015, p720) suggest that all definitions of CT have a common 'focus on the skills, habits and dispositions needed to solve complex problems . . . with the help of computing . . . and computers', but we need to identify the skills, habits and dispositions in more detail to fully understand what CT is and how it might apply in the classroom.

Computing At School attempts to explain this by suggesting that CT is about

> *applying tools and techniques from computing to understand and reason about natural, social and artificial systems and processes. It allows pupils to tackle problems, to break them down into solvable chunks and to devise algorithms to solve them . . . It concentrates on pupils performing a thought process, not on the production of artefacts or evidence. Computational thinking is the development of thinking skills and it supports learning and understanding.*
>
> (CAS, 2015, pp5–6)

After reviewing relevant academic literature, Selby and Woollard (2013) identify the key components of computational thinking when they propose that it is

> *an activity, often product oriented, associated with, but not limited to, problem solving. It is a cognitive or thought process that reflects*

- the ability to think in abstractions,
- the ability to think in terms of decomposition,
- the ability to think algorithmically,
- the ability to think in terms of evaluations, and
- the ability to think in generalisations.

Aho (2012, p832) provides a more succinct summary when stating that computational thinking is 'the thought processes involved in formulating problems so their solutions can be represented as computational steps and algorithms'. Put more simply still, the BBC Bitesize website suggests that 'Computational thinking allows us to take a complex problem, understand what the problem is and develop possible solutions. We can then present these solutions in a way that a computer, a human, or both, can understand' (http://www.bbc.co.uk/education/guides/zp92mp3/revision).

Whichever overall definition of computational thinking makes sense to you, it is still important that you understand each of the component parts, so we will now turn to consider these in more detail, particularly those that are used in the primary school curriculum. Berry (2014) suggests that '[t]here is a degree of consensus around what computational thinking might involve, with much of this making it into the programme of study [in England]':

- abstraction
- decomposition

- patterns or pattern recognition and generalisation
- logical reasoning
- algorithms.

As L'Heureux et al. (2012) point out, even though 'IT-centric industry partners' were influential in developing the computing curriculum, such words may be regarded as 'education-speak' and not ones they use in their typical daily routine. It is thus important that we clearly understand the 'education-speak' definitions of each aspect of computational thinking as they might vary from those used outside education.

Abstraction

L'Heureux et al. (2012, p187) assert that: 'Abstraction reduces information and detail to focus on concepts relevant to understanding and solving problems.' In other words, 'deciding what details we need to highlight and what details we can ignore – underlies computational thinking' (Wing, 2008, p3718). QuickStart Computing (2015, p14) suggests that this means 'identifying what is important without worrying too much about the detail, and . . . [that it] is a way of thinking about systems problems which can be used in many areas of the curriculum'. Such reminders are very important as, if we see computational thinking as a whole series of new skills that need to be learned, it may prove overwhelming in the face of the many other demands of primary teaching across the curriculum. The more we recognise what a particular computing term actually means, the easier it is to find examples of it in what we already do. This helps to show that it is not necessarily something new, but more of an adaption (or renaming) of what we already do. In addition, it also makes it easier to explain to pupils of any age. QuickStart Computing (2015) gives examples, such as a map reducing the complexity of the environment, or how pupils working with word problems in maths need to identify the key information and recognise how to represent it in different arithmetic algebraic forms. In the case of a teacher, they also suggest that a school timetable is an abstraction of the key information needed without listing the more complex level of detail that actually takes place.

Decomposition

Having identified the important information in a problem, it is then necessary to begin to look at ways of solving that problem. An important part of this process is decomposition. In itself, decomposition is at first sight an easy concept to understand as it basically means taking a complex idea and breaking it down into small bits. Berry (2014) gives an interesting analogy when he reports that:

> I remember a former colleague giving an assembly on how to eat an elephant: it's one mouthful at a time. The same approach works for developing software – to solve problems or understand systems involves breaking things down into smaller parts and dealing with each separately.

As with other key concepts discussed here, it may be useful to introduce them in another area of the curriculum and then relate them to computing – as well as to reinforce them later in different areas of the curriculum: for example, making a list in a literacy lesson of the things we need to consider when undertaking an everyday activity, such as brushing teeth or getting dressed. In each of these we could consider in detail when and where we do them, in what order we do things, and so on. We may need to learn new skills for each part (such as tying shoelaces or a tie or baking a cake); this is just the same in computing. However, we may also see that we are applying the same skills or techniques in more than one place (such as kicking a ball in football), which can then use in another context (such as rugby) without the need to learn new ones. This also applies to programming, where code can be used again, but in all instances it may be possible to refine and improve the skill or code.

Pattern recognition and generalisation

From a very early age, pupils in the primary school learn to recognise repeating patterns, such as repeated phrases in nursery rhymes, common rules of spelling or repeating patterns in a piece of music. From this they begin to realise that these patterns can be used to make predictions and create rules, which can then be generalised and used in other contexts. QuickStart Computing (2015, p15) gives the example of learning about area, where pupils 'could find the area of a particular rectangle by counting the centimetre squares on the grid on which it is drawn. But a better solution would be to multiply the length by the width: not only is this quicker, it's also a method that will work on *all* rectangles.' In the context of computing, pupils may be able to recognise how blocks of code can be repeated to save having to write individual commands separately.

Logical reasoning

Another activity that is very common from the early ages in the primary school is asking children to predict what they think will happen and then explain their thinking. Such an approach is inherent in many aspects of science and again represents a familiar approach that has just been given a new name in the computing curriculum. In this context, one example might be where

> *pupils use an appropriate system of rules to plan and evaluate their work. For example in KS1 the national curriculum says use logical reasoning to predict the behaviour of simple programs. A pupil who understood the constraints and rules of a Beebot would know that they only make 90 degree turns and have set distances for each arrow key pressed so will design routes with those parameters in mind.*

(http://code-it.co.uk/csvocab)

TASK

Either on your own or with others make a list of where these skills already are, or could be, applied to other areas of the curriculum to introduce or reinforce their use in computing.

Algorithms

Most children in primary school will have written instructions at some time for simple tasks, such as baking a cake. In essence this is an algorithm and is yet another example of a task from one area of the curriculum, in this case English, being given another name in computing. Essentially, an algorithm is a list of step-by-step instructions in the right order, designed to solve a problem. An everyday example is a recipe from a cookery book. If we take the recipe analogy a little further, you will know that some recipes are better than others, some are easier to follow than others, some use different ingredients in a different order, but they all achieve the same end result. In addition, people often change the recipe based on their experience when they identify things that are not working (bugs), for instance the cake not rising, and experiment to find a solution (debugging) – which in itself can be a valuable educational experience. The same ideas also apply to algorithms, which can be tested, evaluated and improved.

In addition, when preparing a meal you may be following several different algorithms for different components of your meal, but each needs to be done in the correct sequence overall. This is similar to a computer program that uses different algorithms to achieve an overall end result. In the same way, the different parts of a meal can be made in a restaurant by different chefs, and different algorithms can be developed by different people working on the same project, with each working to achieve an overall objective. As such, algorithms precede coding, which is essentially putting the algorithm into a language the computer will understand.

Computer programming

There are many different computer 'languages' and the process of writing in these languages is called programming or coding. It is important to remember, however, that:

> One thing that you will learn quickly is that a computer is very dumb, but obedient.
> It does exactly what you tell it to do, which is not necessarily what you wanted.
> Programming will help you learn the importance of clarity of expression.
>
> (http://www.bfoit.org/itp/Programming.html)

As there are so many resources available to help teach programming or coding (see 'Useful resources' at the end of this chapter), we will not consider it further here, but will move on to consider how it fits into the larger picture of computing in the primary school.

Do I need a computer to develop computational thinking?

Although there are many pieces of software which will help in developing computational thinking, we have already seen that many of the skills are already used by you and your pupils. As such, it is possible to both learn and practise the skills while 'unplugged' from any hardware. This can take the form of games, puzzles and practical activities without any existing programming skills. The CS Unplugged web-site (see 'Useful websites' at the end of this chapter) is a good example of a resource that provides many free activities for classroom and home use. The use of such activi-ties also means that you do not need to invest in any expensive hardware or software to develop computational thinking. There will, of course, come a time where you need to become 'plugged in' to apply new skills, but it is important to identify how these skills can be developed across the whole of the primary curriculum. We will see later in this book that pupils need to recognise that skills have different names in different areas of the curriculum and there may be occasions where you need to explicitly tell them that, for instance, in music we call this one thing but in comput-ing we call it another.

To sum up

Although aimed at KS3 pupils, the BBC Bitesize website (http://www.bbc.co.uk/education/guides/zp92mp3/revision#glossary-zp8thyc) provides an example of the process of computational thinking that could also be useful to teachers. It states that:

> Computational thinking involves taking that complex problem and breaking it down into a series of small, more manageable problems (decomposition). Each of these smaller problems can then be looked at individually, considering how similar problems have been solved previously (pattern recognition) and focusing only on the important details, while ignoring irrelevant information (abstraction). Next, simple steps or rules to solve each of the smaller problems can be designed (algorithms).
>
> Finally, these simple steps or rules are used to program a computer to help solve the complex problem in the best way.

Having established that computational thinking is something that is not entirely new to the primary classroom, we now need to explore other existing skills that children will develop and use in the broader context of their digital literacy or competence.

Digital literacy or competence

We have already seen that different countries use digital literacy and digital com-petence interchangeably, but here we will use the term digital literacy to represent both. There has been a growing emphasis on digital literacy in primary education internationally. For instance, in Norway, digital literacy is the fifth basic skill in the national curriculum that runs through all subjects on all levels (Erstad, 2006; Bjørgen and Erstad, 2015) – in the same way as is proposed in Wales. But, in our multi-literate world, where 'the use of digital technologies has permeated and morphed people's leisure and work' (Henderson, 2011, p152), we do need to consider whether the term digital literacy is sufficient or whether we should refer instead to digital literacies, reflecting the wide range of digital technologies and contemporary forms of commu-nication. The case is made persuasively by Lankshear and Knobel (2006, p17), who suggest that *we should think of 'digital literacy' not as something unitary, and certainly not as some finite 'competency' or 'skill' – or even as a set of competencies or skills. Rather, it means we should think of 'digital literacy' as shorthand for the myriad social practices and conceptions of engaging in meaning making mediated by texts that are produced, received, distributed, exchanged etc., via digital codification. Digital literacy is really digital literacies.*

These literacies can take many forms but can be summarised as the 'knowledge, skills and attitudes required in order to use technology critically and reflectively in the process of building new knowledge' (Instefjord, 2015, p155). We will return to consider this area in more detail in Chapter 8.

Computing

At its simplest in educational terms, we could define computing as 'the tightly focused core knowledge and understanding identified in the National Curriculum programme study' (Turvey et al., 2014, p1). However, given that this varies so much from country to country, it is important to explore a broader definition. To begin with, we can consider the narrow interpretation of, and rationale for, computing outlined in the National Curriculum in England. The current programmes of study (https://www.gov. uk/government/uploads/system/uploads/attachment_data/file/239033/PRIMARY_ national_curriculum_-_Computing.pdf) state that:

A high-quality computing education equips pupils to use computational thinking and creativity to understand and change the world. Computing has deep links with mathematics, science, and design and technology, and provides insights into both natural and artificial systems. The core of computing is computer science, in which pupils are taught the principles of information and computation, how digital systems work, and how to put this knowledge to use through programming. Building on this knowledge and understanding, pupils are equipped to use information technology to create programs, systems and a range of content. Computing also ensures that pupils become digitally literate – able to use, and express themselves and develop their ideas through, information and communication technology – at a level suitable for the future workplace and as active participants in a digital world.

What is immediately obvious from this is that it introduces a range of new terms (such as computational thinking) without defining what they actually mean in any depth. In addition, it is clear that ICT retains an important place within the computing programme of study.

Wing (2008, p3717), an influential figure in this area, defines computing as 'very broadly the field encompassing computer science, computer engineering, communications, information science and information technology'. Within this definition, Wing (ibid., p3719) states that 'operationally, computing is concerned with answering "How would I get a computer to solve this problem?"' We need to remember at all times that a computer cannot (at least not yet) read our minds. This is summed up in a comment from one person in Holloway and Valentine's (2001) study who stated that: 'It's only as stupid as you are.' Or, conversely: 'It's only as clever/creative/imaginative and so on as you are.' This is important for pupils to realise, as we often talk about computers as if they were able to act independently or without agency from a human. Phrases such as 'the computer will work it out' actually mean 'after someone has input some information, the computer will use programming that a human has created, to work out an answer, but only those solutions which the human has allowed to happen when they programmed it'. The concept of artificial intelligence (allowing computers to do things that are normally done by people) is one which many have worked on, and continue to do so, but as yet remains elusive.

In summary, computing 'isn't about understanding how computers work, it's about understanding how *things* work so that we can get computers to do them (although, admittedly, we also need to know a bit about some of the computer's limitations before we can do that)' (Virnuls, 2015).

Computer science

As we have already seen, there is considerable overlap and potential misunderstanding about the differences between computing, computer science and ICT. Therefore, before moving to examine computer science in more detail, it is worth trying to understand the history behind its place in the curriculum today. Brown et al. (2014, p92) report that:

> In the 1980s, computer science was available in schools, under the name Computer Studies, which included hardware, logic, binary, programming and various other aspects of computers . . . Computing in schools slowly became focused on computer use, under the banner of Information and Communication Technology (ICT) . . . In the 1990s, programming and understanding the workings of computers became secondary to using computers and computer applications. While the ICT syllabus was predominantly focused on using computers, there was still mention of programming; but programming was often not covered by schools . . . By the 2000s, ICT was prevalent in schools and focused on using computers (IT skills and digital literacy), while computer science was found primarily at A-Level (the age 16–18 qualification).

As computer science now moves into the primary curriculum, or is at least mentioned in the computing curriculum, we need to understand its relationship with computing and ICT. As the terms computing and computer science seem to be used interchangeably in the primary curricula of many countries, we need to be clear that they are not the same thing. Wing (2006, p34) states: 'Computer science is the study of computation – what can be computed and how to compute it.' As such, we can suggest that computer science, whilst it does include computing, goes beyond coding to look at how it actually works. Figure 1.1 below attempts to show the relationship between the different areas that we have looked at so far.

In this figure we can see that computational thinking can be developed across the primary curriculum as well as being a discrete part of computing within the curriculum. Digital literacy is also developed as one of the many different literacies (reading, mathematical, scientific, musical and so on) pupils develop in the primary school. All

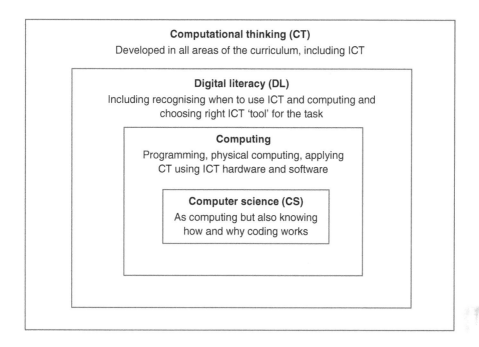

Figure 1.1   Summary of the relationship between computational thinking, digital literacy, computing and computer science

of these skills are applied in computing in the curriculum and lessons learned within computing help develop both computational thinking and digital literacy in the broader context. Computer science, at least in my interpretation, reflects a deeper level of understanding about computing.

All of these areas are also affected by pupils' and teachers' understanding of ICT, which is a fundamental part of digital literacy. Therefore ICT should be built upon, not abandoned, in any move to computing in the curriculum (Turvey et al., 2014). The use of ICT thus remains an essential part of teaching and learning, and we will now turn to consider why we should keep using it in the primary school.

Why use ICT?

Potential for positive impact on learning

We will begin by looking at *why* we really need ICT in the primary school. The first, and perhaps most important, reason for using ICT is that it *can* have a positive effect on attainment. Cox et al. (2003, p3) undertook a comprehensive review of research and concluded that 'evidence from the literature shows the positive effects of specific uses of ICT on pupils' attainment in almost all the National Curriculum subjects'. This claim, however, is immediately qualified by stating that 'there is a strong relationship between the ways in which ICT has been used and pupils' attainment. This suggests that the crucial component in the appropriate selection and use of ICT within education is the teacher and his or her pedagogical approaches.' More recently, Selwyn, Potter and Cranmer (2010, p24) have asserted that 'although there is much anecdotal and case study evidence from classrooms around the world that ICT can be used to support and enhance learning, there is very little rigorous evidence of the educational impact of ICT use on a wide-spread scale'. More recently again, however, the OECD (2015), although claiming 'that the impact of technology in education delivery remains sub-optimal' (p4), nevertheless acknowledge that 'technology can amplify great teaching but great technology cannot replace poor teaching'. In other words, it is essential to realise that just using ICT does not mean it will have a positive impact. As Somekh and Davies (1991, p153) conclude, 'computers, of themselves, are not transforming'. In the years since this was written, it seems probable that we could replace the word 'computers' in that sentence with any of the many new technologies available (IWBs, iPads, and so on) and the claim would still be valid.

What is missing from arguments about the way in which teachers use technology, however, is the impact of pupils' input into the process. This cannot be underestimated, and we will see throughout this book that we need to take account of the skills and knowledge that primary school pupils possess for teaching and learning to be effective. We cannot assume any more that it is only teachers who can influence the course of learning and the use of ICT within it. While it remains essential that teachers need to be aware of the full range of ICT's capabilities, from which they can select the most appropriate uses, pupils will also see ways in which technology can be used as part of their learning.

In a broader sense, this is supported by John and Sutherland (2005, p406), who assert that 'in reality, learning is always distributed in some form between the technology, the learner and the context and there is nothing inherent in technology that automatically guarantees learning'. This theme is developed by Cox et al. (2003, p4), who contend that many studies 'show that insufficient understanding of the scope of an ICT resource leads to inappropriate or superficial uses in the curriculum'. Thus, to ensure its effective use in learning and teaching, teachers need to understand the unique features of ICT and how these can be used as part of a wide range of resources in the classroom.

Unique features of ICT

ICT can offer a range of unique features to teachers and learners that are not available using other means. Although the range of ICT equipment is wide, the following general features are strengths of ICT:

- *speed* – making things happen more quickly than by other methods, both for the individual on a device or for the whole class;
- *automation* – making difficult processes happen automatically, for example filming and editing video on an iPad;
- *capacity* – the storage and retrieval of large amounts of material, including online and outside the classroom;
- *range* – access to materials in different forms and from a wider range of sources than otherwise possible, including outside the classroom;

- *provisionality* – the facility to change content and then change it back (e.g. undo and redo) if necessary, in other words to 'play' with ideas either as an individual or as a whole class or group;
- *interactivity* – in this definition, the ability to respond to user input repeatedly – without getting bored like a person! – and to provide (pre-programmed) feedback based on input from the user.

(Adapted from Kennewell and Beauchamp, 2007)

It is worth considering each of these factors in turn and examining how they could apply to specific hardware and software. As already stated, this book is not a 'how to' guide to hardware and software, so any examples will be generic. They will also primarily relate to teacher use of ICT, but later chapters will consider the importance of allowing pupils to use ICT as a tool for learning.

Speed

ICT can make things happen very fast. Whilst this may be useful at times, for example to gain attention or add pace to a lesson, it should be used with care. As a teacher, it is very useful to be able to move quickly through a prepared series of images, or examples from texts, to present an idea in a variety of contexts or with different forms of presentation. For the learner, however, this may not always be beneficial. Although ICT allows things to happen quickly, the teacher remains central to the *control* of this speed, guided by the needs of the learners. The analogy of an accelerator pedal in a car is useful. No driver would keep their foot on the accelerator without being aware of the conditions around them, any more than a teacher would present information to learners without being aware of the needs and reactions of their pupils. Speed as a feature applies to all ICT devices, but an example in this case would be the IWB. This allows teachers, and indeed pupils, in a synergistic classroom (Beauchamp, 2004) to move from slide to slide, from image to image, or between programs very quickly in a planned or spontaneous manner and applies equally to pupils if they are allowed to use the IWB and have the requisite skills. The dual nature of ICT as a resource for teachers *and* pupils will be considered in detail in later chapters, but here we need to note the importance of the teacher in ensuring that speed is not used at the expense of understanding, whoever is using the ICT.

In addition to presenting information, ICT also allows teachers and learners to very quickly find and edit information, images and data. In this context, speed is a useful feature of ICT, although it does not help pupils, or indeed teachers, to find the best or most appropriate results.

Automation

At the same time, however, this speedy movement through prepared resources (such as a PowerPoint or other file) demonstrates the feature of automation. Before the advent of ICT resources, such as the IWB, teachers would have to produce text in real time (often with their back to the class) or try to illustrate an example with a poster or a drawing. Automation allows teachers to produce whole pages of text or complicated diagrams at the touch of a screen or mouse. The benefits of automation may perhaps be better recognised when something goes wrong with the computer or projector in the classroom and you have to return to writing things on a traditional black/whiteboard or using handheld posters instead of high-quality graphics on the IWB!

WHAT DO YOU THINK?

A class teacher has prepared a PowerPoint for their class. This has taken a long time as it includes text, images and even a short movie. Halfway through the lesson the teacher realises that the first few slides have provoked so much discussion that there is little chance of getting through all the rest of the presentation as originally planned – including some good pictures and the movie. Due to the speed and automation features of ICT, the teacher knows that it is possible to get through all the slides. Should the teacher use these features to finish the slideshow? What are the possible implications of doing so?

Capacity

Automation would be of limited use without the ability to store large amounts of information. There have been rapid advances in recent years in the ability to store and retrieve information quickly, both from physical devices and on school networks, or in the 'cloud' – the latter with automatic back-up and retrieval of deleted files, which can be synchronised across devices. Another important recent development is that storage devices and cloud storage have become both smaller and cheaper. It is now possible to save and access a range of data, even large video files, from very small storage devices or through networks (both wired and wireless). Many of these networks can be accessed from any classroom in a school, thus enabling the easy sharing and re-use of resources within school or even from outside school (for example, to access work teachers have prepared at home) or on school trips. In recent times, these networks have also become virtual and do not always need a wired connection, which enables files to be uploaded, or even programs to be accessed, from anywhere with an internet connection – for example, a teacher from home or on a trip away from school. In reality, teachers are limited only by their imagination in choosing and using effectively a wide variety of content for lessons.

Range

We saw above that ICT can very quickly find a wide range of materials for use by teachers and pupils. These materials can take many forms, such as textual, aural and visual (including still and moving images). These different 'modes' (see more in 'Multimodal and multimedia capability' below) can be accessed separately and in combination, both from existing storage and through search engines and databases. These can be used to supplement or replace existing resources, although, as usual, when making such decisions you need to consider which will best help meet the learning needs of the pupils. For instance, while reading a big book with a class remains an important part of teaching, it is now possible to project large images of the page on a screen using a visualiser, or a scan of the page on the IWB incorporating sound clips of children from the class reading it (made using digital recorders), as well as hyperlinks to pages on the internet illustrating places from the story or to an interview with the author on their own website.

As will become apparent throughout this book, however, an effective teacher should not be seduced by all of the above into using ICT for the sake of it. It may be that reading children a big book is actually the most effective and appropriate strategy, and the ICT becomes an unnecessary distraction creating a barrier between teacher and pupils.

Provisionality

The key aspect of provisionality is the ability to explore ideas by asking the powerful question: *What would happen if?* This question can, of course, be asked without using ICT. Indeed, the central part that dialogue plays in learning and teaching at all ages will be explored later. What we are considering here is how teachers and pupils can use the features of ICT to pose and investigate challenges, and to explore concepts in a way that conventional resources (such as books) cannot.

CASE STUDY

A Key Stage 2 class is exploring different types of food as part of a balanced diet. The teacher set up an Excel spreadsheet with relevant formulas linked from a variety of food groups to a variety of graph formats. This meant that, as pupils entered information from tally sheets they kept as food diaries, the associated graphs would change to reflect the information entered – see below. This spreadsheet was used in the first instance by the teacher on the IWB, but also later on PCs and laptops for individual and group work and to print out individual records.

On the IWB, the teacher was able to explore the impact of how changing the amount of different foods affected the graphs. As well as the real information entered, provisionality also allowed the class to explore how they could change the foods they ate to achieve a better balance and a more healthy diet.

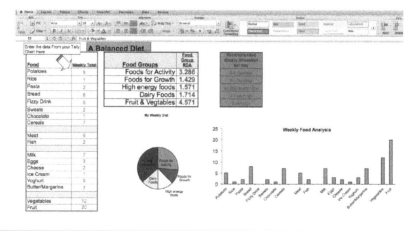

One way of posing 'what if?' questions is to use undo and redo in many formats, from text editing on PCs through to maths work on the IWB. This ability to explore ideas could be considered an element of the beneficial 'playful' use of ICT, but can also lead to situations where pupils 'subvert' the learning intentions by adopting a 'trial and error' approach to solving a problem. Such an approach can lead pupils to concentrate on the product (getting the right answer) rather than the process (the learning) (Beauchamp et al., 2010). It is worth considering whether pupils are adopting this approach whilst using ICT in tasks you set them. It can be easy to find out just by asking them what they are doing!

There is another important facet of provisionality, which arose in a research project, which is leaving, or not leaving, a record of mistakes. Such is the speed of advances in technology that even some students training to become teachers may not have been taught using blackboards, or possibly even wipe-clean whiteboards – but all will have used paper. Whether you are using a blackboard, a wipe-clean whiteboard or paper, it almost impossible to totally erase what has gone before. In all of these examples, some visible evidence of a mistake will be left. On a computer, IWB or tablet device, this is not the case, and it is possible to explore multiple ways of solving problems with no visible evidence of 'wrong' answers. Although this is perhaps more influential in pupils' work, it is also a consideration for teachers – but only if they operate an open classroom where mistakes are accepted as part of the learning process. In this context, the option for the teacher to be 'wrong' in front of the whole class, and to be prepared to explore other options openly, can send a powerful message to learners.

While we have seen above that there are negatives to provisionality, in general terms the provisional nature of ICT has many benefits, particularly when linked purposively to an interactive approach to learning.

Interactivity

The concept of interactivity in learning and teaching will be returned to in more detail later, but a brief overview of the concept is relevant at this stage. Although there is no agreed definition of what constitutes interactive teaching generally (Moyles et al., 2003), in our first encounter with the concept we can define it somewhat narrowly to begin with as ICT's ability to respond contingently (the response depending on the input, but limited to a predefined set of responses – unlike a teacher) in a variety of ways to input from different sources, both human and electronic. So, for instance, a pupil could input a number in a maths software package and the answer would be checked and summative feedback given, or a teacher could bring up a website on the IWB and pupils could use it collaboratively to seek information on a topic. In addition, ICT can make such responses again and again without getting bored! Although this ability does allow pupils (or teachers) to practise new skills (such as addition or multiplication) repeatedly, it also allows them to make the same mistake every time, as, unless they are programmed to do so, ICT resources are not really able to give a response that allows for personalised formative feedback. (See more on this in Chapter 3.)

Hargreaves et al. (2003, p224) classify interactivity in two broad forms. The first form contains classifications that are 'surface' forms of interactive teaching, which are 'associated by some teachers with "gimmicky" techniques such as the use of phoneme fans, various games or whiteboards'. The second form contains classifications that encourage a 'deeper level of engagement with the purposes of interactive teaching, to probe pupils' understanding, to try to ensure reciprocal interaction and the co-construction of meaning, or to enable children to consider or articulate their own thinking strategies'.

These forms will be returned to in more detail in Chapter 2, but at this stage they draw attention to an important consideration for any ICT use: *am I using ICT (in any form) as a 'gimmick' (which will get attention or make my life easier) or as something that is essential to engage, challenge and develop thinking?*

In making these judgements, we should also note the useful distinction made by Smith et al. (2005) between *technical* interactivity (physical interaction with the device) and *pedagogic* interactivity (interaction between students and others in the classroom designed to bring about learning). Mercer, Hennessy and Warwick (2010, p197) define this as 'the distinction between what a piece of technology can do, and what it can be used to achieve educationally'. Although both are important, pedagogic rather than technical interactivity has currently been the focus of most research to date (Beauchamp et al., 2010), suggesting, as we have seen above, that it is not *what* is done with the technology but *why* and *how* it is done that is important.

Multimodal and multimedia capability

The multimodal capability of ICT is another reason to use it, as it allows teachers to present an idea in a variety of different ways to help pupils understand it. It can also make work more interesting or motivating. Multimodal capability describes the facility of ICT to combine various modes – such as visual, sounds and text – which are displayed through a variety of media (multimedia). Twiner et al. (2010, p212) summarise the distinction as mode being 'considered as the form of the content, such as image, writing or talk; while media refers to the vehicle through which information is conveyed, such as television, a book or website'. They also suggest that

> the proliferation of new technologies has led to a culture permeated by multiple
> modes and media, in which communication is becoming increasingly more
> multimodal . . . Increasing recognition of the pervasiveness of digital technologies and
> multimodal experiences in pupils' out-of-school lives therefore is exposing a need to
> incorporate such tools within teaching and learning, to enhance current and evolving
> pedagogic practice.

> (Twiner et al., 2010, p212)

It could be argued that it has always been possible to present information in different modes using older media devices, such as video, photographic slides, overhead projectors and so on. Indeed, all these resources allow users to present ideas in a variety of ways, but when the modes are allied to the features of ICT noted above, things can now be done quicker, from an ever expanding range of sources and in better quality, and can be saved to use or modify later. This is particularly true of the IWB. Hall and Higgins (2005, p106) in the UK found that the Year 6 pupils in their study seemed

> to enjoy in particular the multi-media capabilities of the technology, especially the visual
> aspects (colour and movement), audio (music, voice recordings, sound effects) and being
> able to touch the IWB. All pupil groups mentioned the multi-media aspects of the IWB as
> advantageous especially in engaging and holding their attention.

Although no research has yet been done on this specifically, it may also be true of mobile devices.

The multimodal benefits of using the IWB in primary schools was also highlighted by Littleton, Twiner and Gillen (2010), who noted the potential of the wide range of multimodal resources to engage students' cognitive and imaginative capacities. Although the IWB is much more common in UK classrooms, research in primary schools in Australia (Maher, 2011; Murcia, 2014) also found that the multimodal affordances of the IWB not only engaged the pupils but also helped teachers to assess pupils' under-standing as they engaged with the range of representations used by the teachers on the IWB.

This ability to engage and hold attention may also be enhanced by the ease with which pupils' own work can be used on the IWB, or increasingly through any projector, as work on iPads can be mirrored using devices such as Apple TV. It is now very easy to display and discuss word-processing or picture files, pictures, movies, readings from handheld data collectors, sound files of pupils themselves, and so on. All of these help make the work relevant and real to pupils of all ages. This is particularly true as such devices become smaller and easier to carry and can be used both indoors and out by younger children – and teachers!

Technology-based games in education

The multimodal features of the IWB also make it a good platform for playing games and this was the favourite feature of the IWB in research in a primary school in Spain (Yáñez and Coyle, 2011). The use of games in learning is, in itself, not new to the pri-mary school, but the features of ICT already described above, and the increased capacity of both computers and mobile devices to provide a stimulating and authentic gaming environment, mean that 'digital gaming can form the basis of effective and purposeful education-based interventions' (Crowe and Flynn, 2015, p165) – including with very young children (Lieberman, Fisk and Biely, 2009). This is because 'when we think of games, we think of fun. When we think of learning we think of work. Games show us this is wrong. They trigger deep learning that is itself part and parcel of the fun. It is what makes good games deep' (Gee, 2005, p15). Despite this potential, however, many teachers – including pre-service teachers – are reluctant to use video games as learning tools (Ray, Powell and Jacobsen, 2014). Findings from a Belgian study of 517 secondary school teachers (De Grove, Bourgonjon and Van Looy, 2012) support this, but suggest that two significant factors can lead to successful adoption:

1. curriculum-relatedness, where 'teachers believe that digital games can be fitted into the curriculum, they will also be regarded as tools for learning, which in turn will lead to a higher adoption intention' (ibid., p2028);
2. experience;
3. where 'teachers with more experience will on average consider digital games as more suited to fit the curriculum than teachers with less experience' (ibid., p2029).

WHAT DO YOU THINK?

Do you agree that teachers with more experience are more likely or less likely to use digital games in your experience? Why might be the case or what factors mean that these findings might not apply in schools you are familiar with?

In recent years, interest has grown considerably in the potential for play in general to form the basis for learning. This is especially true in the early years, with developments such as the Foundation Stage in England and the Foundation Phase in Wales. Using the features of ICT outlined above, technology can offer a specific type of play through computer or video games, which can be individual or whole-class activities and may be particularly useful in early years teaching (Morgan, 2010).

Research into the area of using computer games in education has tended to focus on two categories: firstly, the informal use of computer games outside educational settings (often called commercial off-the-shelf software [COTS]) and their potential for use in learning; and secondly, the use of games specifically developed for educational settings. Sandford and Williamson (2005, p1) suggest that games in the second category 'are designed to be as rich and dynamic as their mainstream "cousins", but are intended for particular formal educational outcomes'. The importance of teachers understanding this distinction is underlined by Sutherland, Robertson and John (2009, pp168–9), who draw attention to the potential for teachers and pupils to have 'radically different networks of meaning, resources and practices' when they refer to something as 'like a game'. This might be influenced by the fact that some studies show (although this may change) that, although 85 per cent of children report playing computer games in their leisure time at least once a fortnight, only 28 per cent of teachers do (Sandford et al., 2006). This has profound implications for teachers when they plan to use computer games in lessons. Not only do they have to become familiar with the games, they also have to ensure that they make clear the way in which they want the game to be used. Sutherland, Robertson and John (2009, p169) give an example from a science lesson and suggest that:

> While the students, following the logic of domestic games play, are moving immediately into immersion – expecting to learn to rapid feedback and trial and error from the 'game' – the teacher is asking the students to step back, to reflect upon their decisions prior to starting activity, to carefully observe and document the implications of their choices – to learn from practices of scientific method.

The same difference in expectation could be possible in other areas of the curriculum, and unclear expectations can lead to misunderstandings between teacher and pupil. I have seen one example where pupils were playing a game on an iPad in which they had to pop bubbles (by tapping on the screen) in pairs when the sum and answer matched. Most children were carefully popping balloons using one finger, but one child used all the fingers on both hands to pop everything as quickly as possible and was the first to finish. By chance, some pairs were right, but, when asked, the child explained that the teacher had said it was a game, which he wanted to win, and this was the best way of doing it! This potential subversion of the activity was in fact the child adopting the normal practices he would use when playing a computer game, where winning was perceived as the outcome, rather than a maths activity where accuracy was important.

Once common expectations are established, depending on the ICT resources available and the learning intentions of the teacher, games can be played individually or in small groups on PCs, mobile devices or handheld gaming devices. They can be shared, if necessary, with the whole class or group, through the IWB, a data projector or television screen, or even between schools if they are web-based. Making decisions about how or if games are shared will be guided by the learning intention of the lesson – either academic or social. The type of skills that could be developed by ICT games include:

- strategic thinking
- planning
- communication
- application of numbers
- negotiating skills
- group decision-making
- data-handling.

(Kirriemuir and McFarlane, 2004)

Obviously you need to be familiar with games in order to make decisions about which of these skills they can develop, if any. But while familiarity with games is important, Sandford et al. (2006, p3) suggest reassuringly that 'achieving particular educational objectives through the use of the game was more dependent upon a teacher's knowledge of the curriculum with which they were working than it was on their ability with the game'. Hence, perhaps more than in any other area outlined in this chapter, the role of the teacher in deciding on the appropriate use of games is important to ensure effective learning.

ACTIVITY

Think of a computer or web-based game you have used or seen in the classroom. In pairs or small groups, explain why you chose it and the strengths and weaknesses of it, with reference to a particular age group if necessary. Discuss if there are any common features that would help you choose whether to use an ICT-based game in future teaching.

Computing and games design

The introduction of computing into the curriculum means that primary school children can now design and make their own games to play. These games can come from pupils' own imagination, or can even use characters and settings from books they are reading on their own or with the teacher. There is an increasing range of software available (see 'Useful websites' at the end of this chapter) that will help teachers and pupils. Some schools put these games on their school website when they are complete; this means that pupils see a real purpose, and a potential global audience, for their games. This type of activity makes the learning more active and authentic (as games are meant to be played, not just be exercises in themselves), particularly if the activities are linked to pupils' own experiences of the curriculum or of computer games outside school. In addition, designing computer games not only allows pupils to apply coding in a real context, but also encourages them to be creative. It also develops skills of co-operation, as computing, particularly in business contexts, is normally done by working with others.

Despite the many skills that pupils can develop by designing computer games, CAS (2013, p19) reminds us that:

Games can be very motivating, and pupils often enjoy evaluating each other's work. Remember, though, that such projects are not an end in themselves: the focus should remain on developing knowledge and understanding of computing through such activities, however engaging they may be. Your role as a teacher extends beyond setting the challenge and providing support in projects, to helping pupils understand the ideas that lie at the heart of the creative work in which they're engaged, and to helping pupils make the connection between these concepts.

Mobility

In the early days of personal computers, users were forced to work at a fixed computer. Advances in technology now mean that computers can be taken to the work, and, increasingly, other mobile devices, especially mobile phones and tablets, have very advanced capabilities and can be used to supplement or even replace a laptop computer. This is an advantage with young children, as small devices are easy to carry. Such is the speed of change that by the time they leave primary school pupils may be able to do more things with a phone or tablet than they can with a computer. As we have seen above, the ability to work outside the classroom and carry work around with you is nothing new – a clipboard and a piece of paper can do the same thing. The advantage of using ICT is that the portability of work is complemented by the ability to produce high-quality, collaborative and easily edited work, which can then be both shared easily through resources such as the IWB or sent to other pupils or teachers within the school grounds and beyond. Indeed, with the increasing use of networking and wireless technology (including Bluetooth) there is added scope for collaborating and communicating, which will be discussed below. We will discuss this in much greater detail in Chapter 5.

Communication and collaboration

Having gathered a variety of information in a variety of forms, another feature of ICT is the ability to communicate this information with others and work collaboratively on it. The potential partners who can share information are not limited to the school, as virtual learning environments (VLEs), emails, texts, websites and social media (see more in Chapter 6) are increasingly being used to communicate with parents and other stakeholders locally, nationally and internationally. Again, there is nothing new in the ability to communicate, but what is different is how the features of ICT can be used to do this faster, using a variety of modes and media. The speed of communication is also important in developing interactivity, with responses often possible in real time, allowing a meaningful dialogue to be conducted and lines of inquiry developed without delays interrupting the flow of thought. For instance, developments in videoconferencing, and the ability to use it wirelessly on tablet devices, mean that it is possible not only to share text and speech in real time but also to co-construct a range of materials, such as concept maps or designs, with instant feedback from collaborators – see more in Chapter 8. These collaborations can be between teachers and pupils, between pupils in pairs or groups, and even between teachers. Again, there is nothing new in the idea of collaboration, but what is new is how ICT allows collaboration not only between those physically present, such as pupils anywhere within the school, but also between schools in the same country and even between schools across the world – but do check your time zones (on your computer, of course) before connecting!

Globalisation

The global reach facilitated by ICT allows pupils, individual classes and schools to have a global presence. This is not only restricted to the internet and school websites, but is also available through social networking and other media. There are obvious safety issues implicit in all sharing of information (see the section on e-safety in Chapter 4), but it is now very straightforward for a school or nursery to make itself known around the world. Besides the obvious promotional possibilities, there are also other benefits that can accrue. For teachers, one important benefit is that it is possible to build up online communities of settings that share similar practices (see more in Chapter 6). This may be particularly useful in early years settings and primary schools as outdoor learning approaches, such as the Foundation Phase in Wales (for children aged 3–7 years) and forest schools, become more established. The possibility of teachers and pupils building communities of practice (Wenger, 1998) that share resources and advice is now very real and will be returned to in later chapters.

SUMMARY

This chapter has clarified and provided definitions for a range of terms used in computing and ICT. It has also explored why we should use ICT in learning and teaching in the primary school and have identified a range of features of ICT that are available. We have begun to discuss the ownership and use of ICT resources and how control of these are evolving. In this evolution, however, even if pupils are actively involved in using ICT and have well-developed skills in using it, what they lack is a teacher's understanding of pedagogy that will enable effective learning to take place. Whilst it is important that teachers also maintain and develop their ICT skills, it is even more important that they develop their understanding of how to 'transform' knowledge (Shulman, 1987) using the features of ICT outlined above, and of when it is appropriate to do so. Hence, having established some of the many unique features of ICT and why we should use them, it is now necessary to examine how, when and who should use these features in the primary classroom and early years settings.

References

Aho, A.V. (2012) 'Computation and computational thinking', *The Computer Journal*, 55(7), pp832–5.

Beauchamp, G. (2004) 'Teacher use of the interactive whiteboard (IWB) in primary schools – towards an effective transition framework', *Technology, Pedagogy and Education*, 13(3), pp327–48.

Beauchamp, G. and Kennewell, S. (2010) 'Interactivity in the classroom and its impact on learning', *Computers and Education*, 54, pp759–66.

Beauchamp, G., Kennewell, S., Tanner, H. and Jones, S. (2010) 'Interactive whiteboards and all that jazz: the contribution of musical metaphors to the analysis of classroom activity with interactive technologies', *Technology, Pedagogy and Education*, 19(2), pp143–57.

Berry, M. (2014) *Computational Thinking in Primary Schools*, http://milesberry.net/2014/03/computational-thinking-in-primary-schools/ (accessed 10 June 2016).

Bjørgen, A.M. and Erstad, O. (2015) 'The connected child: tracing digital literacy from school to leisure', *Pedagogies: An International Journal*, 10(2), pp113–27.

Brown, N.C.C., Sentance, S., Crick, T. and Humphreys, S. (2014) 'Restart: the resurgence of computer science in UK schools', *ACM Transactions on Computing Education*. 14(2): Article 9 (June).

CAS (2013) *Computing in the National Curriculum: A Guide for Primary Teachers*, Swindon: Computing At School (CAS), http://www.computingatschool.org.uk/data/uploads/CASPrimaryComputing.pdf (accessed 7 January 2016).

CAS (2015) *Computational Thinking: A Guide for Teachers*, Swindon: Computing At School (CAS), http://community.computingatschool.org.uk/files/6695/original.pdf (accessed 23 November 2015).

Cox, M., Abbott, C., Webb, M., Blakeley, B., Beauchamp, T. and Rhodes, V. (2003) *ICT and Attainment: A Review of the Research Literature*, London: Department for Education and Skills (DfES).

Crowe, N. and Flynn, S. (2015) 'Games and learning: using multi-play digital games and online virtual worlds', in Younie, S., Leask, M. and Burden, K. (eds) *Teaching and Learning with ICT in the Primary School*, 2nd edition, London: Routledge, pp164–70.

DCSF (2009) *Independent Review of the Primary Curriculum: Final Report*, Annesley: Department for Children, Schools and Families (DCSF).

De Grove, F., Bourgonjon, J. and Van Looy, J. (2012) 'Digital games in the classroom? A contextual approach to teachers' adoption intention of digital games in formal education', *Computers in Human Behavior*, 28(6), pp2023–33.

Erstad, O. (2006) 'A new direction? Digital literacy, student participation and curriculum reform in Norway', *Education and Information Technologies*, 11(4), pp415–29.

Gee, J.P. (2005) 'Learning by design: good video games as learning machines', *E-learning*, 2(1), pp5–16.

Grover, S. and Pea, R. (2013) 'Computational thinking in K–12: a review of the state of the field', *Educational Researcher*, 42(1), pp38–43.

Hall, I. and Higgins, S. (2005) 'Primary school students' perceptions of interactive whiteboards', *Journal of Computer Assisted Learning*, 21, pp102–17.

Hargreaves, L., Moyles, J., Merry, R., Paterson, F., Pell, A. and Esarte-Sarries, V. (2003) 'How do primary school teachers define and implement "interactive teaching" in the National Literacy Strategy in England?', *Research Papers in Education*, 18(3), pp217–36.

Henderson, R. (2011) 'Classroom pedagogies, digital literacies and the home-school digital divide', *International Journal of Pedagogies and Learning*, 6(2), pp152–61.

Higgins, S. (2001) 'ICT and teaching for understanding', *Evaluation and Research in Education*, 15(3), pp164–71.

Holloway. S.L. and Valentine, G. (2001) '"It's only as stupid as you are": Children's and adults' negotiation of ICT competence at home and at school', *Social & Cultural Geography*, 2(1), pp25–42.

Holmes, B. and Gardner, J. (2006) *E-learning: Concepts and Practice*, London: Sage Publications.

Instefjord, E. (2015) 'Appropriation of digital competence in teacher education,' *Nordic Journal of Digital Literacy*, Jubileumsnummer, pp155–71.

Israel, M., Pearson, J.N., Tapia, T., Wherfel, Q.M. and Reese, G. (2015) 'Supporting all learners in school-wide computational thinking: a cross-case qualitative analysis', *Computers & Education*, 82, pp263–79.

John, P. and Sutherland, R. (2005) 'Affordance, opportunity and the pedagogical implications of ICT', *Educational Review*, 57(4), pp405–13.

Kennewell, S. and Beauchamp, G. (2007) 'The features of interactive whiteboards and their influence on learning', *Learning, Media and Technology*, 32(3), pp227–41.

Kirriemuir, J. and McFarlane, A. (2004) *Literature Review in Games and Learning*, Bristol: Futurelab.

Lankshear, C. and Knobel, M. (2006) 'Digital literacy and digital literacies: policy, pedagogy and research considerations for education', *Nordic Journal of Digital Literacy*, 1(1), pp12–24.

L'Heureux, J., Boisvert, D., Cohen, R. and Sanghera, K. (2012) 'IT problem solving: an implementation of computational thinking in information technology', *Proceedings of the 13th Annual Conference on Information Technology Education*, Calgary, Alberta, Canada: ACM, 11–13 October 2012, pp183–88.

Lieberman, D.A., Fisk, M.C. and Biely, E. (2009) 'Digital games for young children ages three to six: from research to design', *Computers in the Schools*, 26(4), pp299–313.

Littleton, K., Twiner, A. and Gillen, J. (2010) 'Instruction as orchestration: multimodal connection building with the interactive whiteboard', *Pedagogies: An International Journal*, 5(2), pp130–41.

Luckin, R. (2008) 'The learner centric ecology of resources: a framework for using technology to scaffold learning', *Computers and Education*, 50(2), pp449–62.

Lye, S.Y. and Koh, J.H.L. (2014) 'Review on teaching and learning of computational thinking through programming: what is next for K-12?', *Computers in Human Behavior*, 41, pp51–61.

Maher, D. (2011) 'Using the multimodal affordances of the interactive whiteboard to support students' understanding of texts', *Learning, Media and Technology*, 36(3), pp235–50.

Mayes, T. and de Freitas, S. (2007) 'Learning and e-learning: the role of theory', in Beetham, H. and Sharpe, R. (eds) *Rethinking Pedagogy for a Digital Age*, London: Routledge, pp13–25.

Mercer, N., Hennessy, S. and Warwick, P. (2010) 'Using interactive whiteboards to orchestrate classroom dialogue', *Technology, Pedagogy and Education*, 19(2), pp195–209.

Morgan, A. (2010) 'Interactive whiteboards, interactivity and play in the classroom with children aged three to seven years', *European Early Childhood Education Research Journal*, 18(1), pp93–104.

Moyles, J., Hargreaves, L., Merry, R., Paterson, F. and Esarte-Sarries, V. (2003) *Interactive Teaching in the Primary School: Digging Deeper into Meaning*, Maidenhead: Open University Press.

Murcia, K. (2014) 'Interactive and multimodal pedagogy: a case study of how teachers and students use interactive whiteboard technology in primary science', *Australian Journal of Education*, 58(1), pp74–88.

OECD (2015) *Students, Computers and Learning: Making the Connection*, PISA, Paris: Organisation for Economic Co-operation and Development (OECD) Publishing.

QuickStart Computing (2015) *Computational Thinking*, http://primary.quickstartcomputing. org/resources/pdf/comp_thinking.pdf (accessed 7 January 2016).

Ray, B.B., Powell, A. and Jacobsen, B. (2014) 'Exploring preservice teacher perspectives on video games as learning tools', *Journal of Digital Learning in Teacher Education*, 31(1), pp28–34.

Sandford, R., Ulicsak, M., Facer, K. and Rudd, T. (2006) *Teaching with Games: Using Commercial Off-the-Shelf Computer Games in Formal Education*, Bristol: Futurelab.

Sandford, R. and Williamson, B. (2005) *Games and Learning: A Handbook from Futurelab*, Bristol: Futurelab.

Selby, C.S. and Woollard, J. (2013) *Computational Thinking: The Developing Definition*, http://eprints.soton.ac.uk/356481/7/ Selby_Woollard_bg_soton_eprints.pdf (accessed 3 January 2016).

Selwyn, N., Potter, J. and Cranmer, S. (2010) *Primary Schools and ICT: Learning from Pupil Perspectives*, London: Continuum International Publishing Group.

Shulman, L.S. (1987) 'Knowledge and teaching: foundations of the new reform', *Harvard Educational Review*, 57(1), pp1–22.

Smith, H.J., Higgins, S., Wall, K. and Miller, J. (2005) 'Interactive whiteboards: boon or bandwagon? A critical review of the literature', *Journal of Computer Assisted Learning* 21, pp91–101.

Somekh, B. and Davies, R. (1991) 'Towards a pedagogy for information technology', *The Curriculum Journal*, 2(2), pp153–70.

Sutherland, R., Robertson, S. and John, P. (2009) *Improving Classroom Learning with ICT*, Milton Park, Abingdon and New York: Routledge.

Turvey, K., Potter, J., Allen, J. and Sharp, J. (2014) *Primary Computing and ICT: Knowledge, Understanding and Practice*, 6th edition, London: Sage.

Twiner, A., Coffin, C., Littleton, K. and Whitelock, D. (2010) 'Multimodality, orchestration and participation in the context of classroom use of the interactive white-board: a discussion', *Technology, Pedagogy and Education*, 19(2), pp211–23.

Virnuls, A. (2015) 'What is computing?', *TES*, 27 November 2015, https://www.tes.com/news/blog/what-computing (accessed 1 December 2015).

Voogt, J., Fisser, P., Good, J., Mishra, P. and Yadav, A. (2015) 'Computational thinking in compulsory education: towards an agenda for research and practice', *Education and Information Technologies*, 20(4), pp715–28.

Vygotsky, L. (1978) *Mind in Society*, Cambridge, MA: Harvard University Press.

Wenger, E. (1998) *Communities of Practice: Learning, Meaning, and Identity*, Cambridge: Cambridge University Press.

Wertsch, J.V. (1991) *Voices of the Mind: A Sociocultural Approach to Mediated Action*, Hemel Hempstead, Harvester Wheatsheaf.

Wing, J. (2006) 'Computational thinking', *Communications of the ACM*, 49(3), pp33–5.

Wing, J.M. (2008) 'Computational thinking and thinking about computing', *Philosophical Transactions of the Royal Society A: Mathematical, Physical and Engineering Sciences*, 366(1881), pp3717–25.

Yáñez, L. and Coyle, Y. (2011) 'Children's perceptions of learning with an interactive whiteboard', *ELT Journal*, 65(4), pp446–57.

Further reading

CAS (2013) *Computing in the National Curriculum: A Guide for Primary Teachers*, Swindon: Computing At School (CAS), http://www.computingatschool.org.uk/data/uploads/CASPrimaryComputing.pdf (accessed 7 January 2016).

CAS (2015) *Computational Thinking: A Guide for Teachers*, Swindon: Computing At School (CAS), http://community.computingatschool.org.uk/files/6695/original.pdf (accessed 23 November 2015).

Holloway. S.L. and Valentine, G. (2001) '"It's only as stupid as you are": Children's and adults' negotiation of ICT competence at home and at school', *Social & Cultural Geography*, 2(1), pp25–42.

Sandford, R. and Williamson, B. (2005) *Games and Learning: A Handbook from Futurelab*, Bristol: Futurelab.

Vee, A. (2013) 'Understanding computer programming as a literacy', *Literacy in Composition Studies*, 1(2), pp42–64.

Useful websites

Computer Science Terminology for Primary Teachers: http://code-it.co.uk/csvocab This page attempts to define may computational terms.

Computer Science Without a Computer – Computing Unplugged: http://csunplugged.org/ This site provides a range of free activities to develop computer science skills without a computer.

Education Scotland – Games Design and Learning: http://www.educationscotland.gov.uk/learningandteaching/approaches/ictineducation/gamesbasedlearning/

gamedesign/ This site from Education Scotland provide examples of the tools and packages that could be used by pupils and teachers to design their own computer games.

Google for Education: https://www.youtube.com/watch?v=SVVB5RQfYxk See the video 'Solving problems at Google using computational thinking'.

Useful resources

Computational thinking

CAS (2015) *Computational Thinking: A Guide for Teachers*, Swindon: Computing At School (CAS). Available at http://community.computingatschool.org.uk/files/6695/original.pdf.

Berry, M. (2015) *QuickStart Computing: A CPD Toolkit for Primary Teachers*, Swindon: Computing At School (CAS). Available at http://primary.quickstartcomputing.org/resources/pdf/qs_handbook.pdf. This QuickStart resource is focused on Key

Stages 1 and 2 and claims to 'give you the essential subject knowledge you need, with a framework and guidance for planning, teaching and assessing progress'. It provides many specific examples and a wide range of further resources that can be used in the primary school. Although aimed at serving teachers, it is equally relevant to those training to be teachers and others with an interest in developing their understanding of computing in the primary school.

ICT in the primary classroom: how, when and who?

In this chapter we will consider how and when ICT should be used and who should use it. We will consider the affordances of ICT and how they can contribute to personalised learning, interactive and dialogic teaching. Finally, we will consider how Shulman's (1987) model of pedagogical reasoning and action relates to ICT use in the primary classroom.

Let us begin this chapter by imagining the start of a lesson where you have carefully prepared an interactive whiteboard (IWB) activity in which you guide the children through an example of drawing a graph. As you change variables, the graph changes in real time according to the input. A few minutes after you begin, a pupil puts up their hand and says, 'But what about if you put a three there instead of a two?' This seemingly innocuous question actually poses a series of fundamental questions about the role of the teacher and the learner, including who is in control of the learning and do pupils have a voice or role in their own learning?

When responding to the question, you are faced with a number of options, including:

- ignore the child and carry on;
- put the new number there yourself and show the class what would happen;
- ask the pupil to come to the IWB and explore what would happen for themselves;
- ask the class what they think would happen and then invite someone to come and try.

The choice you make will depend on your pedagogical beliefs, your subject knowledge and understanding of the topic (with resultant confidence in dealing with unexpected questions), or, more pragmatically, if you are having a good or bad day! Assuming you are able to rise above a bad day, and having made the decision (why) to use ICT in the first place, by choosing your course of action you are beginning to address *how* and *when* ICT should be used and *who* should use it.

In order to help make these decisions, it is useful to consider the different roles that ICT can play, which will help in allocating these roles to different actors (people in the classroom). I have suggested elsewhere (Beauchamp, 2011) that a useful categorisation might the one shown in Table 2.1.

Table 2.1 The different roles that ICT can play

Category of use	End product	Your choice?
a. A *passive tool* for interactions: ICT provides a way of completing a practitioner-directed task or a practitioner uses ICT to demonstrate or model an activity	• Practitioner-led demonstration (normally to whole class) or modelling of task with some limited opportunities for pupils to clarify • Practitioner control of ICT • Minimal dialogue/discussion about the nature of task	• Ignore the child and carry on • *If you chose this option, you would continue to use the IWB to finish your prepared activity and not allow the pupils to come and use the board, or influence the course of the lesson.*
b. The *object* of interaction: ICT provides something to interact about (e.g. video clip or pupil's work) and the practitioner usually provides the structure for interactions	• Dialogue/discussion *about* the digital 'object'	• Put the new number there yourself and show the class what would happen • *If you chose this option, you would add the suggested number but crucially you would then discuss the outcome – the new graph is the 'object' of the interaction.*
c. A *participant* in interaction: ICT 'joins in' the activity (the activity couldn't be done without ICT) and often sets the tasks and provides immediate feedback (such as a game, quiz or simulation)	• Completed task – and perhaps discussion to complete task if more than one person	• Ask the pupil to come to the IWB and explore what would happen for themselves • *If you chose this option, you would allow the IWB and graphing software to 'join in' and become a participant in the interaction. Again, discussion of the outcome remains important.*
d. An *active tool* for interaction: ICT allows children to communicate and/or build ideas (e.g. email/chat, annotation, mind-mapping) and	• Dialogue/discussion/ learning/co-construction of knowledge	• Ask the class what they think would happen and then invite someone to come and try • *If you allow the same pupil or others to try different options, the IWB continues to participate in the interactions. The key change*

learners usually provide the structure for interactions, e.g. by choosing the tool and/or who (people) or what (technology) to interact with	*here is that the pupils (learners) are providing the structure for the interactions by choosing inputs – albeit within your prepared activity. In addition, if the pupils wanted to look at other graphs on a website, or within another program, and you allow it, the tools remain 'active' in helping to develop learning.*

In the example above, you could choose between all of these categories, on their own or in combination. However, in making such choices, you are making a fundamental decision about the locus of control in the classroom and hence who has power over of the direction of learning – you or the pupil. In the split second in which you make this choice, it is very unlikely you will consciously use the categorisation above, but if you are aware of it, it may influence you subconsciously – or at least cross your mind when you evaluate the lesson and consider what you could have done differently.

One of the main purposes of this book is to bring to your attention a wide range of pedagogic ideas relating to ICT, all informed by research and classroom experience. You may use some ideas in this 'pedagogic toolkit' more than others, but the key idea is that you have the tools and that you know how to use them and what they do. At the same time, you will be developing practical skills in, and knowledge of, how particular hardware or software works. As programs evolve, you will need to keep updating these practical skills, but you will also need to do the same thing for your ICT and computing pedagogic skills. At times, one can inform or trigger the other. In some research projects I have undertaken with primary teachers, showing them a new facet of a program results in an immediate recognition of how it could work in a lesson: 'Oh, I didn't know you could do that, but I could use it for . . . '.

Conole and Dyke (2004, pp114–15) suggest that:

We believe that a better understanding of the nature and properties of technologies will lead to a more systematic application of the use of ICT for learning and teaching . . . evidence suggests that practitioners are still unclear about how to use technology appropriately, and its application is often based on common sense rather then [sic] being theoretically informed by pedagogical theory.

To encourage greater use of research-informed pedagogic theory ('I am doing this because I have researched it and several researchers, using sound methods, have found that it is effective'), rather than 'common sense' ('I am doing this because it seems the obvious/ easiest thing to do and I haven't got much time'), this chapter will examine a range of ideas that influence ICT pedagogy.

Affordances

The first of these ideas relates to seeing the possibilities that ICT can offer to both teacher and pupils. The idea of 'affordance' is normally attributed to Gibson (1986) in the first instance, but it has been used by many others since then in many areas of the curriculum (for example, Kennewell, 2001; Conole and Dyke, 2004; John and Sutherland, 2005; Webb, 2005; Warwick and Kershner, 2008). Essentially, an affordance 'refers to the perceived and actual properties of a thing, primarily those functional properties that determine just how the thing could possibly be used' (Pea, 1997, p51). Alternatively, Kennewell (2001, p106) suggests that affordances are the 'attributes of the setting which provide potential for action'. As such, affordances can be considered as preconditions for activity, but, even though they are there, this does not mean that activity will take place, as the affordances need to be perceived by, in our context, the learner or teacher. As Hammond (2010, p206) points out, 'the affordance is there, it has always been there, but it needs to be perceived to be realised . . . The world is full of potential, not of things.' As such, we need to make the distinction between *'real'* (*actual*) and *perceived* properties (Norman, 1999). In other words, some affordances may be much more obvious than others and different people may see different affordances in the same object.

Put more simply, one example could be the handle on a door, which has many affordances – although, perhaps, little educational value beyond allowing access to the classroom. For instance, you could hang your coat on it, or even tie a skipping rope to it and have a tug of war with the door! In reality, the two main affordances are opening and shutting the door. In the same way, ICT hardware and software have many affordances and pupils are not afraid to 'play' to find these out – see more later in this book. The role of the teacher in this context is to be sure that the most suitable (educational) affordances of all resources (especially in this context of ICT) are identified and used, but also to provide the opportunity for pupils to see and use others. In doing this, however, you will need to be aware that affordances are not the same for everyone and different affordances can be seen by different people – some of your pupils might enjoy the challenge of door tug of war and see it as an obvious thing to do with the door handle! Perhaps the key thing to remember is that 'in an ICT-supported learning environment affordances are provided by interactions between the hardware, software, other resources, teachers and other students' (Webb, 2005, p707).

Considering the affordances of ICT (in terms of both hardware and software) can also be useful in many ways, particularly in taking into consideration how you are going to differentiate activities for different pupils or in different subjects – again, more on the latter will follow in later chapters. You will need to take account of several factors as the affordances for each may vary. These could include the age of the pupils, their level of maturity or independence, any special needs, or their knowledge of how to use a particular piece of software or hardware.

ACTIVITY

Consider a piece of software that you know well and identify the affordances it offers and how they could be used with a class you teach or are familiar with.

Person-plus – distributed cognition

The affordances outlined above form part of the surroundings in the classroom and are resources to be used. The importance of using these surroundings is stressed by Perkins (1997, p89), who makes the distinction between the *person-solo*, 'the person without resources in his or her surround', and the *person-plus*, 'the person plus [their] surround'. This theory suggests that 'thinking and learning for the person-plus depend only on what might be called the "access characteristics" of relevant knowledge – what kind of knowledge is represented, how it is represented, how readily it is retrieved, and related matters – and not whether the knowledge is located in the person or the surround'. The question posed to support this suggestion is this: if a pupil can access information about a specific thing from a notebook 'because they have organised it so well, does it really matter whether the ideas lie inside or outside the student's cranium?' (Perkins, 1997, p90). It is easy to see that ICT in many forms could replace the notebook in this example.

This idea is intended to help achieve an 'information flow analysis' in a person-plus situation, where thinking and learning are distributed between the pupil and their surroundings. The learner picks up information from various points in the system and uses it. The four components of this framework are discussed below.

Knowledge

For teachers, this involves factual and procedural knowledge, including knowledge of ICT hardware and software, as well as higher-order knowledge, such as problem-solving strategies, explanation, and knowledge and understanding of pedagogy. In this context, it is the teacher – rather than the pupils or the surroundings – who has much of the higher-order knowledge. This *teacher-solo* would have a 'rich technical repertoire' (of teaching) in long-term memory, but the teacher also needs more:, the 'plus' provided by things such as books, videos, ICT, and indeed the pupils themselves.

Representation

This relates to how the knowledge is represented, in particular, in ways that make it easily picked up, transported in the system, and recoded. In terms of ICT, this could be how ICT allows you to represent models of complex subjects, which Perkins suggests is of most benefit to 'less able learners'. The *teacher-solo* will have mental images, but the *teacher-plus* has other ways of representing and exploring ideas – and multimedia and multimodality may be particularly useful for this. This can range from pen and paper to using the various features of ICT. (See also use 'Representation' below, p43.)

Retrieval

Retrieval concerns whether the system can find the knowledge representations in question, and how efficiently it can do this. Perkins contends that knowledge can exist in a system, but may not have suitable 'retrieval characteristics' for it to be used effectively. Besides conventional ways of retrieving information from books, ICT allows quick and easy retrieval of information from a range of resources such as CD-ROMs, searchable databases and websites and, increasingly commonly, internet search engines such as

Google – although with these searches there are resultant issues of literacy to which we will return in Chapter 8.

Construction

This relates to the (knowledge-processing) system's capacity to assemble the pieces of knowledge retrieved into new knowledge structures. Perkins draws attention to the importance of this in view of problems caused by limitations in short-term memory, which make some concepts inaccessible to learners. It is suggested that a well-designed surround, including ICT, can provide a 'surrogate short-term memory' to support learners in mastering these concepts.

Perkins suggests that it should be possible for pupils to make better use of the cognitive resources around them to make their own 'personal-plus'. This includes their use of ICT resources, which would accord with theories of child-centred learning examined elsewhere in this book. The key message about the best use of ICT in the person-plus model is that it should allow learners to do more than they can do alone or with other non-ICT resources in the classroom. As Selwyn (2011, p82) states, 'the ability to passively retain information is less important than the skills to access and actively augment information stored elsewhere when required'. We will now consider where this information may be stored in both human and physical form.

Distributed cognition

As well as ICT resources, the primary classroom has many other resources, both human and physical. As Angeli (2008, pp271–2) asserts: 'Cognition in technology-enhanced classrooms is distributed throughout the system, which includes teachers, students, tools, and various artifacts . . . Thus, distributed cognitive systems should be considered as hybrid systems comprised of humans and physical artifacts.' These systems of learning, however, are dynamic, and are part of what Schwartz (2008, p389) calls 'a dynamic transaction between mind, materials, outcomes, and goals'. In these learning transactions your role as teacher can be made easier if you realise that you do not need to be the source of all knowledge (although you may need to know where to find it), and you need to be careful to use all aspects of your school environment (including classroom assistants, parents, governors, colleagues and indeed pupils) to help you and your pupils. An interesting example of using the whole primary school community is the way in which teachers are willing to learn from their pupils how to use the iPad. Beauchamp, Burden and Abbinett (2015, p173) report that 'in the classroom, teachers and pupils provided support to each other, and both were prepared to involve other family members and friends as "consultants" in solving problems'. In this instance, the cognition is distributed not only within the school, but also in the home and community – a theme we will return to in Chapter 10.

Interactive teaching

The interactions a pupil has with teachers, adult helpers, other pupils and their surroundings form the basis of the concept of interactivity. In Chapter 1 we began to consider the notion of teaching as a socio-cultural activity, where actions are mediated by tools (including ICT), with language being the most important. Nevertheless, the features of the setting and the pedagogic beliefs of teachers play an important role. As we have discussed above, the features of the setting can include resources that are physical (the classroom itself and equipment within it), human (everybody in the classroom) and intellectual (the belief system of the people). The pedagogic beliefs of the teacher will play an important role in deciding how these factors are used and by whom. Traditionally, the teacher will organise, or orchestrate, the features of the setting. The idea of orchestration is set in a socio-cultural perspective on activity, where, as we saw in Chapter 1, people and objects interact and provide the context for the activity. Beauchamp and Kennewell (2010, p760) suggest:

> *The people involved will include teachers, support staff, and students; objects commonly employed include books, pens, stories, ICT resources. Orchestration is a conscious and contingent arrangement, dynamic re-arrangement, and emphasis of these elements and their affordances in order to facilitate the achievement of goals. It may be carried out by the teacher, the students, or even ICT resources, often in combination.*

In this context, the 'role of the teacher is one of orchestrating and supporting the learner's exploration rather than directly providing instruction' (Selwyn, 2011, p74), and 'the successful learner can be seen as someone who is able to appropriate and deploy these resources in their actions' (ibid., p77). Allowing pupils to 'appropriate and deploy' resources forms part of interactive teaching. This is a commonly used phrase and has been advocated widely in official policy documents in recent years. Despite this extensive use, however, it is very difficult to find an actual definition of the term in these documents. In the academic literature, there have been many attempts to define interactive teaching, but a commonly accepted definition still remains elusive. This situation is complicated due to the many different types of interactivity that are possible within whole-class, group and individual work, especially in the primary classroom. What does emerge from the literature are attempts to characterise the features of interactive lessons. Burns and Myhill (2004) suggest the following characteristics:

- reciprocal opportunities for talk that allow children to develop independent voices in discussion;
- appropriate guidance and modelling when the teacher orchestrates (organises) the language and skills for thinking collectively;
- environments that are conducive to student participation;
- an increase in the level of student autonomy.

In lessons that display these characteristics, Hargreaves et al. (2003) suggest it is possible to identify different levels of interactivity, which may be broadly classified into two groups:

- *'Surface' interactivity* – engaging pupils, practical and active involvement or participation, collaborative activity, emphasising recall, conveying knowledge.
- *'Deep' interactivity* – assessing and extending knowledge, emphasising understanding, attention to thinking and learning skills (Hargreaves et al., 2003).

As we have seen above, ICT can contribute to both of these levels of interactivity, from engaging pupils with a new, but not necessarily challenging, feature of the technology (such as writing your name in smiley faces with your finger on the IWB) (surface), through to posing cognitively challenging activities designed to focus attention on thinking and learning skills (deep). It is suggested that most meaningful teaching at all ages should aim to move beyond surface to deep interactivity. One way of doing this is to combine effective talk with the use of ICT.

Dialogic teaching with ICT

We have already seen that language remains the most important tool in the classroom context. Alexander (2008, pp37–8) makes a compelling case for raising further the profile of talk in the classroom, but argues

> not for more of the same kind of classroom talk that children already encounter, but for a particular kind of interactive experience which we call dialogic teaching. Dialogic teaching harnesses the power of talk to engage children, stimulate and extend their thinking, and advance their learning and understanding. Not all classroom talk secures these outcomes, and some may even discourage them.

He goes on to outline the five most important principles of dialogic teaching; there are obvious overlaps with the features of interactive teaching already outlined above. Dialogic teaching is:

- *collective* – teachers and pupils work together;
- *reciprocal* – teachers and pupils listen to each other, share ideas and discuss different viewpoints;
- *supportive* – pupils speak freely, are not afraid of 'wrong' answers, and help each other to develop common understandings;
- *cumulative* – teachers and pupils build on each other's ideas and develop them into clear lines of thinking and enquiry;
- *purposeful* – teachers plan for and steer classroom talk with specific educational goals in view.

WHAT DO YOU THINK?

Consider a recent lesson you have seen or been part of and decide if it could be described as dialogic teaching. As you think about it, also consider what role, if any, ICT played. *If it was dialogic, what did the teacher do to make it so; if it was not, what needed to be done to make it dialogic?*

In making decisions about what constitutes dialogic teaching, it can be useful to contrast it with an 'authoritative' approach (Scott, Mortimer and Aguiar, 2006) – in which the views of the teacher dominate – and with 'dialectic' teaching – with an emphasis on overcoming disparities between students' thinking and formal knowledge (Wegerif, 2008). Beauchamp and Kennewell (2010, p760) suggest that 'effective teaching, however, is likely to demonstrate a variety of these characteristics in an appropriate combination; in particular, there is an important interplay between dialogic and dialectic forms of interaction, although the relative importance of each will depend on what is to be learned'.

From this perspective, and using the range of possible approaches considered above, we have now arrived at a point where we can consider in more detail how to transform them into tangible outcomes in the classroom, using ICT as appropriate. In the remainder of this chapter, we will examine how ICT can develop deep interactivity in the context of Shulman's (1987) model of pedagogic reasoning, as well as how it can be used in the context of dialogic and dialectic teaching in the primary classroom or early years setting. We will continue to adopt a generic perspective and will not yet consider in detail the potential impact of subject- or age-specific (especially early years) pedagogy, but this will be considered in later chapters. In doing so, we will be fulfilling in part the requirements for student teachers to have a knowledge and understanding of a range of teaching and learning strategies and to know how to use and adapt them. We will also, however, be moving beyond knowledge and understanding to develop a critically evaluative mindset that can be applied at all stages of a teacher's career.

Pedagogic reasoning and ICT in the primary classroom

The cycle of planning, teaching, assessing and evaluating is familiar to all teachers. In 1987, Shulman proposed a model of pedagogical reasoning and action that outlined the knowledge needed during this cycle:

- comprehension
- transformation
- instruction
- evaluation
- reflection
- new comprehensions.

In each of these categories there is a role for ICT, from your use of the internet to help your own comprehension, to providing affordances to help you transform what you have to teach, to providing many possible ways (multimodal and multimedia) to represent ideas or present analogies, and even to helping you record an evaluation of lessons. The decision to use ICT, however, and the sophistication of its use, can range from very simple to very complex depending on the age and ability of the class and your own ability to recognise the unique contribution that ICT can make. We will consider each stage of Shulman's model of pedagogic reasoning in more detail and suggest how ICT can contribute to each.

Comprehension

The first stage is comprehension. This is defined as comprehension of:

- purposes
- subject matter structures
- ideas within and outside the discipline.

From this list, it becomes apparent that it is not just understanding the subject, but, as Shulman (1987, p15) states, 'the key to distinguishing the knowledge base of teaching lies at the intersection of content and pedagogy, and the capacity of a teacher to transform the content knowledge he or she possesses into forms that are pedagogically powerful and yet adaptive to the variations in ability of background presented by the students'. Shulman makes it clear that teachers should understand what they teach and, when possible, to understand it in different ways, not only to reinforce comprehension but also to allow them to think of different forms of representation later in the process. In the primary and early years classroom or setting, it is also important to consider how your understanding, or comprehension, in one area of learning or in one subject can be integrated into and reinforce other areas. Although guidance is given by many official sources, and many books offer 'subject knowledge', there is still some freedom for teachers to develop their own understanding and how it can apply in the primary classroom. Having said this, the role of ICT in comprehension is perhaps rather limited, although it can play a part in developing your subject knowledge, especially the use of internet sources – although, as with its use with pupils, you need to be selective to ensure that you get information (and hence understanding) that is accurate.

Transformation

The next stage in the process is transforming your understanding into a form that can be understood by your pupils. Perhaps more than any other part of the process, the features and capabilities of ICT that we looked at in Chapter 1 offer unique ways of transforming and representing ideas. Shulman (1987, p16) suggests that transformations 'require some combination or ordering' of the following processes:

- preparation
- representation
- selection
- adaptation and tailoring to student characteristics.

It is important to note that these processes may not all be needed and should not be considered as sequential. As we have seen before, the teacher remains central to the success of using this model. It is the teacher who decides what will be combined with what and how this will be ordered, not the ICT. ICT can help mechanically in the process, but it cannot help with pedagogic decisions. You need to apply your own professional judgement when selecting from your curricular and ICT 'repertoire', which will increase throughout your career. This will apply particularly in 'preparation', when you consider how you can structure and segment your understanding into a suitable sequence of ideas as you transform your understanding of one 'big' idea into a series of smaller ones that can be understood by pupils. In this, you will be guided by your knowledge of how the features of ICT can effectively represent or demonstrate your analogies or examples. You will also consider how ICT can help you organise and manage your teaching. In addition, you will also need to reflect on how ICT can then be used, or not used, to meet the needs of your pupils. From this, it becomes obvious that there is no logical sequence to be followed, as it may be that a particular feature of ICT (for example, automation) triggers a thought about how to represent an idea, which in turn will guide how you organise your lesson. Or it could be that the needs of your pupils have to guide all other considerations. We will consider each process in more detail to establish how ICT can help.

Preparation

- Critical interpretation and analysis of 'texts', structuring and segmenting, development of a curricular repertoire, and clarification of purposes.

The word 'text' in this context can be considered as your starting point for the teaching activity. It could literally be a written text or could take any other form of material or idea that you need to interpret critically and/or analyse to use in teaching. Although researching with ICT can help in this, perhaps its most relevant use in this stage is in helping to structure and segment ideas. This feature is inherent in presentation programs such as PowerPoint, which, although perhaps a more functional use of ICT, forces you to consider the structure and sequence of ideas (using, for example, the 'slide sorter' view) as you organise and reorganise segments of a lesson or even a sequence of lessons. An important part of this process is deciding when you are going to leave the 'presentation' facility of ICT to make best use of another feature, or deciding not to use ICT at all, for example to undertake a practical activity. In addition, it is important to plan opportunities for talk and other interactions to develop dialogic and interactive lessons.

Representation

- Use of a representational repertoire, which includes analogies, metaphors, examples, demonstrations, explanations, and so forth.

A particular strength of ICT in this process is that it can meet Shulman's contention (1987, p16) that 'multiple forms of representation are desirable'. In Chapter 1 we discussed the potential of the multimedia and multimodal capabilities of ICT, and this is one area where they may be very useful. However, just because ICT *can* do this, it does not mean that it *should* be used. The main questions are the following:

1. Do the features of ICT allow it to provide representations (e.g. analogies, metaphors or examples) well and/or in a better way than any other resources?
2. Will this work for *my class* (with my ICT resources)?

The importance of the second question will be returned to in 'Adaptation and tailoring' below, but the first question is perhaps the most important. By considering each of the features of ICT (see Chapter 1), you can decide if one, or a combination of them, makes ICT the best choice of tool or medium to transform and organise your understanding into something meaningful for your class. The caveat here is that just using ICT will not be enough on its own – it will remain just part of your repertoire of teaching to be used in conjunction with other resources in a dialogic or interactive context.

Selection

Consideration of the use of ICT is part of the 'selection', which Shulman suggests is making a choice from among an 'instructional repertoire' that includes modes of teaching, organising, managing and arranging. The ability to do this will depend of your level of experience and will continue to evolve at all stages of your career. Modes of teaching could include whole-class and other types of grouping. Again, we will need to consider the best use of ICT within each of these contexts. For instance, much research has been done which shows that the IWB can be very effective in whole-class teaching (for example, Somekh et al., 2007), but it may be more appropriate to use laptops or iPads in group work – although there is no reason why the IWB cannot be used for a group activity on its own or as part of a 'circus' of activities. In addition, you may be more confident in certain types of classroom organisation at different points in your training or career, and this might be reflected in your ability to select from a 'repertoire' and your confidence in doing so.

Adaptation and tailoring to student characteristics

- Consideration of conceptions, preconceptions, misconceptions and difficulties, of language and culture, of motivations, social class, gender, age, ability, aptitude, interests and self-concepts, and of attention.

When making a 'selection', it is necessary to take account of the needs of your pupils. Although all teachers need high expectations of *all* pupils, it is important to acknowledge that not every group of learners is the same, as shown by the fact that teachers need to differentiate work in all lessons, even if doing the same lesson for two classes of the same age. Although there is a pragmatic use of ICT in accessing records of prior work and checking previous achievements (for example, difficulties and misconceptions), 'adaptation and tailoring' work to pupils perhaps make less use of ICT than other parts of this model of teaching, but remain central to effective lessons. As many of the features of adaptation and tailoring are covered in great detail in more generic teaching texts, and as we will be examining the impact of a pupil's age later in this book, we will consider here the potential impact of adapting and tailoring the ICT resources you have available.

As already mentioned, the first consideration is who is in control of the ICT. If the pupils are used to making use of ICT as an active tool through which to interact (see Beauchamp, 2011, and Table 2.1 on p34), you can tailor your use of ICT to this. If they are not used to this approach, you need to adapt ICT use (by you and the pupils) accordingly. In addition, you need to tailor your use of ICT to the relevant skills that you and your pupils possess in different areas of the curriculum. This can range from knowledge of the affordances of a particular piece of software to knowing how to manipulate a particular piece of hardware, such as the IWB or how to mirror a tablet device on the IWB. It is worth mentioning here that you also need to adapt your work to the version of the software used by the school, if relevant. It is very frustrating when you have used a newer version of software to develop ICT work at home, only to realise that the school uses an older version that will not open your files – especially if you are a student teacher and your tutor (or external examiner), or inspector, is watching you!

ACTIVITY

In groups, or on your own, decide on a topic, idea or concept that you are going to teach. Identify its 'big' ideas and organise these into the sequence in which they need to be taught to ensure sound understanding. Next, thinking of a class you are familiar with, break down each 'big' idea into smaller ideas that will need to be taught as part of this idea. Continue this process as necessary, and then decide which of these can be taught as they stand and which will need to be 'transformed'. When these ideas have been identified, split them into those that will use the features of ICT well, and those that are better done using other resources. Finally, decide how you will use ICT for some or all of the ideas.

Presentation packages, such as PowerPoint, can be useful for sequencing ideas. You can add slides for smaller ideas and also use the 'slide sorter' view to see the flow of ideas and to reorganise them as appropriate.

Instruction

- Management, presentations, interactions, group work, discipline, humour, questioning, and other aspects of active teaching, discovery or inquiry instruction, and the observable forms of classroom teaching.

When you reach the instruction stage, you have moved beyond the planning stage (which can take place anywhere) to actually being with a class of pupils ready to begin a lesson. You will already have checked that all the hardware and software are compatible and functioning, all the pupils are there, and you are ready to start your lesson. Although there are lots of pedagogic issues to be considered in the 'instruction' phase, many of them are related to generic classroom management. As above, these are covered in many existing texts on classroom teaching, so we will concentrate on how ICT can be used effectively in this context in a generic sense – we will consider its use in different subjects and areas of learning in later chapters.

We have already considered different types of interactions, so let us first consider management and presentation. ICT provides a good tool to manage and organise your lesson content through a variety of software. ICT also provides a wide range of media to present or share your lesson content, such as computers or visualisers, through a wide variety of modes, including movie and sound files. ICT also allows you the opportunity to use humour (an unexpected effect, image, movie clip or sound file) and pose questions or stimulate debate through unusual images. This can take many forms and is not always restricted by the limitations of a program if you are prepared to try new ideas and consider how the features of ICT can be used effectively or creatively.

CASE STUDY

PowerPoint has many limitations, and is ultimately a presentation program, but one teacher used it to show her class two contrasting automated slide shows of images, both accompanied by the Louis Armstrong song 'What a wonderful world'. The first showed some of the wonders of the world, such as the diversity of life in a rain forest, pyramids, waterfalls and so on; the second, with the same song in the background, was of devastated rain forests, polluted seas, war zones and so on. The rest of the lesson concentrated on a discussion of the content. ICT had served its purpose, to do something it was good at, and was not used again.

Evaluation

- Checking for student understanding during interactive teaching.
- Testing student understanding at the end of lessons or units.

ICT tools in general are not good at helping you reflect on your lessons; an exception, perhaps, is video recordings of lessons used on some training courses. What it can do is provide a quick way of testing pupils' understanding through the use of tests or other activities and of keeping a record of outcomes. The limitation of this is ICT's inability to provide formative feedback beyond pre-programmed responses. Again, you need to make decisions about why you are using ICT and decide if it serves a purpose to advance learning.

Evaluating one's own performance and adjusting for experiences: reflection and new comprehensions

In addition to evaluating the outcome of the lesson for the pupils, we also need to evaluate our own performance as a teacher. As mentioned above, video-recording lessons can be useful and ICT can help you record your thoughts and your new understanding, but in reality it is possibly less useful here than in other parts of this process.

SUMMARY

In this chapter we have considered how and when ICT should be used and who should use it. We have examined the concepts of interactive and dialogic teaching and how ICT can allow both teachers and learners to become active partners (co-constructors of knowledge) in the learning process. We have also considered some of the strengths of ICT in relation to Shulman's model and the different roles it can play in the classroom for both teachers and pupils. As the role of the teacher changes to facilitate greater pupil autonomy (at all ages), the next chapter will consider how this can be developed in the context of the primary classroom.

References

Angeli, C. (2008) 'Distributed cognition', *Journal of Research on Technology in Education*, 40(3), pp271–9.

Beauchamp, G. (2011) 'Interactivity and ICT in the primary school: categories of learner interactions with and without ICT', *Technology, Pedagogy and Education*, 20(2), pp175–90.

Beauchamp, G., Burden, K. and Abbinett, E. (2015) 'Teachers learning to use the iPad in Scotland and Wales: a new model of professional development', *Journal of Education for Teaching: International Research and Pedagogy*, 41(2), pp161–79.

Burns, C. and Myhill, D. (2004) 'Interactive or inactive? A consideration of the nature of interaction in whole class teaching', *Cambridge Journal of Education*, 34(1), pp35–49.

Conole, G. and Dyke, M. (2004) 'What are the affordances of information and communication technologies?', *ALT-J: Research in Learning Technology*, 12(2), pp113–24.

Gibson, J.J. (1986) *The Ecological Approach to Visual Perception*, Hillsdale, NJ: Lawrence Erlbaum Associates.

Hammond, M. (2010) 'What is an affordance and can it help us understand the use of ICT in education?', *Education and Information Technology*, 15(3), pp205–17.

Hargreaves, L., Moyles, J., Merry, R., Paterson, F., Pell, A. and Esarte-Sarries, V. (2003) 'How do primary school teachers define and implement "interactive teaching" in the National Literacy Strategy in England?', *Research Papers in Education*, 18(3), pp217–36.

John, P. and Sutherland, R. (2005) 'Affordance, opportunity and the pedagogical implications of ICT', *Educational Review*, 57(4), pp405–13.

Kennewell, S. (2001) 'Using affordances and constraints to evaluate the use of ICT in teaching and learning', *Journal of IT and Teacher Education*, 10(1&2), pp101–16.

Norman, D.A. (1999) 'Affordance, conventions, and design', *Interactions*, 6(3), pp38–43.

Pea, R.D. (1997) 'Distributed intelligence and designs for education', in Salomon, G. (ed.) *Distributed Cognitions: Psychological and Educational Considerations*, Cambridge: Cambridge University Press, pp47–87.

Perkins, D.N. (1997 [1993]) 'Person-plus: a distributed view of thinking and learning', in Salomon, G. (ed.) *Distributed Cognitions: Psychological and Educational Considerations*, Cambridge: Cambridge University Press, pp88–110.

Schwartz, N.H. (2008) 'Exploiting the use of technology to teach: the value of distributed cognition', *Journal of Research on Technology in Education*, 40(3), pp89-404.

Scott, P.H., Mortimer, E.F. and Aguiar, O.G. (2006) 'The tension between authoritative and dialogic discourse: a fundamental characteristic of meaning making interactions in high school science lessons', *Science Education*, 90, pp605–31.

Selwyn, N. (2011) *Education and Technology: Key Issues and Debates*, New York: Continuum International Publishing Group.

Shulman, L.S. (1987) 'Knowledge and teaching: foundations of the new reform', *Harvard Educational Review*, Feb., pp1–22.

Somekh, B., Haldane, M., Jones, K., Lewin, C., Steadman, S., Scrimshaw, P., Sing, S., Bird, K., Cummings, J., Downing, B., Harber Stuart, T., Jarvis, J., Mavers, D. and Woodrow, D. (2007) *Evaluation of the Primary Schools Whiteboard Expansion Project: Summary Report*, Manchester: Manchester Metropolitan University, Centre for ICT, Pedagogy and Learning.

Warwick, P. and Kershner, R. (2008) 'Primary teachers' understanding of the interactive whiteboard as a tool for children's collaborative learning and knowledge-building', *Learning, Media and Technology*, 33(4), pp269–87.

Webb, M. (2005) 'Affordances of ICT in science learning: implications for an integrated pedagogy', *International Journal of Science Education*, 27(6), pp705–35.

Wegerif, R. (2008) 'Dialogic or dialectic? The significance of ontological assumptions in research on educational dialogue', *British Educational Research Journal*, 34(3), pp347–61.

Further reading

Alexander, R. (2008) *Dialogic Teaching*, 4th edition, York: Dialogos.

Beauchamp, G. and Kennewell, S. (2010) 'Interactivity in the classroom and its impact on learning', *Computers and Education*, 54, pp759–66.

Shulman, L.S. (1987) 'Knowledge and teaching: foundations of the new reform', *Harvard Educational Review*, Feb., pp1–22.

3 ICT and the child: theories of learning

In this chapter we will focus on learners and how they learn. After a brief examination of *why* children need to learn, we will continue to examine a range of learning theories and relate them to the role and purpose of ICT.

So far we have discussed theories of ICT pedagogy, but we now need to explore how these are based upon more generic theoretical perspectives on how children learn. This process is not straightforward, as these perspectives are informed by, and situated in, complex and contested views of the nature and purpose of education itself. Bartlett and Burton (2007, p11) sum up the views of many when they suggest that 'the meaning of the term "education" and its purpose is not universally fixed and is not the same for all of us'. They suggest that it is shaped by factors including individual experiences and a range of beliefs and values. Perhaps the most important of all in terms of their impact are the beliefs and values of decision makers (including leaders at both national and local levels) and their resultant vision of the role of ICT in education. As such, although there is not space to explore all the relevant issues in depth, it is necessary to consider briefly the role and purpose of education in its widest sense and how ICT may fit within this to see how these views may be formed.

What is education for and what is the role of ICT within it?

We can begin by acknowledging that there exist many different, and sometimes irreconcilable, ideologies of education and that these emphasise different targets, such as:

- *the individual* – an emphasis on individual development based on the needs of the learner;
- *formal knowledge* for its own sake – either in subjects or in a less prescribed format;
- *society* – the importance of education to the economy or to democratising or reshaping society.

There is a role for ICT in all of these systems and sometimes it can even influence the direction of education. As Kelly (2009, p5) points out, when considering the major changes in education in recent years, it is not surprising that

the nature and structure of our education system should have been changing so
extensively at a time when we have been experiencing social change of an equally
dramatic kind, much of it prompted by a rapid technological advance . . . the education
system is a social institution which should be expected to change along with other such
institutions.

One rather extreme view of the impact of ICT, or more specifically computers, was offered in the late 1970s by the influential writer Seymour Papert (1993, p9) when he suggested that 'schools as we know them today will have no place in the future. But it is an open question whether they will adapt by transforming themselves into something new or wither away and be replaced.' One of the premises of this book is that the creative and imaginative use of ICT will allow teachers and pupils to transform primary schools into something new. Many of the ideas discussed, however, apply just as well to the use of ICT within a virtual environment, with no physical structure or location that pupils attend. Indeed, many primary schools increasingly use new technologies to transform the classroom *and* use virtual learning environments (VLEs) to provide both a real and a virtual approach to schooling, hence resolving Papert's dichotomy above.

Other less radical views of the importance and role of ICT reflect the educational ideologies discussed above and are summarised in Table 3.1.

What is immediately apparent from this table is that primary schools have a role to play in all of these categories. What is also evident is that some areas are addressed by the curriculum and others by extracurricular activities. Even within the curriculum, some areas, such as I(C)T skills, may be specific to one subject in the first instance, but then applied across different areas of learning or subjects – see more later.

If we accept that, whatever justification is adopted, children will need to be educated, we now need to consider how they will actually learn and how ICT can contribute. We need to be aware, however, that even theories of learning can be subject to the same

Table 3.1	Three purposes of education	
Individual	**Formal learning**	**Society**
ICT provides the means to: • increase attainment and/or achievement through personalised learning • enhance access, especially for those with special educational needs (SEN) • provide access to remote learners, teachers and content	• ICT provides access to a large body of knowledge with information available directly from primary sources – and some less reputable sources! • This information can be retrieved quickly and in a variety of formats	Children need to learn ICT skills: • as a necessity for economic competitiveness in a knowledge society • as preparation for the world of work • to access information and learning that allow children of all backgrounds to develop and succeed and to develop greater economic activity in the longer term through increased e-commerce

ideological influences. This does not make them less valuable, and while the advocacy of a particular theory examined below may be based on ideological influences at a meta-level (such as the government) or at a micro-level (such as an individual teacher in the classroom), decisions are made to use many, or even all, theories based on the needs of individual children.

ICT and how children learn: learning theory and learners

What is learning?

As with trying to define the purpose and nature of education, it is difficult to come up with an agreed definition of learning. Therefore, it is perhaps best to work with a broad conception of what happens when someone learns something. Woolfolk, Hughes and Walkup (2008, p244) suggest that, broadly speaking, learning occurs when 'experience causes a relatively permanent change in an individual's knowledge or behaviour'. They suggest that these changes are not the result of maturation and propose that temporary changes caused by, for example, illness or fatigue should be excluded (as you do not learn to be hungry just because you do not have food). This definition, however, highlights one of the essential difficulties with studying learning in that we can *see* changes in behaviour, but it is much harder to assess what someone knows or understands – particularly when they may not be able to express themselves clearly due to maturational, linguistic or other factors. As Meadows (2004, p142) points out, 'we do not directly observe thinking or other cognitive processes, we infer them from observable behavior'. Nevertheless, it is this emphasis on observable behaviours that brings us to the first of our learning theories: behaviourism.

Behaviourism

Although it dates from the Enlightenment period, behaviourism is a 'philosophy, theory and pedagogy' which was a 'strong force' in education from early in the twentieth century until the mid-1970s (Woollard, 2010, pp1–2). It is predicated on the idea that all behaviours are the result of conditioning, caused by interactions with the environment. Behaviourists suggest that if the resultant behaviours are observed in a systematic way, there is no need to consider consciousness or internal states. Although we necessarily need to summarise the key ideas of behaviourism, in order to see how this theory can be applied to ICT in education we need to consider the distinction between the two major types of conditioning: classical and operant or instrumental.

Classical conditioning

In classical conditioning, the key idea is the linking of stimulus and response. The most famous example, and the foundation for much that followed, was the work of Pavlov (1927). Pavlov found that dogs could be taught to salivate at a given signal that food was about to arrive. The response was not to the unconditioned stimulus provided by the food, but to the conditioned stimulus (to the signal, such as a buzzer) and 'when the response is elicited only from the conditioned stimulus, it is regarded as a conditioned response' (Jarvis, Holford and Griffin, 2003, p27). These ideas were extended to humans by Watson (1925). For our purposes, we need to understand that, although some dispute whether this approach results in learning, as it is simply reflexive, it can have an impact in some situations – how many teachers feel thirsty or need to visit the toilet when a bell goes for break time!

Operant conditioning

In operant conditioning, the central idea, originating from the work of Skinner (1938), is the linking of reward and punishment with behaviour, resulting in an association between a type of behaviour and the consequence of it. The name derives from the idea that a person can act, or operate, on their environment to attain the outcome they desire. There are three components to this process: the antecedents (what comes before), the behaviour and the consequences (Yeomans and Arnold, 2006). The consequences (such as the reaction of a teacher or indeed a computer) can encourage or discourage and are labelled as reinforcers or punishers accordingly. In classroom terms, and for the purposes of how these ideas apply to ICT, this may simply be regarded as praise or punishment – the latter being interpreted as covering many approaches, such as sanctions, adopted in a school's behaviour management policy, rather than merely any physical act.

An extension of operant conditioning that we must also consider briefly is the concept of programmed learning. Despite the obvious contemporary link with computing in the name, this idea was not originally related to computer use but was a more general view on how learning could be developed. An example of this approach could be where children have been given some information that is then tested. Next,

> a correct response was rewarded in some way (typically with praise); an incorrect response would lead to their being given either a repeat of the original information, or an alternative (simpler) presentation. Programmed learning was often implemented in expensive 'teaching machines' which presented the materials in the appropriate sequence.

> (Long, 2007, p15)

One of the implications of the rapid advances in ICT technology discussed above is that such 'machines' (in the form of computers or other devices) are now readily available in the classroom, and indeed in many homes, at an affordable cost. In this context, we need to consider carefully when, or if, it is appropriate to use them as 'teaching machines' in the process of computer-assisted learning (CAL).

The distinction between classical and operant conditioning

Although there are many more subtle distinctions, the key difference between classical and operant conditioning for our purposes is the nature of the response. In classical conditioning the response is involuntary and not under conscious control (such as heart rate), whereas in operant conditioning the response is voluntary and under conscious control (such as the behaviour of a child to get praise from a teacher).

Behaviourism, learners and ICT

Transmission

In a behaviourist view of learning, the 'minds of learners are seen as spaces to be filled, their objective is to accumulate knowledge of this world and the teacher's task to interpret and transmit this to the learners' (Cook, 2010, p39). The idea of 'transmission' of information is central to understanding this model of learning and how it links to ICT. In earlier chapters we have already seen that ICT is good at transmitting information (such as through a video) and we have also noted that ICT can do this quickly, using a range of different modes and media. However, just because ICT can do this, it does not necessarily make it suitable for use in learning and teaching. While there are times when teachers need to 'transmit' information (such as the details of a task), in most contemporary primary classrooms this would be limited. One of the main reasons for this is the belief of many teachers that the classroom should be a more democratic place (see 'Experiential learning' below).

WHAT DO YOU THINK?

When, if ever, is it appropriate to 'transmit' information or ideas? In deciding this you may want to consider if it varies depending on the age of the pupils, the subject or area of learning, the location (e.g. in the classroom or outside) or other school factors (such as approaching tests).

Stimulus and response

The other central idea of behaviourism we need to consider in relation to ICT is that of stimulus and response, which we will look at alongside programmed learning. As above, this is also an area where the features of ICT (see Chapter 1) can make it very effective, but can also impose limitations. Unlike humans, a computer's ability to respond time and again is limited only by technical reliability, rather than by boredom or other more human factors. This can also, however, be a fundamental limitation. Anyone involved in interactions with a learner in a primary classroom would not want to keep responding in the same way. They would realise that they need to modify their response to take account of a range of factors, such as the level of learner engagement or their ability to understand what was being asked of them. Indeed, the sheer variety of responses offered by an experienced classroom practitioner, and the subtle nuances of response they can adapt to, cannot be matched (at least not at the moment!) by a computer or by another ICT resource, however well programmed. Hopefully, the result is that the learner remains interested, rather than potentially becoming bored or disenchanted by the programmed responses of a computer. Indeed, Papert (1993, p19) provides an important warning about the dangers of 'computer programming the child' in a situation where 'the computer is used to put children through their paces, to provide exercises of an appropriate level of difficulty, to provide feedback and to dispense information'.

Advances in technology mean that this warning now applies to many other ICT devices as well as computers, and as teachers we must be mindful that we are selecting ICT resources that allow children some control over their own learning.

Reward and sanction

We have seen above that rewards and sanctions are an essential feature of operant conditioning in human behaviour, but the ability to offer these is not restricted to humans. One of the ways in which ICT resources help to avoid boredom (and potentially increase motivation) is through the use of rewards, and even sanctions. The rewards can range from reaching a new level, taking ownership of a new monster or printed certificates, while sanctions can range from repeating a level through to more prosaic sound effects.

This should not be taken to mean that there is no place for stimulus and response with rewards and sanctions. What is suggested is that this use of ICT must be matched closely to the likely effectiveness. It may be that in learning, or assessing, basic number bonds or times tables, a limited use of this approach may be suitable; although it should not be offered as a replacement for more effective or creative approaches and its effectiveness should be closely monitored. One reason for monitoring closely, which is a direct outcome of the features of ICT (especially through experience of using computer and console games – see Chapter 1), is the fact that a learner can achieve an answer, or a solution to a problem, through trial and error rather than through logic or reasoning. It is suggested that the likelihood of trial and error being used increases the longer a learner is left unsupervised or not monitored.

Constructivism

We have seen above that in behaviourist theories the learner is acted upon by others to achieve learning. The central idea of constructivist views of learning is that, although still focusing on the individual (as opposed to more social models of learning), the learner takes a central role in constructing their own knowledge and understanding. The distinction is neatly summed up by Jones and Mercer (1993, p15), who state that:

> whereas in operant conditioning the emphasis is on the learner 'being shaped' by the instructor (or computer) through selective reinforcement, here [constructivism] the learner is seen as an active participant, who, in the course of learning, is structuring his or her experience or knowledge.

As with behaviourism, we need to consider briefly two main areas of constructivism – cognitive constructivism and social constructivism – in general terms before moving to examine how they apply to ICT.

Cognitive constructivism

Much of the work in this area is based on the ideas of Piaget and the early work of Bruner in the first half of the twentieth century. Cognitive constructivists consider how the individual learner develops knowledge, as opposed to social constructivism, which is based on examining social relations in learning – see more below. For our purposes, we will concentrate on the views of Piaget and his stages of cognitive development – 'ages and stages'. We do not need to cover each stage in detail, as this has been covered by many writers elsewhere, but we do need to recognise the key principles of this stage theory:

- Each stage has specific characteristics and is associated with a specific age range from birth to age 15.
- A child cannot 'jump' stages but must pass through all of them.
- As children grow older their ability to conceptualise develops.

In this theory, learning is closely linked to the stage of development and is a cumulative process. Given that each stage is built upon the preceding one, and 'if, therefore, cognitive frameworks depend on what had preceded, it is important to regulate the difficulty level and order of presentation of material' (Child, 2007, p103). The judgement about difficulty may be a professional one, but there is a role for ICT in helping to order the presentation of material.

In terms of ICT, it is not difficult to see the influence of stages of development in the labelling of software as age specific, for instance.

WHAT DO YOU THINK?

Should we, as teachers, accept such labels, or should we make our own judgement based on ability or experience? Or, indeed, should we allow children to make their own judgements?

In terms of differentiation, it is also important to note that children with additional learning needs may not fit such categories neatly. Overall, the theoretical Piagetian link between age and development may be less important in making decisions about the use of ICT resources, such as a piece of software, than professional judgement based on the reality of the child in your class, regardless of their age – particularly given the increasing exposure of very young children to sophisticated ICT in the home prior to formal schooling (this is examined in Chapter 4).

To explore further how Piaget's theory can be linked to ICT, it is necessary to also examine his views on the way in which knowledge is structured in schemata. Each schema allows a child to hold a cognitive representation of something. These concepts vary from child to child, but are based on perceived important properties of the idea represented. For instance, a bird schema may be that birds can fly, and have two wings and two legs. As the child adds new knowledge to the bird schema – for instance by seeing high-definition pictures of the shapes of different bird wings through the use of ICT – a process of assimilation takes place. Such a process will not change the fundamental property that birds have two wings. There will, however, also be occasions when a child discovers something, such as a bird that does not fly, which does not fit into the properties of the existing schema and means it must be changed. These changes are known as accommodation and can again be influenced by experience gained through ICT, by, for instance, seeing movies of penguins on the interactive whiteboard (IWB).

Although hugely influential, Piaget's theories have also been criticised because, among other reasons, they assume a close relationship between achievement and biological age, rather than considering the influence of the wider world in which the child lives and how this may impact at any age. This may be particularly true of experience of ICT, where children's ICT skills may be well in advance of other skills and greater than we may expect of someone their age. The impact of the wider world, and those who inhabit it, led to the development of social constructivist theories.

Social constructivism: socio-cultural theory

When considering behaviourist and cognitive theories, it should be noted that both theories focus on the leaner as an individual, isolated from their social context – even if working with others. In reality, as Jones and Mercer (1993, p20) rightly assert, learning 'may seem a solitary endeavour, but in practice nearly all learning (of computer skills or anything else) is in some sense a social experience: some person – colleague, tutor, manual author – is involved as well as the learner'. They continue to suggest that we cannot just consider theories of learning, but need to examine theoretical frameworks that take account of 'teaching-and-learning'. In this model of teaching-and-learning, great emphasis is placed on the ability of all involved to communicate with each other. In this book, this includes the ability to do this using a variety of communication tools in order to work with others who may not be physically present, using both synchronous (in real time) and/or asynchronous (at different times) technologies. The advantages of real-time communication (such as immediate responses) are perhaps more apparent, but Conole and Dyke (2004) also point out the advantages of asynchronous technologies, such as blogs, which are being used in primary schools today. They suggest that such technologies have 'the potential for encouraging reflection and critique, with users engaging in discussions over a longer time frame than is possible in face-to-face discussions. In addition, users are able to access and build on archived material available from earlier discussion' (Conole and Dyke, 2004, p118).

We should note that in these situations those involved in the learning are not communicating with, or expecting a response from, the computer (or other ICT tool), but with and from another learner – the ICT is not the object of the interaction, but a tool through which to interact. The ICT resource, although capable of giving pre-programmed responses or lots of information, is a medium that 'reorganises interactions among people, creating new environments in which children can be educated and grow by gaining access to the world around them' (Jones and Mercer, 1993, p23). With recent advances in using ICT, such as voice recognition, touch-sensitive screens and gesture recognition, such opportunities are available to children of all ages and abilities.

The ideas of socio-cultural theory, in particular the work of Vygotsky, provide a suitable framework to analyse and discuss how ICT can contribute to a socio-constructivist view of teaching and learning.

Vygotsky

Although relatively little known in the West until after his death in 1934, Vygotsky's influence has grown in recent years. (McIntyre, 2000) He was familiar with behaviourist theories and with the work of Piaget but

> *took issue with the Piagetian view that from the time of their birth children learn independently by exploring the environment, and with the behaviourist view that adults are entirely responsible for shaping children's learning by the judicious use of rewards and punishments.*

(Williams and Burden, 1997, p39, cited in Pachler, 1999)

One of the key differences with the ideas of Piaget is that Vygotsky draws attention to the *potential achievement* of a child, particularly when collaborating with others, rather than his or her *independent achievement*. Unlike Piaget's conception that cognitive development precedes learning, Vygotsky (1978, p90) suggests that 'the development process lags behind the learning process; this sequence then results in zones of proximal development' (ZPDs). Although these zones may differ in size between individuals (an important part of this theory for teachers to remember), the key idea is that the learner has the potential to make progress if working with 'adult guidance or in collaboration with more capable peers' (ibid., p86). As such, Jarvis, Holford and Griffin (2003, p37) propose that 'we cannot draw inferences from what individuals do independently. We need to try and see their potential rather than their achievements.' When considering the use of ICT in the primary school, or indeed at any stage of learning, we need to consider how it can facilitate this type of collaboration, and hence help fulfil potential. It is suggested, however, that this change in the role of ICT does not diminish the role of the teacher in any way; in fact, it may even call for greater skill or the development of new skills. The ability to judge the size of the ZPD for each child, as well as making judgements about who might be classified as a more capable peer, or when to use adults instead, call for both skill and professional judgement on the part of the teacher, as well as an understanding of how ICT can be used effectively in this context.

Constructivism, learners and ICT

It was noted earlier that it is sometimes hard to see evidence of what learners know and how they learned it. Although children can be explicitly asked to explain an answer or a viewpoint, there may be many barriers (depending on age and ability) that may prevent them giving an explanation which reflects their true understanding. This is particularly true when an answer has been arrived at in collaboration with others. One of the features of using ICT in the primary school in a constructivist approach, however, is that it can help make visible things that children know – for instance, through the use of the IWB in a class discussion or a concept mapping exercise – which would not be apparent otherwise. Recent studies (for example, Warwick and Kershner, 2008; Mercer, Hennessy and Warwick, 2010) have shown that using the IWB in particular (and other ICT resources) can be a very valuable way of supporting pupils' learning through, for instance, increased participation, motivation and the sharing of ideas.

CASE STUDY

A Key Stage 2 class was studying the Second World War. A local landmark had been bombed and the class had a copy of a letter from a child who had lived near enough to see what happened. The teacher used the IWB flipchart software to display a section of the letter showing what the child had written describing the events and the aftermath – the pupils would later get paper copies of the whole letter. In the text of the letter, the teacher had inserted hyperlinks to images of the landmark before and after the bombing and other links to images of local landmarks that were mentioned in the letter. The teacher had also inserted a link to a map of the area on another page of the flipchart. The teacher had got another child in the school to read the extract and had digitally recorded it so that when the text was clicked on the IWB the extract was read by a child of the same age as the writer. This was used at the beginning of the lesson to introduce the topic. The pupils then clicked on the links to view the images. At the same time, the teacher used a blank page of the flipchart for the pupils to write key words and phrases for later written work. The pupils then used the IWB pens to annotate the map, showing where the bombs had been dropped based on the evidence from the letter. They discussed how this would have affected the area and the people who lived there throughout this work with the IWB. This dialogue and participation were the main focus of the lesson, but the ICT tools motivated and enhanced it. Most of the same things could be done using posters, printed pictures and bits of paper, but the ICT automated this process, allowing the work to be quicker, with better-quality images that could be seen by the whole class, with participation by all, and done in one place with the IWB as a 'digital hub'– see more in Chapter 5 – for accessing a variety of modes and media.

The use of ICT in collaborative work can also facilitate tasks addressing the ZPD, as identified by Vygotsky, although this can also be done with more traditional resources. The guiding principle is that, as stated before, ICT should be used when it can do things better and/or quicker than other resources.

Experience-based learning – John Dewey

The idea that learners can take an active role in supporting each other, for instance in the ZPD activities noted above, is also a feature of democratic pedagogy, originating from the ideas of the American John Dewey in the late nineteenth and early twentieth centuries. Alexander (2008, p80) sums up democratic pedagogy as follows:

[It rejects] the traditional domination–subordination relationship between teacher and taught, makes knowledge reflexive rather than disciplinary, the child an active agent in his or her own learning, and the classroom a workshop or laboratory. In all these aspects the classroom seeks to enact the ideals of the wider democratic society. Negotiation thus stands in conscious antithesis to both transmission and induction.

Dewey's influence, particularly in America, was significant as part of what became known as the Progressive movement. In *The School and Society*, published in 1899, Dewey proposed a 'new education' based on a 'conception of experience-based practical learning [which would] form habits of inquiry and co-operation securing democratic life' (Waks quoted in Dewey, 2001, p387). The concept of negotiation is central to understanding this theory, and learners take an active role in their own learning and have the ability to influence decisions. This idea was to influence constructivist and other theories that followed. In 1921, Schneider (1921, p136, cited in Brehony, 1997, p429) introduced Dewey's idea to British readers as follows:

The emphasis on natural development is supposed to come directly from Rousseau. The idea of 'learning by doing' is attributed largely to Pestalozzi. The educational use of play is attributed largely to Froebel and the idea of freedom to Montessori.

By building on these ideas, Dewey suggested that children should learn in a democratic classroom through

purposive and conscious activity; not Froebel's 'drawing out' nor Herbart's 'putting in' but rather the giving of direction to pupils' activities. These activities were held to arise from impulses or instincts which could be classified into four groups which were available for guidance in the school. These Dewey labelled, the social instinct, the instinct of making, the instinct of investigation and the expressive impulse.

(Brehony, 1997, p435)

What should be apparent by now is that the features of ICT can cater for all of these groups and, indeed, they provide an appropriate framework for classifying ICT activities.

ACTIVITY

Using the following headings, identify ICT activities in different areas of learning or subjects:

The social instinct	The instinct for making	The instinct for investigation	The expressive impulse

Experiential learning

Dewey's ideas contributed to the centrality of the learner's experience in their own learning, developing the notion of child-centred learning. The concept of experiential learning, however, is on one level very simple (in that we will apprehend the world around us as we learn, whether planned or unplanned), but also complex (each person's experience is different and subjective). In examining the ideas of Dewey, we have taken a slightly narrow view of experiential learning, but this is deliberate as we are accepting Jarvis, Holford and Griffin's (2003) suggestion that *all* learning is experiential in some way. They suggest, rightly, that the term 'experiential learning' has become a 'new orthodoxy' and, as such, is largely redundant except when educators deliberately plan learning 'in which the learners have primary experience of the external world' (ibid., p67). In this view, ICT may appear to have little to offer, except when the ICT forms part of the real world – although this does reinforce the importance of presenting ICT and computing in 'real' contexts. If we accept only primary experience, however, we are losing important experiences that can be gained through mediated experience. It is in this context that ICT can play an important part in experiential learning.

Multiple intelligences – Gardner

The four instinct groups identified above when considering the ideas of Dewey also provide an early precursor to the idea that children may have instincts, or intelligences, in more than one area. Much later, in 1983, Howard Gardner published *Frames of Mind*, which, he later stressed, he wrote as a 'psychologist and [he] thought that he was addressing principally his colleagues in psychology. He devoted little of the book to educational implications and never expected that his ideas would be picked up by educators, first in the United States and then, eventually, in many countries across the globe' (Gardner, 2008, p1). Despite this, his 'theory of multiple intelligences' (MI theory) – rather than a single, unitary intelligence – has become very influential in educational settings. As much has been written on this elsewhere, for our purposes it is only necessary to list his original intelligences:[1]

1. Linguistic intelligence
2. Logical-mathematical intelligence
3. Musical intelligence
4. Bodily-kinaesthetic intelligence
5. Spatial intelligence
6. Intrapersonal intelligence
7. Interpersonal intelligence.

It is important to note immediately, however, that due to the popularity of Gardner's ideas in educational circles, there have been many interpretations of his original ideas. As he did not consider himself an educator, Gardner (2008) asserts that he 'did not lay out – and indeed never has laid out – a program for the education of multiple intelligences'. However, to mark the twenty-fifth anniversary of his ideas, and to counter some 'radical abuse' of them, he wrote about 'the various myths and misunderstanding of MI theory – for example, confusing an intelligence with a learning style, or asserting that all children are strong in at least one intelligence'. Given the common use of VAK (visual–audio–kinaesthetic) ideas in primary school, often based on the assumption that MI can help identify learning styles, some may be surprised by the first myth, but it should encourage us to read first-hand materials wherever possible – see more in Chapter 4.

For the purposes of this chapter, it is also important to note that Gardner (2008) continues to suggest that he

> *now believes that any serious application of MI ideas should entail at least two components:*

1. An attempt to individuate education as much as possible. The advent of personal computers should make this goal much easier to attain.
2. A commitment to convey important ideas and concepts in a number of different formats. This activation of multiple intelligences holds promise of reaching many more students and also demonstrating what it means to understand a topic thoroughly and deeply.

While the role of ICT in the first component is explicit (and should not be restricted to computers), we should also recognise from previous chapters that the ability to present ideas and concepts using a variety of modes and media is also a strength of ICT. Perhaps the most important idea to take forward to the next chapters is that Gardner's ideas relate to the *potential* existence of more than one intelligence, and the role of ICT should be to *activate* these intelligences, rather than be employed trying to satisfy or facilitate supposed learning styles. Indeed, Gardner himself (2008) suggests that one of the ways in which MI theory could expand is in the 'devising of computer software and virtual realities that present or teach the same topics via the activation of several intelligences'.

Even if you do not believe in the existence of multiple intelligences, using them as a framework to ensure that you exploit all the facilities of ICT may be a useful activity. In Figure 3.1, a start has been made on such an exercise.

ACTIVITY

In groups, or on your own, add more ICT activities, resources or programs to the outer boxes in Figure 3.1.

Goals of instruction – theory into practice

Given the multitude and complexity of the theories explored above, it is should be obvious that no one theory will cater for every situation. As in all aspects of teaching, in reality you will start with the learning you want to achieve and then decide the best way of attaining it. Although aimed at those designing educational software, Dabbagh (n.d.) provides a useful summary of how the theories examined above can

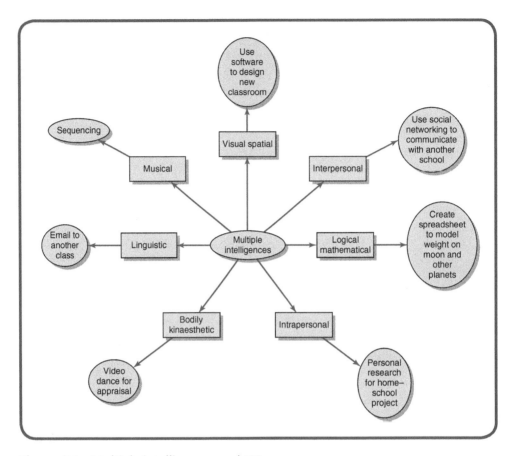

Figure 3.1   Multiple intelligences and ICT

be linked to the outcomes of lessons using ICT – see the website for more information. Dabbagh uses three competing schools of thought summarised by Dede (2008, p45) as follows:

1. Objectivism posits that reality is external and is objective, and knowledge is gained through experiences. Behaviourists believe that, since learning is based on experience, instruction centres are manipulating environmental factors to create instructional events, inculcating content and procedures in ways that alter students' behaviours.
2. Pragmatism posits that reality is mediated through cognitively developed representations, and knowledge is negotiated through experience and thinking. Cognitivists believe that, since learning involves both experience and thinking, instruction centres on helping learners develop interrelated, symbolic mental constructs that form the basis of knowledge and skills.
3. Interpretivism posits that reality is internal, and knowledge is constructed. Constructivists believe that, since learning involves constructing one's own knowledge, instruction centres on helping learners to actively invent individual meaning from experience.

None of these schools of thought should be regarded as a single unified theory; they are a collection of theories loosely related by a common set of fundamental assumptions. The major theorists for each school of thought, which have been examined above, are listed in Table 3.2 – see Dabbagh (n.d.) for more theorists and the full version of the table.

Although there may be times when the teacher uses all of these schools of thought, it is suggested that most ICT use (especially in an interactive or dialogic classroom) will be based on the constructivist views listed in the final column.

Table 3.2 Dabbagh's Instructional Design Knowledge Base (IDKB)		
Principal theorists		
Objectivism/ Behaviourism	**Cognitivism/ Pragmatism**	**Constructivism/Interpretivism**
Pavlov Skinner	Gardner	Bruner Dewey Papert Piaget Vygotsky
Goals of instruction		
Objectivism/ Behaviourism	**Cognitivism/ Pragmatism**	**Constructivism/Interpretivism**
• Communicate or transfer behaviours representing knowledge and skills to the learner (does not consider mental processing)	• Communicate or transfer knowledge in the most efficient, effective manner (mind-independent, can be mapped onto the learner)	• Build personal interpretations of the world based on individual experiences and interactions (constantly open to change, cannot achieve a predetermined, 'correct' meaning, knowledge emerges in relevant contexts)
• Instruction is to elicit the desired response from the learner who is presented with a target stimulus	• Focus of instruction is to create learning or change by encouraging the learner to use appropriate learning strategies	• Learning is an active process of constructing rather than acquiring knowledge
• The learner must know how to execute the proper response as well as the conditions under which the response is made	• Learning results when information is stored in the memory in an organised, meaningful way	• Instruction is a process of supporting knowledge construction rather than communicating knowledge

(continued)

Table 3.2   *(continued)*

• The learner acquires skills of discrimination (recalling facts), generalisation (defining and illustrating concepts), association (applying explanations), and chaining (automatically performing a specified procedure)	• Teachers/designers are responsible for assisting the learner in organising information in an optimal way so that it can be readily assimilated	• Learning is not structured for the task, but the learner is engaged in the actual use of tools in real-world situations
		• Learning activities should be authentic and should centre around the 'problematic' or 'puzzlement' as perceived by the learner
		• The focus is on the process not the product
		• The role of the teacher is as a mentor not a 'teller'
		• Encourage reflective thinking, higher-order learning skills
		• Encourage testing of the viability of ideas and seeking of alternative views

Source: Adapted from Dabbagh (n.d.) at http://tinyurl.com/zh6jwx7.[2]

SUMMARY

In this chapter we have focused on learners and how they learn. This has been set in the context of how ICT can contribute to the needs of both an individual and the society in which they live, as well as the need in some cases to gain formal knowledge for its own sake. In achieving these diverse aims we have also examined a range of learning theories and have related them to a range of ICT. From this, it has become apparent that ICT can contribute to personalised, socially situated and experiential learning by providing a range of tools and by enhancing motivation. Overall, it is suggested that no single theory of learning can be applied to all learners, but that ICT can be applied to a greater or lesser extent in all. It is suggested that the effectiveness of its use can be increased if teachers consider carefully the theoretical context in which it is being used.

Notes

1. Gardner added an 'eighth (naturalist) intelligence and continues to speculate about a possible ninth (existential) intelligence' (Gardner, 2008).
2. All references from this page onwards use www.tinyurl.com to shorten very long URLs to a more manageable length. This can be useful in presentations.

References

Alexander, R. (2008) *Essays on Pedagogy*, Abingdon: Routledge.

Bartlett, S. and Burton, D. (2007) *Introduction to Education Studies*, 2nd edition, London: Sage.

Brehony, K.J. (1997) 'An "undeniable" and "disastrous" influence? Dewey and English education (1895–1939)', *Oxford Review of Education*, 23(4), pp427–45.

Child, D. (2007) *Psychology and the Teacher*, 8th edition, London: Continuum.

Conole, G. and Dyke, M. (2004) 'What are the affordances of information and communication technologies?', *ALT-J: Research in Learning Technology*, 12(2), pp113–24.

Cook, D. (2010) 'Views of learning, assessment and the potential place of information technology', in McDougall, A. (ed.) *Researching IT in Education: Theory, Practice and Future Directions*, London: Routledge, pp39–45.

Dabbagh, N. (n.d.) 'Select instructional models/theories to develop instructional prototypes', Instructional Design Knowledge Base, http://cehdclass.gmu.edu/ndabbagh/Resources/IDKB/models_theories.htm (accessed 19 July 2016).

Dede, C. (2008) 'Theoretical frameworks influencing the use of information technology in teaching and learning', in Voogt, J. and Knezek, G. (eds) *International Handbook of Information Technology in Primary and Secondary Education*, Volume 20, New York: Springer, pp43–62.

Dewey, J. (2001) 'The educational situation: as concerns the elementary school', *Journal of Curriculum Studies*, 33(4), pp387–403.

Gardner, H. (1983) *Frames of Mind: The Theory of Multiple Intelligences*, New York: Basic Books.

Gardner, H. (2008) 'The 25th anniversary of the publication of Howard Gardner's *Frames of Mind: The Theory of Multiple Intelligences*', http://www.howardgardner.com/Papers/papers.html (accessed 10 October 2011).

Jarvis, P., Holford, J. and Griffin, C. (2003) *The Theory and Practice of Learning*, 2nd edition, London: RoutledgeFalmer.

Jones, A. and Mercer, N. (1993) 'Theories of learning and information technology', in Scrimshaw, P. (ed.) *Language, Classrooms and Computers*, London: Routledge.

Kelly, A.V. (2009) *The Curriculum*, 6th edition, London: Sage.

Long, M. (2007) *The Psychology of Education*, London: RoutledgeFalmer.

McIntyre, D. (2000) 'The nature of classroom teaching expertise', in Whitebread, D. (ed.) *The Psychology of Teaching and Learning in the Primary School*, London: RoutledgeFalmer, pp1–14.

Meadows, S. (2004) 'Models of cognition in childhood: metaphors, achievements and problems', in *The RoutledgeFalmer Reader in Psychology of Education*, London: RoutledgeFalmer.

Mercer, N., Hennessy, S. and Warwick, P. (2010) 'Using interactive whiteboards to orchestrate classroom dialogue', *Technology, Pedagogy and Education*, 19(2), pp195–209.

Pachler, N. (1999) 'Theories of learning and ICT', in Leask, M. and Pachler, N. (eds) *Learning to Teach Using ICT in the Secondary School*, London: Routledge.

Papert, S. (1993) *Mindstorms: Children, Computers, and Powerful Ideas*, 2nd edition, New York: Basic Books.

Pavlov, I. (1927) *Conditioned Reflexes*, Oxford: Milford.

Skinner, B. (1938) *The Behavior of Organisms*, New York: Appleton Century Crofts.

Vygotsky, L. (1978) *Mind in Society*, Cambridge, MA: Harvard University Press.

Warwick, P. and Kershner, R. (2008) 'Primary teachers' understanding of the interactive whiteboard as a tool for children's collaborative learning and knowledge-building', *Learning, Media and Technology*, 33(4), pp269–87.

Watson, J.B. (1925) *Behaviorism*, New York: People's Institute Publishing Company.

Woolfolk, A., Hughes, M. and Walkup, V. (2008) *Psychology in Education*, Harlow: Pearson.

Woollard, J. (2010) *Psychology for the Classroom: Behaviourism*, London: Routledge.

Yeomans, J. and Arnold, C. (2006) *Teaching, Learning and Psychology*, London: David Fulton.

4 ICT and the teacher: pupils, planning and inclusion

In this chapter we will consider how teachers use ICT based on the needs of *all* pupils, who have grown up in a world surrounded by technology. We will examine the potential impact of this under the headings of planning and preparation in an e-inclusive classroom. The chapter ends with an examination of e-safety.

Start with the child

Given the huge growth in both the number and variety of ICT devices available, coupled with their relatively low price, it is inevitable that children arrive in school with some experience of ICT. Indeed, Sefton-Green, Nixon and Erstad (2009, p121) suggest that 'young people gain most of their experiences and knowledge in relating to digital technologies *outside* the formal institutions of knowledge building'. In Chapter 7 we will examine the implications of this for early years classes, but there are also issues that need to be considered throughout the primary school. One of the most important of these is the potential for children in the class to have greater personal experience of, and capability in, the use of ICT than their teachers, due to their exposure to ICT from birth.

Any figures provided in this chapter regarding how many children have access to ICT resources will become outdated very quickly. Therefore, to represent a baseline on both the scale and range of devices used, and with the assumption that numbers will only increase, we will consider the findings of Selwyn, Potter and Cranmer (2009), who conducted research with 612 pupils in five primary schools in the London and West Midlands regions of England during the 2007–08 academic year. The results are important as the schools were selected to force variation in terms of pupils' ethnicity, geo-demographic and socio-economic backgrounds and included two inner-city schools and two suburban schools in London and one school in a medium or small town located in the West Midlands. Overall, Selwyn, Potter and Cranmer (ibid., p922) report that:

> 89% (n = 543) of respondents reported having access to a computer that was available to them to use if they required. Eighty-six per cent (n = 523) of respondents reported having access to a games console (e.g., Wii, Xbox, PS3), 61% (n = 376) access to their own television in their bedroom and 51% (n = 314) a mobile phone that they could use if required . . . these levels of access increased by the age of the respondent, with older children more likely to report access to all four of these ICTs.

This type of wide access to ICT suggests that we need to consider the disputed concept of children as 'digital natives'. The term was first used by Prensky (2001) as a result of his view that rapid advances in ICT represented a 'singularity': that is 'an event which changes things so fundamentally that there is absolutely no going back. This so-called "singularity" is the arrival and rapid dissemination of digital technology in the last decades of the 20th century' (ibid., p1). Prensky was writing about the generation of children who were in education (from nursery to university) at the time of writing (15 years ago at the time when *this* book was written), who had grown up with ICT around them from birth, and, as a result, were 'all "native speakers" of the digital language of computers, video games and the Internet' (ibid., p1). As all of these children will be at least 20 by now (some in university at the time will be approaching 40), it may be that you are one of them! He continued to suggest that this generation had a fundamentally different approach to thinking and processing information compared with the rest of the population, who he labelled 'digital immigrants'. He suggested, rather provocatively, that if digital immigrants wish to teach digital natives effectively, they have to 'stop their grousing' (ibid., p6) and change.

It has to be said, however, that not everybody, including me, agrees with the concept of digital natives. For instance, Guo, Dobson and Petrina (2008, p235) contend that 'the digital divide thought to exist between "native" and "immigrant" users may be misleading, distracting education researchers from more careful consideration of the diversity of ICT users and the nuances of their ICT competencies'. Others also suggest that age alone is a rather simplistic measure of ICT confidence and competence and does not take account of other factors. For instance, Brown and Czerniewicz (2010) find 'the concept of the "digital native" especially problematic, both empirically and conceptually . . . age is not a determining factor in students' digital lives; rather, their familiarity and experience using ICTs is more relevant'. Bennett, Maton and Kervin (2008, p776) also suggest that, while more 'dispassionate research' is needed, 'the picture beginning to emerge from research on young people's relationships with technology is much more complex than the digital native characterisation suggests. While technology is embedded in their lives, young people's use and skills are not uniform' (ibid., p783).

ACTIVITY

Do you consider the children you teach to be 'digital natives'?

Consider this question on your own, or discuss with others. You may wish to reflect on what factors (such as age or social background) affect your decision and whether the ICT resources available to pupils in school either exacerbate or improve this situation. You may also wish to consider whether *you* are a digital native (in nursery or university in 2001, according to Prensky's definition) and the impact of this on the way you see technology being used in teaching.

Computer use in the home

For technology to become embedded in the lives of pupils, they must be using it both inside and outside school. Indeed, studies suggest that pupils' use of technology outside school is more advanced than in school (Wang et al., 2014). This may in part be due to the fact that as well as an increasing number of households having access to computers, they also have access to a wide variety of other ICT devices, both static and mobile – although social inequalities remain (OECD, 2015). When allied to the increased availability of high-speed broadband internet connections, children have access to a range of networks both within the home and beyond.

The ways in which these ICT resources are used, however, can present a tension between parental aspirations, for instance to support homework (Cranmer, 2006), and children's actual use – with a preference for gaming among boys and online communication for girls (Ofcom, 2014). This relative freedom in ICT at home can lead primary children to make negative comparisons with more constrained ICT use in educational settings. In a study of Key Stage 2 children, Selwyn, Boraschi and Özkula (2009, p924) found that the children's views 'reflect clearly the restrictions of the schools and the (relative) freedoms of the home, as well as the oppositional relationship between the "work" of learning in school and the "play" of using digital media at home'. Nevertheless, even within the 'restrictions' of school ICT use, Kerawalla and Crook (2002, p751) found that school technology

> is well placed to extend children's opportunities for learning. However, computers are versatile tools: they support a wider range of activities than those that are prominent in classrooms. Whatever parents who purchase computers may hope to encourage at home, research suggests that, for most children, game playing becomes the predominant form of domestic use.

Whichever view you take on the issues above, it is impossible to dispute that rapid, and ever more sophisticated, developments in ICT resources will have an impact of some kind on learning and teaching, especially for teachers who have to adapt to an increasing range of technology. To provide the structure for the rest of this chapter, we will consider the potential impact of these changes – and possible solutions – under the headings of planning and preparation.

Planning

There are many styles and formats of planning, but for our purposes we need to consider how ICT can be used effectively in the planning process and what factors we need to consider to use ICT effectively. It is important, however, that we reflect on the use of ICT in the context of broader issues that need to be considered in the planning process. The first of these is the concept of learning styles and ICT.

Learning styles – fact or fiction?

Although not a theory of learning, when planning we need to reflect on the impact of the use of learning styles in education and the role of ICT within them. A learning style may be defined as 'a set of learner characteristics that influences their response to different teaching approaches' (Howard-Jones, 2009, p29). The main problems when considering learning styles include not only the abundance of models but also the competing academic and commercial benefits of their successful use, which can lead to their promotion at the expense of proven merit providing an 'illusory legitimacy' (Rohrer and Pashler, 2012, p635).

Coffield et al. (2004, p2) identify 71 different models and highlight that 'beneath the apparently unproblematic appeal of learning styles lies a host of conceptual and empirical problems'. Coffield (2012, p219–20) has since written (in a book chapter tellingly entitled 'Learning styles: unreliable, invalid and impractical and yet still widely used') that 'research into learning styles can, in the main, be characterized as small-scale, non-cumulative, uncritical and inward looking . . . In short, the research field of learning styles is theoretically incoherent and conceptually confused.' Pashler et al. (2008, p105) support this and conclude that, 'at present, there is no adequate evidence base to justify incorporating learning styles assessments into general educational practice'. They also add a slightly barbed caveat when they state that 'given the lack of methodologically sound studies of learning styles, it would be an error to conclude that all possible versions of learning styles have been tested and found wanting; many have simply not been tested at all' (ibid., p105).

Perhaps the most popular categorisation of learning styles occurs when learners are allocated to one of three types of learning styles or modalities: visual, auditory or kinaesthetic (VAK). However, in a summary of research on neuroscience and education for the Teaching and Learning Research Programme, Howard-Jones (2007, p16) states that 'some believe that presenting material in a way that suits an individual's preferred learning style can improve their learning . . . However, there is a considerable scarcity of quality research to support the value of identifying learning styles.' Indeed, the whole concept of VAK learning in particular has many critics. Sharp, Byrne and Bowker (2008, p91) go so far as to assert that 'to the best of our knowledge, independently verified quasi experimental and longitudinal studies producing conclusive evidence pointing unequivocally to such a close relationship between VAK and children's academic performance at primary school do not exist'. This is supported by Goswami and Bryant (2007, p20), who conclude that:

> *Learning by the brain depends on the development of multi-sensory networks of neurons distributed across the entire brain. For example, a concept in science may depend on neurons being simultaneously active in visual, spatial, memory, deductive and kinaesthetic regions, in both brain hemispheres. Ideas such as left-brain/right-brain learning, or unisensory 'learning styles' (visual, auditory or kinaesthetic) are not supported by the brain science of learning.*

In this context, although ICT can indeed provide high-quality visual or aural stimuli, the justification for their use should not just be that they match a single learning style, particularly using a VAK model. Nevertheless, as Howard-Jones (2007, p16) concludes,

> *of course, this does not detract from the general value for all learners when teachers present learning materials using a full range of forms and different media. Such an approach can engage the learner and support their learning processes in many different ways, but the existing research does not support labelling children in terms of a particular learning style.*

This is supported by Rohrer and Pashler (2012, p635), who conclude that *there presently is no empirical justification for tailoring instruction to students' supposedly different learning styles. Educators should instead focus on developing the most effective and coherent ways to present particular bodies of content, which often involve combining different forms of instruction, such as diagrams and words, in mutually reinforcing ways.*

The facility of ICT to provide just such a full range of modes or forms of communication is one of its strengths and we should therefore 'focus on the content's best modality – not the student's' (Willingham, 2005).

Differentiation

Differentiation is a complex area, but is broadly conceived here as the ability to match the level or type of task to the known level, or potential level (see Vygotsky in Chapter 3), of each child. In broad terms, we can also divide this into physical and cognitive differentiation, but in the primary school differentiation can take many forms – see Kerry and Kerry (1997) for a detailed discussion of the pros and cons of many methods. Medwell (2007) suggests that these forms include:

- presentation
- context
- resources
- grouping
- task
- support.

In this list, ICT could be regarded as a resource, but the use of ICT can also contribute to other items – for example, how content is presented or provides a context for the work. In addition, ICT use can also facilitate group work (e.g. a laptop for music composition, a digital voice recorder for interviewing, or an interactive whiteboard (IWB) for planning a design task). The choice of whether or not to use ICT can in itself be an act of differentiation, either to support less able learners or to stretch the more able, but this is only effective in a classroom where pupils are confident in using ICT independently. This type of pupil-centred learning environment with ICT is advocated by Smeets and Mooij (2001, p416), who suggest that:

Teachers need to create learning environments that are adapted to the needs, abilities, and interests of individual pupils, thus stimulating pupils to be active, to co-operate and to take more responsibility for the learning processes. ICT may not be expected to contribute to creating innovative, pupil-centred learning environments unless the teachers involved pay attention to the potential of ICT to facilitate curriculum differentiation. Teachers should adopt the role of a coach who actually hands over a substantial part of the responsibility for the learning processes to the pupils.

If this approach is required, much work needs to be done at the planning stage, bearing in mind that just using ICT will not be enough. Instead, you need to remember the features of ICT previously discussed and decide to use only those features that make ICT a better choice than any other resource. In addition, having made the choice to use ICT, you need to make decisions based on the individual needs and abilities of your class. Just as the actual work they may be undertaking needs to be differentiated, so too does the type of ICT selected, the features to be used and the ways in which they will be accessed (e.g. overlay keyboards to change letters from upper to lower case – see also 'ICT as an enabler' below, p74).

Preparation

Classroom design and ICT resources

When visiting schools, it is obvious that the design and layout of both schools and classrooms vary immensely, dictated by many factors including their age, adaptations and equipment present. The physical layout of a classroom will obviously have an impact (both positive and negative) on opportunities for interaction. Some class-rooms provide discrete areas for discussion in groups, while others provide large open spaces with easy access for pupils (and teachers) to move around and interact or hold whole-class discussions, and others still (such as an L-shaped classroom) make inter-actions (pupils–pupil, pupil–teacher and pupil–technology) much more challenging. This 'architecture shaped discourse' (Beauchamp, 2011) and subsequent interactions need careful consideration. Unfortunately, not many teachers are in a position where they can choose to design and build a new classroom, so they have to make decisions about the best use of the space they have available. This is especially true of how they facilitate the use of ICT in the classroom, or make decisions to use it elsewhere. In some instances, the position of network points or power sockets makes it difficult to achieve significant change, but this only applies to fixed resources, such PCs or IWBs. The increasing use of mobile technologies and their ability to connect wirelessly to remote devices (such as printers and network storage), or to store work remotely on a network, or even to access programs remotely using cloud computing makes the flex-ible use of ICT much easier.

WHAT IS CLOUD COMPUTING?

Cloud computing (or technology) allows users to access applications, resources or applications through a web browser rather than from software installed on whatever device they are working on. In addition, work can be saved remotely to ensure access from anywhere with an internet connection. In reality, the 'cloud' is a network of computers that host the relevant software, which means that much less space is needed on the hardware devices. This leaves space available for other features and enables manufacturers to produce devices with less memory and hence smaller machines. Some cloud services are managed and therefore have cost implications, but this also means that support is provided when things go wrong – and problems can be resolved remotely as that is where the fault will lie. There are many advantages to such an approach, but also some drawbacks, the most fundamental being that if you lose your internet connection, you lose your access to the software or other resources or any work saved there. This may be less of a concern in fixed computers with wired network connections, such as in many classrooms currently, but may be more of an issue with mobile access to the internet. In addition, there may also be security concerns, as with any internet-based work.

This increased flexibility should also help pupils to take more control over their learning as advocated above, as it will increase their ability to make decisions about not only what technology they use but also where they use it. To artificially restrict pupils to one location, based solely on the availability of a power supply, seems rather contrary. In addition, given the location of many classroom computers, the thoughts of Stephen Heppell are worth considering: he states that 'sitting facing the wall was formerly a punishment and just adding a bit of technology doesn't change the social isolation and exclusion much' (http://rubble.heppell.net/places/#physical). Based on experience in many countries, Heppell (see previous link and http://www.heppell.net) has many suggestions for modifying learning spaces (and for wider ICT issues), ranging from simply adding mirrors to the wall behind computers (so that both learners and teachers can make eye contact without turning around) to significant changes in classroom design and furniture.

In reality, most teachers will probably be faced with making the most of specific fixed ICT resources, before considering mobile devices. Perhaps the most common fixed resource will be the IWB, and the first step in preparing lessons with an IWB is to check that it can be seen from all positions where pupils will sit. It is surprising how often pupils are too polite to say they can't see! Even if you have sat in their seat to check that the IWB can be seen (an easy first step), the fact that you are taller means you can see when they can't. The same concerns apply to the position of text (or anything else they need to see, such as pictures) on materials you are presenting. In presentation tools such as PowerPoint, it is possible to change the slide template you use to ensure that text does not appear below the line of sight – this is well worth considering. In addition, Egerton, Cook and Stambolis (n.d.) suggest that 'students should be able to face the board straight on without having to angle their heads, to avoid reduced levels of concentration and the risk of muscle strain (see also Miller, Glover and Averis, 2004; Sharp, 2006). They need clear access to the IWB – anything that limits students' access to it may affect their inclination to contribute (Higgins, Beauchamp and Miller, 2007).'

ICT and inclusion

Another important part of planning and preparing for lessons is to consider inclusion and how ICT can contribute, particularly with pupils with SEN (special educational needs, often now referred to as additional learning needs or ALN). Becta (2003) suggests that ICT can support inclusion by enabling learners to communicate, to increase their participation in lessons and to learn more effectively. It is suggested that the general benefits are that ICT:

- enables greater learner autonomy – for example, by improving independent access to education at their own pace;
- unlocks hidden potential for those with communication difficulties;
- enables students to demonstrate achievement in ways that might not be possible with traditional methods;
- enables tasks to be tailored to suit individual skills and abilities – for example, 'interactive technologies can provide personalised help on a daily basis in a way that is difficult to achieve in a demanding classroom environment' (Royal Society, 2011, p7).

To understand how ICT can achieve these benefits, we need to examine both the idea of inclusion itself and how its current understanding was arrived at.

Inclusion as a concept is deeply rooted in liberal and progressive thinking. Thomas, Walker and Webb (2005, p18) suggest that the 1944 Education Act, as well as providing free education for all, 'constructed a highly segregative post-war education system with its ten categories of handicap for which special schools would cater'. This resulted in a minority of pupils being placed in 'special' schools with the majority in 'mainstream' schools – although the selection process at age 11 (the '11-plus') ensured that even these schools were not part of a 'comprehensive' education system. The next move was to try to 'integrate' pupils with special needs into the mainstream system. The term 'integration' was first used in education in 1988 (Thomas and Vaughan, 2004), but, since then there has been a move away from 'integration' towards 'inclusion' for *all*, reflecting wider concerns over rights, participation and social justice outside education. To be clear about the distinction between integration and inclusion, and how this may affect the use of ICT, we need to briefly consider them in more detail. Jones (2004, p12) states that integration can be regarded as a 'state', which involves 'putting someone in where they were originally excluded'; but does just doing this mean they will be truly integrated? Integration can also be regarded as a 'process', with 'planned and continuous interaction with other children within common educational systems and settings' (ibid.). But, in the context of this book, we need to be aware that this ignores other interactions, for example with ICT. Inclusion, on the other hand, may be:

- *an attitude or principle* – redefining 'normality' as accepting and valuing diversity;
- *an end-product* – a non-segregated system of education (ibid., p13).

Both of these ideas also work at a class level, where work can be planned for pupils to have continuous interactions (between both human and other resources) in a classroom environment, where all are regarded as equal and having a right to equal access. The distinction between integration and inclusion is summed up by Woolfson (2011, p175): 'with inclusion the mainstream school reorganises its structures to accommodate children regardless of their needs. Integration on the other hand leaves the school structure unchanged and the child's task is to assimilate into an unchanged school environment.'

ICT as an enabler

In this context, ICT can be an aid to moving from integration to inclusion. Rahamin (2004) makes the important point that ICT has a long tradition of supporting pupils with SEN in the mainstream classroom, by allowing such pupils to achieve something that would be very difficult or even impossible to achieve in any other way. This assistive, or enabling, technology includes touch screens, large track balls instead of a mouse, adjustable trolleys so computers can be lowered for wheelchair users, 'talking' word processors and dictation software. Such changes as also known as technical accommodations and could also include 'assistive devices to help a student to communicate or to produce work output (e.g. modified keyboard, a computer with a visual display and touch screen or with voice synthesiser, braillers for blind students, greatly enlarged text on a computer screen for a student with partial sight, radio-frequency hearing aids for students with impaired hearing)' (Westwood, 2005, pp155–6).

ACTIVITY

Discuss the use of any such devices you have witnessed in the classroom. Why have they been effective, if they have, and what factors can positively or negatively impact on their use?

If you have not seen or used such devices, undertake some research into as many as possible and share and discuss your findings with others.

A distinctive feature of ICT as an enabler for pupils with SEN is how it provides access, which Meiring and Norman (2005) suggest can take three forms: physical, cognitive and supportive. Physical access can range from overlay keyboards and text-to-speech readers to text magnification. Cognitive access is provided by presenting the curriculum in different ways; as we have seen, this is one of the strengths of ICT. Finally, supportive access is provided by the way in which technology supports a pupil in a particular area of difficulty – we will return to this later.

E-inclusion

The whole area of using ICT to help with learning difficulties is complex, but could perhaps be summed up as trying to encourage what Abbot (2007) calls e-inclusion, which aims to use digital technologies to minimise the problems that pupils with learning difficulties experience. This is based on the social model of disability, where learning difficulties are created by the social context, rather than a medical model that sees the difficulties as biologically determined. Such a model resonates with collaborative models of learning with ICT explored in this book, and Abbot outlines three categories for using digital technologies for e-inclusion:

- using technology to train or rehearse;
- using technology to assist learning;
- using technology to enable learning.

We have already considered the limitations of using technology to train or rehearse, but we will now explore how technology can assist and enable learning. Although it is necessary to read the full report to gain a complete understanding, Abbot (2007, p2) concludes that

> *it is possible to recognise the limitations of drill and practice software and the potential of socially collaborative use of digital technologies. Although computers have been used to some effect to assist learners to practise skills, it is only when they have been employed to enable learning that the full potential of e-inclusion has begun to be revealed.*

To ensure that this happens as much as possible, it is essential to use a diverse range of teaching styles and resources. This may be easier with some ICT resources than others, but even apparently beneficial ICT resources can have disadvantages. A good example of this is the IWB, which can present a range of multimodal resources (thus potentially allowing access for some pupils with SEN), but also requires a level of fine motor control to use, particularly if it requires a pen; this then counts against it being included in an interactive teaching style with some pupils with SEN unless adaptations are made. In a review of IWB use with children with autism and complex learning disabilities, Egerton, Cook and Stambolis (n.d.) concluded that, although the IWB motivated such pupils,

> *students with ASD and severe and complex learning disabilities often do not have the expressive communicative skills or executive skills to demonstrate or present understanding by ways other than physical manipulation of the IWB or the physical resources they are working with. Additionally, these students' need to focus on one aspect of learning at a time can dictate a linear and prescriptive teaching style. However, by employing a cumulative 'layering' approach whereby learning experiences in different modes are consecutively built up and, where possible, eventually combined, teaching staff can enrich students' learning experience.*

In reality, as above, there will be barriers that make inclusion with, and of, ICT difficult; these may be categorised as situational, institutional and dispositional (Harrison, 1993). Teachers, unless they are senior managers, may find it difficult to directly influence institutional policy, but they can deal with the situational (the classroom, including ICT use) and the dispositional (professional characteristics and relations with pupils, including a willingness to allow pupils to use ICT even if the teacher lacks confidence). If we assume that everyone reading this book has suitable dispositional characteristics, we can turn to consider situational factors.

In the classroom context, ICT can be used in a variety of ways, and each needs to be considered when planning. We have considered many factors in earlier chapters, but specifically in relation to inclusion we will consider how ICT can:

- be used to tutor or to explore;
- be applied as a tool;
- be used to communicate.

In addition, in SEN, ICT is also used for assessment and management purposes (Means, 1994) – we will return to this below.

ICT as tutor

ICT can offer individual(ised) instruction, but its effectiveness will depend on the match of this instruction to the needs of the learners. Indeed,

> in an extensive review of the literature on technology research in special education, Woodward and Rieth (1997) reported mixed results for the use of computer programs to generate feedback to pupils with SEN. They concluded that, on its own, Computer-assisted Instruction (CAI) was insufficient for teaching pupils with SEN. However, individualised learning programs retain their appeal, particularly as a supplementary support for learners with special educational needs.
>
> (Florian, 2004, p11)

ICT as tool

In Chapter 1 we discussed the use of ICT as a tool, but a specific example to help develop inclusion is the use of mobile devices – which we will consider for wider use in Chapter 5. Although mobile devices can be used with all pupils, Bauer and Ulrich (2002, cited in Florian, 2004, p14) found that the use of handheld computers helped pupils with SEN to stay organised. They also found that the portability of the devices helped to reduce anxiety in children in Year 6 about knowing what they needed to do or losing papers. In addition, handheld computers 'offer social support, as pupils can share programs with each other and send information to friends' (ibid., p14). We could conjecture that the same may be true of more recent incarnations of handheld devices, such as iPads. Given this potential benefit, it is unfortunate that some writers suggest that there is a lack of research into the ways in which ICT can be used for people with SEN (Williams, Jamali and Nicholas, 2006).

ICT to communicate

ICT can also help inclusion in that it can provide ways to enhance, or even facilitate, communication through:

- rich and engaging materials for learning – presentation using the multimodal and multimedia features of ICT;
- new forms of writing (e.g. speech recognition);
- augmentative and alternative communication (AAC) – 'any means by which an individual can supplement or replace spoken communication' (Chiner et al., 2001, cited in Soan, 2004, p184).

All of the above provide opportunities to accommodate different learners, but challenges remain. Florian (2004, pp18–19) asserts that these could include the 'adaptations that may have to be made for learners to acquire or use the tools of technology. The opportunities lie in the way that technology can then be used to ameliorate the effects of what would otherwise create a barrier to learning or participation in an interactive activity.'

All of the above can help with differentiation leading to effective inclusion, and to what we could call *inclusive differentiation*. In adopting this approach, there is, as with most ICT use, a commitment required from the teacher to ensure that not only are such options known about and considered, but, if they are adopted, they are used effectively.

Perhaps the key idea in all of this is that ICT use should not be regarded as the preserve of the more able, or indeed the less able, or of the teacher, but that, as far as possible, expectations of ICT use should be the same for *all* pupils.

ACTIVITY

Working in a group, or on your own, consider a topic you will be teaching and, using a suitable planning format, record how ICT could be used in different phases of the whole lesson (e.g. the introduction, main activities and plenary) to encourage inclusive differentiation. Part of this process would also include non-ICT resources, and a key part of this activity is considering which resources are best to use on the basis of their 'fitness for purpose'. It may be that this would vary according to the group, so some may use ICT and some may not. Obviously, if you know the class well you can target individual real groups, but, if you do not know a class well, you can still consider both ICT and non-ICT resources and decide on what may be appropriate to use in general terms.

E-safety

Finally, having made all other decisions about ICT use, we need to consider e-safety, which may in turn lead you to *not* use ICT after all! However, it is necessary to put concerns about e-safety in context to avoid such drastic measures. There is much hyperbole around this issue, and although Cranmer, Selwyn and Potter (2009) suggest that primary pupils' views of e-safety are at odds with official definitions, pupils' views do reflect the reality of their everyday experiences. Cranmer, Selwyn and Potter (ibid., p140) continue to state that official policy should 'first focus on meaningful and grounded elements of children's everyday ICT experiences. Only when likely risks and dangers are established should discussion move towards messages of "risk" which focus on the more extreme concerns of stranger danger, paedophiles and other risks of the unknown "other".'

Shipton's research findings are summarised in Figure 4.1, which provides 'an overview of what works in terms of improving and raising e-safety awareness in primary schools' (2011, p5).

Most primary schools will have a policy regarding e-safety, but they are likely to reflect official policies and perhaps not the reality of pupils' lives, as discussed above. Despite this, however, they will all hopefully be based on the key idea that e-safety is not about *restricting* children, but about *educating* them. In the first instance you may have to restrict pupils, but with the ultimate aim that they will become educated to make judgements themselves. This is supported by the views of Ofsted (2010, p8), which states that 'in the best practice seen, pupils were helped, from a very early age, to assess the risk of accessing sites and therefore gradually to acquire skills which would help them adopt safe practices even when they were not supervised'. To develop this best practice, however, it is important that *you* are also educated in this area.

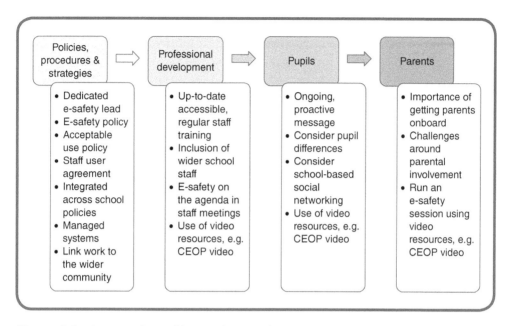

Figure 4.1   An overview of improving e-safety in primary schools

Note: CEOP – Child Exploitation and Online Protection Centre (see https://www.ceop.police.uk/).

We have already established that greater exposure to ICT (rather than age) will lead to greater understanding of its use, and it is vital that teachers engage with new technologies not just to enhance their teaching but also to try to keep up with their pupils. The importance of this was underlined some years ago by Becta (2007, p9), which asserted that:

> *For primary school children, certainly in the lower year groups, some of the risks might appear to be outside their level of ICT use. However, as the research shows, children engage with technology at an ever-younger age, and their knowledge and use of technological services, tools and devices can quickly outstrip that of their parents, carers and teachers.*

This concern is contextualised by figures from Ofcom (2015), which reports that 83 per cent of UK households have access to fixed broadband, allied to an increase in accessing the internet through a mobile device.

To help you address e-safety, there are many primary school resources available (see 'Useful websites' below for a few). It is not necessary here to cover this area in great depth (although we will return to aspects of it in Chapter 6 when we consider social media), except to stress the importance of considering e-safety whenever ICT is used. What we do need to reflect on in broad terms is how to integrate e-safety in planning and preparation. We will do this under three headings:

- filtering
- moderation
- supervision.

Filtering

Most filtering will be done by school or local authority firewalls that will block access to certain sites. You may also need to make your own 'filtering' judgements based on the age of the children you are teaching.

> ### TIP
>
> You need to be aware of this if you are planning to access sites for lessons, as some firewalls can be very restrictive – just because you can access a site at home does not mean that you can access it at school. In addition, just because you can access a site in one school, it does not follow that you can in all schools – for instance, different counties have different levels of access. You always need to access the site from your classroom before using it in a lesson. This is an essential part of preparing for a lesson that uses internet resources.

Moderation

Moderation of web-based content is largely done reactively ('post-moderation' rather than 'pre-moderation'), which, although helpful, is time consuming and cannot prevent inappropriate content. This does, however, ensure that pupils are able to contribute freely, for instance to blogs, and be 'empowered'. An alternative, and part of the educational process, is to peer-assess contributions before they are published online or communicated electronically. In addition, with older children in the primary school, involving them in moderating sites can be a useful way of educating them about what is and is not acceptable.

Supervision

Finally, in planning and preparing lessons, we will consider the role of supervision and who will provide it. This is particularly important in early years settings and when you have support from other adults. In this context, it would not be appropriate to use a more able child (as in Vygotsky's zones of proximal development, discussed previously), as the 'supervisor' is being asked to make moral judgements rather than to help scaffold the task. It is essential that the 'supervisor' shares both the school's and your expectations of their role. In reality, this will probably be a joint role in supporting learning and as 'moral guardian'. The role of the supervisor will be especially important with young children and those with particular needs that may affect their ability to interpret text, language, gesture or emotion.

Engaging parents

However good the education a school provides about e-safety, it is vital that both the school and you as a teacher engage with parents on this issue. This includes both obvious examples, such as informing them about how the school uses social networking (see more in Chapter 5), as well as helping them understand less obvious forms of communication that pupils can use at home, such as gaming machines (for example PlayStation); the latter allow direct, unmoderated communication between users if connected to the internet, which most can do using a wired or wireless connection.

Parents may also need help in understanding the range of ways pupils may be tempted to communicate with others. For instance, there are many chatrooms available (websites that provide a venue to communicate about areas of common interest in real time). Many may not be suitable for primary age children to access, but, rather than trying to discourage their use totally, it might be better to inform parents of the increasing number of 'safe' networking sites available which are specifically aimed at children. These mirror the characteristics of 'real' chatrooms, but allow children to learn how to use them safely with the involvement of their parents. The support and involvement of parents in helping their children learn about the safe use of the internet is essential, as Sharples et al. (2008, p5) assert that:

> Currently, most children are prevented from engaging in any social activity on the web at school. While this may remove the immediate danger to children and protect the school or local authority against lawsuits, it may also store up further problems for society at large. Now that most children have home access, safe behaviours are essential, but a strongly protected online environment at school may not provide the opportunity to learn these.

ACTIVITY

In groups, discuss if primary children should be allowed, or even encouraged, to use suitable social networking sites in school time.

If so, what are the benefits, both personally and in terms of the curriculum? If not, how can children learn safe behaviours?

If all else fails . . .

Despite the best planning and preparation, on occasion things may go wrong. For instance, as Ofsted (2010) reports, it is possible to begin searching for information on the Holocaust and end up on Nazi propaganda sites. Although all the precautions taken above should prevent this, Ofsted (ibid., p9) concludes that:

> The most successful schools visited in terms of their e-safety ensured that pupils knew what to do when things went wrong. Three primary schools visited, for example, made sure that if pupils came across an unsuitable site they could activate a cartoon character which covered the screen; it meant that they did not have to look at the site and had the opportunity to tell an adult.

Although the provision of such a character (or similar options) would be the responsibility of the school, it is your responsibility to ensure that the pupils know how and when to use it, and what to do next.

SUMMARY

In this chapter we have considered the role of ICT in planning and preparing lessons for pupils who have grown up in a world surrounded by technology. We have explored how classroom design can enable effective use of ICT in planning and preparing lessons, to ensure that *all* pupils are included in activities. An important facet of this is how ICT can encourage 'e-inclusion'. Such an approach uses digital technologies as tools to explore and communicate ideas to minimise the problems that pupils with learning difficulties experience. In lessons, teachers are faced with a large and diverse range of learning styles and it is important that the full range of ICT resources are used effectively to engage different learner characteristics. Finally, it is important that all this work takes place in a safe 'e-environment', where pupils are educated about potential dangers and know what to do when things go wrong.

In the next chapter we will examine the implications of this for classroom teaching.

References

Abbot, C. (2007) *E-inclusion: Learning Difficulties and Digital Technologies*, London: Futurelab.

Beauchamp, G. (2011) 'Interactivity and ICT in the primary school: categories of learner interactions with and without ICT', *Technology, Pedagogy and Education*, 20(2), pp175–90.

Becta (2003) *What the Research Says About ICT Supporting Special Educational Needs (SEN) and Inclusion*, Coventry: Becta.

Becta (2007) *Signposts to Safety: Teaching E-Safety at Key Stages 1 and 2*, Coventry: Becta.

Bennett, S., Maton, K. and Kervin, L. (2008) 'The "digital native" debate: a critical review of the evidence', *British Journal of Educational Technology*, 39(5), pp775–86.

Brown, C. and Czerniewicz, L. (2010) 'Debunking the "digital native": beyond digital apartheid, towards digital democracy', *Journal of Computer Assisted Learning*, 26(5), pp357–69.

Coffield, F. (2012) 'Learning styles: unreliable, invalid and impractical and yet still widely used', in Adey, P. and Dillon, J. (eds) *Bad Education: Debunking Myths in Education*, Maidenhead: Open University Press, pp215–30.

Coffield, F., Moseley, D., Hall, E. and Ecclestone, K. (2004) *Learning Styles and Pedagogy in Post-16 Learning: A Systematic and Critical Review*, London: Learning and Skills Research Centre.

Cranmer, S. (2006) 'Children and young people's uses of the internet for homework', *Learning, Media and Technology*, 31(3), pp301–15.

Cranmer, S., Selwyn, N. and Potter, J. (2009) 'Exploring primary pupils' experiences and understandings of "e-safety"', *Education and Information Technologies*, 14, pp127–42.

Egerton, J., Cook, J. and Stambolis, C. (n.d.) 'Developing a model of pedagogical best practice in the use of interactive whiteboards for children with autism and complex learning disabilities: implications for initial teacher training', Stourbridge: Sunfield Research.

Florian, L. (2004) 'Uses of technology that support pupils with special educational needs', in Florian, L. and Hegarty, J. (eds) *ICT* and Special Educational Needs: A Tool for Inclusion, Maidenhead: Open University Press, pp7–20.

Goswami, U. and Bryant, P. (2007) Children's Cognitive Development and Learning, Primary Review Research Survey 2/1a, Cambridge: University of Cambridge Faculty of Education.

Guo, R.X., Dobson, T. and Petrina, S. (2008) 'Digital natives, digital immigrants: an analysis of age and ICT competency in teacher education', Journal of Educational Computing Research, 38(3), pp235–54.

Harrison, R. (1993) 'Disaffection and access', in Calder, J. (ed.) Disaffection and Diversity. Overcoming Barriers to Adult Learning, London: Falmer Press.

Higgins, S., Beauchamp, G. and Miller, D. (2007) 'Reviewing the literature on interactive whiteboards', Learning, Media and Technology, 32(3), pp213–25.

Howard-Jones, P. (2007) Neuroscience and Education: Issues and Opportunities. A Commentary by the Teaching and Learning Research Programme, London: Teaching and Learning Research Programme.

Howard-Jones, P. (2009) Neuroscience, Learning and Technology (14–19), London: Becta for Deep Learning Project.

Jones, C.A. (2004) Supporting Inclusion in the Early Years, Maidenhead: Open University Press.

Kerawalla, L. and Crook, C. (2002) 'Children's computer use at home and at school: context and continuity', British Educational Research Journal, 28(6), pp751–71.

Kerry, T. and Kerry, C.A. (1997) 'Differentiation: teachers' views of the usefulness of recommended strategies in helping the more able pupils in primary and secondary classrooms', Educational Studies, 23(3), pp439–57.

Means, B. (ed.) (1994) Technology and Education Reform: The Reality Behind the Promise, San Francisco: Jossey-Bass.

Medwell, J. (2007) Successful Teaching Placement: Primary and Early Years, Exeter: Learning Matters.

Meiring, L. and Norman, N. (2005) 'How can ICT contribute to the learning of foreign languages by pupils with SEN?', Support for Learning, 20(3), pp129–34.

Miller, D., Glover, D. and Averis, D. (2004) 'A worthwhile investment? The interactive whiteboard and the teaching of mathematics', Keele: Keele University.

OECD (2015) Students, Computers and Learning: Making the Connection, Paris: PISA and Organisation for Economic Co-operation and Development (OECD) Publishing.

Ofcom (2014) Children and Parents: Media Use and Attitudes Report, London: Ofcom, http://stakeholders.ofcom.org.uk/binaries/research/media-literacy/media-use-attitudes-14/Childrens_2014_Report.pdf (accessed 15 February 2016).

Ofcom (2015) The Communications Market Report, London: Ofcom, http://stakeholders.ofcom.org.uk/binaries/research/cmr/cmr15/CMR_UK_2015.pdf (accessed 15 February 2016).

Ofsted (2010) The Safe Use of New Technologies, Manchester: Ofsted.

Pashler, H., McDaniel, M., Rohrer, D. and Bjork, R. (2008) 'Learning styles: concepts and evidence', Psychological Science in the Public Interest, 9(3), pp106–16.

Prensky, M. (2001) 'Digital natives, digital immigrants', On the Horizon, 9(5), pp1–6.

Rahamin, L. (2004) 'From integration to inclusion: using ICT to support learners with special educational needs in the ordinary classroom', in Florian, L. and Hegarty, J. (eds) ICT and Special Educational Needs: A Tool for Inclusion, Maidenhead: Open University Press, pp35–45.

Rohrer, D. and Pashler, H. (2012) 'Learning styles: where's the evidence?', Medical Education, 46, pp630–5.

Royal Society (2011) 'Brain Waves module two: neuroscience: implications for education and lifelong learning', London: The Royal Society, https://royalsociety.org/~/media/Royal_Society_Content/policy/publications/2011/4294975733-Printer-Friendly.pdf (accessed 15 February 2016).

Sefton-Green, J., Nixon, H. and Erstad, O. (2009) 'Reviewing approaches and perspectives on "digital literacy"', Pedagogies: An International Journal, 4(2), pp107–25.

Selwyn, N., Boraschi, D. and Özkula, S.M. (2009) 'Drawing digital pictures: an investigation of primary pupils' representations of ICT and schools', *British Educational Research Journal*, 35(6), pp909–28.

Selwyn, N., Potter, J. and Cranmer, S. (2009) 'Primary pupils' use of information and communication technologies at school and home', *British Journal of Educational Technology*, 40(5), pp919–32.

Sharp, C. (2006) 'Becoming a research-engaged school: using whiteboards and ICT', *Practical Research for Education* (NFER), 35 (May), pp56–61, https://www.nfer.ac.uk/nfer/PRE_PDF_Files/06_35_09.pdf (accessed 11 June 2016).

Sharp, J.G., Byrne, J. and Bowker, R. (2008) 'The trouble with VAK', *Educational Futures*, 1(1), pp89–97.

Sharples, M., Graber, R., Harrison, C. and Logan, K. (2008) *E-safety and Web 2.0 Technologies for Learning at Key Stages 3 and 4*, Coventry: Becta.

Shipton, L. (2011) *Improving E-safety in Primary Schools: Guidance Document. Final Report*, Sheffield: Sheffield Hallam University, Centre for Education and Inclusion Research.

Smeets, E. and Mooij, T. (2001) 'Pupil-centred learning, ICT, and teacher behaviour: observations in educational practice', *British Journal of Educational Technology*, 32(40), pp403–17.

Soan, S. (ed.) (2004) *Additional Educational Needs: Inclusive Approaches to Teaching*, London: David Fulton.

Thomas, G. and Vaughan, M. (2004) *Inclusive Education: Reading and Reflections*, Maidenhead: Open University Press.

Thomas, G., Walker, D. and Webb, J. (2005) 'Inclusive education: the ideals and the practice', in Topping, K. and Maloney, S. (eds) *The RoutledgeFalmer Reader in Inclusive Education*, London: RoutledgeFalmer, pp17–28.

Wang, S., Hsu, H., Campbell, T., Coster, D.C. and Longhurst, M. (2014) 'An investigation of middle school science teachers and students use of technology inside and outside of classrooms: considering whether digital natives are more technology savvy than their teachers', *Educational Technology Research and Development*, 62(6), pp637–62.

Westwood, P. (2005) 'Adapting curriculum and instruction', in Topping, K. and Maloney, S. (eds) *The RoutledgeFalmer Reader in Inclusive Education*, London: Routledge Falmer, pp145–59.

Williams, P., Jamali, H.R. and Nicholas, D. (2006) 'Using ICT with people with special education needs: what the literature tells us', *Aslib Proceedings*, 58(4), pp330–45.

Willingham, D.T. (2005) 'Do visual, auditory, and kinesthetic learners need visual, auditory, and kinesthetic instruction?', http://www.readingrockets.org/article/do-visual-auditory-and-kinesthetic-learners-need-visual-auditory-and-kinesthetic-instruction (accessed 15 February 2016).

Woolfson, L.M. (2011) *Educational Psychology: The Impact of Psychological Research on Education*, London: Pearson.

Further reading

Adey, P. and Dillon, J. (eds) (2012) *Bad Education: Debunking Myths in Education*, Maidenhead: Open University Press.

Becta (2007) *Signposts to Safety: Teaching E-Safety at Key Stages 1 and 2*, Coventry: Becta. *As well as covering the area of e-safety in general, this resource also includes advice*

on 'Embedding e-safety issues into the curriculum at Key Stages 1 and 2'.

Brown, C. and Czerniewicz, L. (2010) 'Debunking the "digital native": beyond digital apartheid, towards digital democracy', *Journal of Computer Assisted Learning*, 26(5), pp357–69.

Egerton, J., Cook, J. and Stambolis, C. (n.d.) 'Developing a model of pedagogical best practice in the use of interactive whiteboards for children with autism and complex learning disabilities: implications for initial teacher training', Training and Development Agency for Schools R&D Award (SEN) 2, Stourbridge: Sunfield Research. *A useful summary of research literature on the IWB, but, more importantly, a guide to how to use the IWB for a range of learning disabilities.*

Florian, L. and Hegarty, J. (eds) (2004) *ICT and Special Educational Needs: A Tool for Inclusion*, Maidenhead: Open University Press. *An edited collection covering a range of issues relating to ICT and SEN.*

Lewis, L., Trushell, J. and Woods, P. (2005) 'Effects of ICT group work on interactions and social acceptance of a primary pupil with Asperger's syndrome', *British Journal of Educational Technology*, 36(5), pp739–55.

Ofsted (2010), *The Safe Use of New Technologies*, Manchester: Ofsted.

Useful websites

E-safety

Child Exploitation and Online Protection Centre: http://ceop.police.uk/ Information for teachers and pupils from the UK police.

Childnet: http://www.childnet-int.org/kia/primary/teachers.aspx

Educational myths

Centre for Educational Neuroscience – 'Neuro-hit or neuro-myth?': http://www.educationalneuroscience.org.uk/?page_id=861

CHAPTER 5

Mobile technologies in the primary classroom

In this chapter we begin by defining what mobile technologies are and how they can be used within mobile learning (or m-learning). We will then examine the potential of mobile technologies in the primary classroom and consider how specific examples of mobile devices can enhance teaching and learning in the primary school. We will conclude this chapter by considering how mobile devices can be used in assessment and to support learning outside the classroom, both in the school grounds and beyond.

One thing all primary teachers know is that technology changes quickly, and there are occasional innovations, such as the iPad and other tablets, which can radically change the way we teach. The growth in the availability of small, affordable, reliable, networked mobile devices is one such example, and 'the wide availability of these portable, powerful, networked technologies has changed how we work, learn, spend our leisure time, and interact socially' (McNaughton and Light, 2013, p107). Webb (2014, p276) develops this idea and suggests that the 'internet and mobile technologies in particular have led to radical changes in the ways that young people socialize and learn'. Pupils in the primary school are not exempt from these changes, no matter how young they are. Indeed, research suggests that: 'Young children between the ages of 3 and 6 years old [are] able to quickly learn to use the tablet computer as a medium for representing their ideas and learning' (Couse and Chen, 2010, p93).

Such changes in education, however, are also embedded in changes in society as a whole. In particular, where, why, how and when we want access to information and ideas, and the speed we want them, have changed dramatically in recent years. Bauman (2005) suggests that, in the past, the much slower pace of change allowed society to become 'solid' as ideas were given time to 'solidify'. By contrast, Bauman (ibid., p303) makes the claim that now 'society is being transformed by the passage from the "solid" to "liquid" phase of modernity, in which all social forms melt faster than new ones can be cast. They are not given enough time to solidify, and cannot serve as the frame of reference for human actions and long-term life-strategies'.

If we accept Bauman's ideas, one example is society's attitude towards the guardianship of knowledge and how we gain access to it. Previously, society may have expected a teacher to 'own', or at least be the guardian of, knowledge (which may itself have been regarded as 'solidified' and fixed) and then to decide how and when to pass it on to others. Bauman (2005, p316) suggests that, as the result of 'liquid modernity', there is a 'marked shift of emphasis from "teaching" to "learning." Transferring to individual students the responsibility for the composition of the teaching/learning trajectory (and, obliquely, for its pragmatic consequences) reflects the growing unwillingness of learners to make long-term commitments that constrain the range of future options and limit the field of manoeuvre.'

One of the logical consequences of allowing learners to take control of *what* they learn is that they should also have a choice of *where* they learn, *what* resources they use to help them learn, *how* they learn and even *who* they learn with. In making such choices, it is inevitable that learners will be influenced by how they learn in school, but also by how they learn outside school as part of a 'changed and mobile society' (Traxler, 2010, p153). In other words, the ICT resources and approaches to learning that a child uses at home, or in play, may well be their first choice in a school setting if they are available. In addition, they may decide that they learn better not seated at a desk or in a classroom but outside the classroom or even outside the school building. As such, mobile devices could become what Sharples calls 'disruptive devices' as they 'have the potential to support learning any time anywhere, but also to disrupt the carefully managed environment of the classroom' (2002, p504). This does not mean, however, that we should not use them. In a primary school there are obviously restrictions as a consequence of school rules and resources, but we must at least consider allowing pupils the option to make choices about where, when and how they learn. The key implication for us here is that, if learning becomes mobile, then the technology used also needs to be mobile.

On a philosophical level, this may mean a change in pedagogy to allow learners greater autonomy, but it also means changes in more pragmatic arrangements, such as *where* resources (including ICT) are kept, *when* they can be accessed and *who* controls access to them. This does not need to be complicated: it can, for instance, involve simple changes such as keeping iPads on a classroom bookshelf alongside books and allowing children to choose what to use, rather than in a cupboard or other container. But this apparently simple change, if allied to a change in pedagogic thinking, can send a powerful message to learners about their ability to take control of their own learning.

As every school has different resources, and individual devices and related software change over time, in this chapter we will consider how mobile technologies in general (rather than specific devices) can be used effectively in the primary classroom. As before, we are therefore more concerned here with the thinking behind their use (the *why?*) rather than providing instructions on their use (the *how?*).

What are mobile technologies?

I am sure you will have noticed that I have been referring to mobile technologies, rather than mobile technology. In the past, it may have been appropriate to refer to 'mobile technology' as so few ICT devices could be moved easily, but, in recent years, the number of devices and Wi-Fi availability in schools and elsewhere have increased dramatically, so we will refer to all these devices as mobile technologies. Nevertheless, as is usual with educational jargon, there are many different interpretations of the term and so we must consider different definitions of mobile technologies to arrive at a common understanding.

> ### ACTIVITY
>
> Before reading the views of others, in groups, or on your own, develop a definition of mobile technology (or technologies). Decide if this would be suitable for primary children and, if not, develop age-appropriate definitions you can use in the classroom. (If you are in a school, why not ask the children themselves?)

A generic definition is provided by Price (2007, pp34–5):

the use of handheld technologies enabling the learner to be 'on the move', providing anytime anywhere access for learning. We can make a distinction between desktop computing and mobile computing at a very general level of description, in that 'mobile' technologies provide the potential to be used away from a fixed location.

Keengwe and Bhargava (2014, pp737–8) highlight the network capabilities of mobile technologies when they define them as

all those technological devices, which are portable and lightweight and either through the data cables or through wireless connections have Internet capability such as mobile phones, PDAs, iPads, and smart phones.

Hassler, Major and Hennessy (2016, p139) remind us that we should not forget computing devices and should also consider 'specialised handheld devices such as data loggers, phones and smartphones, low-power computers such as the Raspberry Pi and tablets'.

A more succinct and generic definition is provided by Turvey et al. (2014, p198), who define mobile technologies as 'ICT equipment that is small enough to be carried around conveniently'. Ciampa and Gallagher (2013) make a further distinction between 'mobile handheld' devices such as tablets, and 'portable devices' such as laptops. If we combine these we arrive at a definition of mobile technologies as mobile handheld and portable devices small enough to be carried around conveniently.

This definition, however, misses a fundamental advantage of mobile technologies which is their ability to wirelessly network with others, both locally and globally, using the internet or other capabilities such as Bluetooth. This ability to connect with others brings 'new opportunities for learners to be more intensely connected, either face to face or at a distance, extending one's learning community to friends, teachers, mentors, parents, and beyond' (Roschelle, Sharples and Chan, 2005, p159). Although this feature might not be used every time a mobile device is used, it is an essential feature in the use of mobile technologies in the primary school and needs to be incorporated into our definition. Hence, a revised definition of mobile technologies is networkable mobile handheld and portable devices small enough to be carried around conveniently. This broad definition will also therefore incorporate the growing use of near field technologies and devices, such as iBeacons, which we will return to later.

Having defined mobile technologies, we now need to consider what we mean by mobile learning (or m-learning).

What is mobile learning?

In 2004, Futurelab predicted a future in which 'Learning will move more and more out-side of the classroom and into the learner's environments, both real and virtual, thus becoming more situated, personal, collaborative and lifelong' (Naismith et al., 2004, p5). The idea of learning becoming mobile does not, however, need the use of technology. This dilemma lies at the heart of problems in defining the term 'mobile learning' – or m-learning, as it is sometimes called. It could be argued that learning has always been mobile – certainly in the primary school – but in the past it was much harder to move technology due to factors such as size, battery life and so on. With the advent of smaller, lighter and more powerful devices, the term 'mobile learning' has become associated with the use of this type of technology. However, 'the concept of mobile education or mobile learning is still emerging and still unclear . . . [and is] still a relatively immature field' (Traxler, 2007).

Kukulska-Hulme (2009, pp158–9) highlights the ambiguity of the word 'mobile' in this context, and asks

> *does it relate to mobile technologies, or the more general notion of learner mobility? In fact both aspects are currently important; in addition, the mobility of content is often highlighted. Mobility needs to be understood not only in terms of spatial movement but also the ways in which such movement may enable time-shifting and boundary-crossing . . . learners tend to move between using desktop computers and mobile devices, and maybe touch-screen displays in public areas, often for different parts of a learning task. Interactions mediated by technology are interspersed with direct interactions with people.*

As such, mobile learning should not be seen as a single entity, but rather as one part of a more complex set of learner interactions, with teachers and learners each being able to influence the direction of learning. This fits well with Bauman's idea of liquid modernity we discussed above. In this situation, decisions about what mobile technologies to use, when to use them and who uses them reflects a more fluid pedagogy, where m-learning works best as part of a blend of approaches (Duncan-Howell and Lee, 2007).

Given the complexity of ideas about mobile learning, it may be best to use a simple definition such as the one provided by Kearney et al. (2012): 'M-learning is . . . the process of learning mediated by a mobile device.'

Mobile devices – why bother? The potential of mobile learning

Having defined mobile learning, we can now consider the potential benefits of learning mediated by mobiles devices: the '*why?*' we discussed earlier. A key distinction we need to make before we start is between learning *with* and learning *from* the mobile device (Al Hamdani, 2014). I would suggest that both are important in the primary school, but we need to be clear about the role of the device from the start and consider carefully when planning lessons with mobile devices.

To return to why we should use mobile technologies, we can begin with evidence from a wide-ranging critical review of research by Hassler, Major and Hennessy (2016, p139), who conclude that, although evidence is limited and there is a 'scarcity of rigorous studies', mobile devices can

enhance, extend and enrich the concept of learning in a number of ways . . .

(1) contingent mobile learning and teaching (where learners can respond and react to their environment and changing experiences, and where learning and teaching opportunities are no longer predetermined);
(2) situated learning (where learning takes place in surroundings that make it more meaningful);
(3) authentic learning (where learning tasks are meaningfully related to immediate learning goals);
(4) context-aware learning (where learning is informed by the history, surroundings and environment of the learner); and
(5) personalised learning (where learning is customised for the interests, preferences and capabilities of learners).

Some of these ideas are already familiar to us, and others we will return to in later chapters (such as authentic learning in modern foreign languages), but perhaps the most important is the idea of contingent, 'no longer predetermined', learning and teaching. This not only reflects the concept of liquid modernity, but also challenges us to develop a new pedagogy reflecting the opportunities provided by m-learning.

Further opportunities are identified by Duncan-Howell and Lee (2007, p228), who suggest that m-learning:

- reaches places traditional learning cannot;
- makes learning more user-centred;
- works best if perceived as another tool that can be used to fit a learning need;
- can be used to remove some of the formality that non-traditional learners may find unattractive;
- increases motivation and engagement with learning;
- is ideal for facilitating collaboration and communication;
- makes the learning process quicker, easier, more attractive and more acceptable to disenfranchised learners;
- can enhance the growing shift from instructor-centred classroom teaching to constructivist, learner-centred educational settings.

Many of these suggestions are self-explanatory but it is worth noting that the final idea, that primary pupils should take more control over making (or constructing) meaning, has been a recurring theme in this book – and one we will return to in other chapters.

Kress and Pachler outline more advantages of m-learning:

- *Flexibility and portability* – devices are relatively small, readily portable and usable anywhere, anytime. They offer connectivity and allow resources to be edited on the move.
- *Multi-functionality and technical convergence* – mobile devices bring together more than one function that previously needed separate devices: for instance, listening to

music, viewing images and videos, keeping and updating a calendar and contacts, reading and replying to emails, looking at files from computers using different programs, and viewing web pages in real time.

- *Multimodality* – they allow users to view and create content using different modes: for example, text, image and video.
- *Nonlinearity* – the use of hyperlinking, and, more recently, switching easily between programs or apps, allows users 'interconnectedness' whereby they are able to explore ideas in a way that suits them, rather than working through a fixed, linear sequence.
- *Interactivity and communicative potential* – users can create new relationships using text and speech that can be recorded to allow real-time (synchronous) or delayed (asynchronous) communication between a large number of users, if necessary. This meta-collaboration, however, needs to develop knowledge of 'when, where, and with whom (not) to collaborate and to understand its consequences' (Kress and Pachler, 2007, p15).

This final point again reinforces the need to consider e-safety in all aspects of ICT.

In a review of research literature, Domingo and Garganté (2016) identify five further benefits of using mobile technology: providing new ways to learn; increasing engagement with learning; 'fomenting' (developing) learning; promoting collaborative learning; and facilitating access to information. The final suggestion can be a benefit, but it can also be a problem if pupils find too much information or do not understand the information they find. Nevertheless, Traxler (2007) suggests that we may be in new situation where '[f]inding information rather than possessing it or knowing it becomes the defining characteristic of learning generally'.

WHAT DO YOU THINK?

The idea of finding information, rather than possessing it (memorising or knowing it), links to the concept of person-plus we encountered in Chapter 2. How do you feel about this idea? Is it enough that your pupils do not need to 'know' everything (do you?), but instead should be taught the skills to know where to find it?

Finally, as well as technical and pedagogical benefits, mobile technologies also offer opportunities to develop social interactions. For instance, in a small-scale study with grade 6 pupils (11 years of age) in Canada, Ciampa (2014, p93) found that 'students identified teamwork and opportunities to work with other students as important motivational factors. It is in these venues that individuals can share thoughts and ideas and become active participants in a digital society and develop the skills of cooperation and collaboration.'

Having considered a range of benefits for mobile learning in general, we will now consider specific types of mobile technology in more detail.

Examples of mobile devices in the primary school

Tablets as digital hubs

In the same way that previous research on the interactive whiteboard (IWB) noted its potential to be a 'digital hub', the idea of 'multi-functionality and technical convergence' in the list above suggests that mobile devices, particularly tablets such as the iPad, have the same potential. As Clary, Kigotho and Barros-Torning (2013, p51) state, 'as well as their computing power, mobile devices offer flexibility and mobility. For example, they function as digital cameras, video and audio recorders, e-book readers, as well as tracking and mapping devices.' This, of course, offers many potential benefits that can be recognised by both teachers and pupils. For instance, in a recent study of iPads in primary schools in Scotland and Wales, Beauchamp, Burden and Abbinett (2015) reported that pupils recognised the iPad as a digital hub and listed ways they would use it as such. In this study, one Year 5 (9–10 years) pupil summed up the views of others by stating that: 'It [the iPad] is so fun because you can do everything on [the iPad] . . . you can read books, play games, get images, record videos all on one piece of technology' (ibid., p172). Beauchamp, Burden and Abbinett (2015, p172) conclude that '[t]his allows pupils (and indeed teachers) to combine actions more effectively, including switching modalities, as they make decisions about how they will use the various features available.'

We see here again the potential of passing control to pupils, as users of the device, to exploit their own knowledge of devices to make choices about the best tool to use – they may see affordances that you do not! However, as we have seen before, this potential can be limited as 'the characteristics of (the effective use of) new digital technologies revolve around a combination of technology- and user-related factors' (Kress and Pachler, 2007, p13). If the teacher does not let it happen, it will not.

Multimodal capabilities

The multimodal aspects of the iPad, or similar tablet, mean that pupils are to access, construct, modify, display and share a wide range of modes from one device. Without using any specific extra apps, but just the core built-in features of the iPad or other tablet, you and your pupils can create text and images and record still and moving images and sound. It is important to know the potential of these before moving on to consider what apps can add to or improve these functions. For instance, in a dance lesson in the school hall you could record dance sequences by different groups, make notes for assessment purposes, take photographs and even record interviews with the pupils as they reflect back on their performance – or pupils could do this for you! The videos can then be shown on the IWB back in the classroom for evaluation and planning for improvements, or kept as evidence for visitors (such as inspectors or advisers), built into a portfolio or used to show another class next year.

The same approach could be used in a games lesson where you are teaching a specific technique, such as throwing, catching or kicking and you decide to find a free slow-motion app so that a more detailed appraisal can be made by the pupils of their performance and how to improve it. In this instance, the app *adds* something to the core functions – and this can then be used in other areas of the curriculum, such as science. There is a big danger when the iPad is introduced that it is overloaded with unnecessary apps, rather than them being added slowly based on an identified need and the strength of a particular app.

In addition, it may be that the iPad cannot do what you want it to do *without* an app. For instance, to read QR (quick response) codes you need to add a reader app, but the decision to add this would be based on an identified need, such as the potential of QR codes to support learning.

Figure 5.1   An example of a QR code

QR (quick response) codes

QR codes look like the example on the left (Figure 5.1) – which you can scan with a QR reader app to find out more about me!

QR codes enable you to print a code, and when it is scanned on an iPad (or other device) with an internet connection, it will link to many things including web pages, YouTube videos, Google map locations, social media pages and even plain text, such as instructions or even individual letters. Like many ICT activities, you need to explore the capabilities of these codes, which will in turn trigger your pedagogic imagination about what you can do with them with your class.

CASE STUDY

Use of QR codes: spelling in the early years

In an early years class, the pupils were learning to spell three-letter words. They had worked on these previously and the teacher wanted to do a group assessment activity, so made QR codes for each individual letter. For each word the QR code was a different colour. The codes were placed around the classroom and the pupils went on a letter hunt with their iPads to find the red codes, then the blue and so on – it did not matter in what order they collected the coloured codes, but the teacher could have asked the groups to collect the colours in a particular order (displayed as colours next to the group name on the IWB) to prevent overcrowding around each code. Each time they scanned a code, the letter appeared on the iPad. When they had collected three letters, they had to write the word on paper before going on to the next colour. The teacher also made an extra coloured QR code that linked to a picture of what the word was (cat, for example). These were put on a display board and used only if the pupils could not work out the word.

> **TIP**
>
> The use of coloured QR codes can also be used for differentiating work between groups (the red group finds the red codes and so on) without making it too obvious, or for adding extension activities (when you have finished blue, go on to red). If they're laminated, the codes can be used again – but use a matt finish as a gloss one sometimes reflects light and makes it hard for the iPad to read the code.

Green screen technology

Another example of an app using and extending an existing feature of the iPad is the use of the camera in the device and an app that allows you to work with a green screen. In essence, this is basically filming something or someone in front of a green, or even blue, background. You can then add a moving or still image in place of the green background using an app or computer program. You will have seen them used in weather forecasts on the television or elsewhere in films. They allow you to be anywhere in the world, or even beyond, and the more you use this technology, the more ideas you will have about how you can use it across the curriculum at all ages.

Like many forms of technology, you can make this as complicated or as simple as you want. Personally, I would start with the simpler and cheaper options, and then work my way up to more expensive ones if needed. To begin, you need a camera, a green background, and possibly some extra lighting – although I have seen this used very effectively in a normal classroom without extra lighting. The green background can normally be made using cheap green fabric or green sugar paper, or even by painting a section of the wall green. You may want to consider if the green needs to extend down to floor level – for instance, if you would like pupils to be standing within a background image. If you are filming only their head and shoulders, for instance in a 'news broadcast', this is not necessary. In addition, you also need to make sure that nobody is wearing green (as that will become the background as well), unless you want this to be a special effect! Depending on the age of the pupils, the whole process from filming to editing can be done by the pupils with support from adults or older children – such as the 'digital leaders' found in some primary schools. At this stage, if you want to share your films more widely, you may also need to consider where you are going to store (host) the videos. This can either be within the school system or through a third party such as Vimeo or a private YouTube channel – with the normal considerations about privacy taken into account.

Green-screening can be done on separate devices (e.g. a digital camera and computer), but this is a good example of a digital hub where everything can be done on one device, such as an iPad using the iPad camera and a green screen app. We will consider the actual process of constructing a green screen video below, but before that we can consider some examples suggested by Fox (2012) of how green screen technology can be used across the curriculum, and in other aspects of school life, in the primary school:

- Creating a short, narrative film for a local film competition
- Performance poetry

- A weekly 'praise pod' in which the school media team interviews the children who received the 'head teacher's award'
- A Sky Sports-style video for the school football team
- Interviews with children taking part in out-of-school sports
- Macbeth is interviewed live on the *Jemima Kyle Show*
- A 'live' debate about a section of *Pig Heart Boy*
- A report on the Masai tribe in geography
- Instructions.

If you conduct an internet search for green-screening in primary school, you will find many other examples of work across the curriculum that you can use as inspiration for your own work.

Constructing a green screen film with your class

Although many children will be familiar with green-screening from the TV weather forecast or films, it might be best to show them examples made by other pupils their age – which can be easily found in an internet search. If pupils do not know how to use the iPad camera for both video and photos, you will need to teach them the relevant skills before beginning work. However, the first thing to do is choose the topic or area of the curriculum you are going to cover and decide how this will fit into your planning and the class timetable, if you have one.

Making the film will not be a one-off and will need to be planned over a series of lessons as suggested in the sequence below. It may be a class activity the first time, but could become a group activity as pupils become more confident. The sequence below provides a potential starting point for your planning, but please do not assume that each stage will be one lesson or session:

1. *Introduce the green screen and make sure all pupils can use the camera* – you might need to buy a cheap iPad stand to hold it still and in place; this also allows it to be used by younger pupils who may find it difficult to hold the iPad for long periods of time.
2. *Develop ideas, plan and storyboard the film* – there are apps that can be used for this. Decide a choice of background (moving or still image) and find any necessary costumes or props.
3. *Make the green screen backdrop* – consider, for instance, if you want to include the floor as well (if you want the pupils standing in the background) and the maximum number of pupils who need to fit onto the screen (you may need to revisit this as filming progresses).
4. *Rehearse* – you may want to consider the use of an autocue or teleprompter on a laptop or another iPad. (See 'Useful websites' at the end of this chapter.)
5. *Filming* – this can be done within some green screen apps but it is easier to do with the camera and then edit and import later.
6. *Review and edit* as necessary.
7. *Share* – within the classroom via Apple TV or a similar mirroring device or with a wider audience on the school website or class blog.

ACTIVITY

Search for some examples of green screen use in primary schools. Discuss how these might work in your classroom and then identify areas of the curriculum or topics where you think this type of activity would be beneficial, focusing on how it will help to achieve a learning outcome, rather than just being fun.

Emerging technologies

Having discussed some more established uses of mobile technology, we can now turn to what may be considered emerging fields: near field communication (i.e. iBeacons) and augmented reality.

Near field communication (NFC)

Anyone who uses a tap-and-go service, such as paying for goods with a phone or watch, is using near field communication (NFC). Like many technologies that begin as business services, NFC is being adopted within education, although at present it is in its relative infancy and hence may present more challenges for primary teachers until it becomes more established.

Essentially, NFC is a form of contactless communication, where small amounts of data are transferred between NFC devices when in close proximity. NFC has similarities with QR codes in that information is embedded in one form of technology and is transferred to another. However, whereas the QR code uses a scanner, an NFC just has to be near the source of information. As such, it is able to provide location-specific information, such as instructions on how to do a book review when a pupil enters the school library or classroom reading area with an iPad. They can thus help create learning zones within the classroom or school – or indeed anywhere the device is placed. This means that, as pupils move around the school, classroom or school grounds, they can engage with a variety of different content.

It is not necessary to use a pairing code (as with Bluetooth), as it is the close proximity of the two devices to each other that triggers the communication. This means, in essence, that data is pushed from one device to the other as the receiving NFC device comes close to the transmitting device. In this instance, the NFC transmitting device is passive but it contains information that other devices can read (very similar to a sign on a wall). We will focus on the use of passive devices here, where one device (such as an iPad) picks up information from another device, to give examples of how this may be used in the primary school.

Within education, perhaps the most well-known NFC device is the iBeacon. This is a battery-powered device that can be programmed (the tricky bit) to provide specific content for your class. This can then be read by a relevant app on an iPad. The actual programming of these devices is not within the remit of this book, but as this technology is relatively cheap it might be worth exploring and it does present new opportunities to engage pupils in their learning.

Augmented reality

In the same way that a NFC device can be triggered as it comes close to another device, it is also possible to trigger 'augmented reality' information using a trigger image, as long as the device has an internet connection. O'Malley and Fraser (2006, p8) explain that 'in AR [augmented reality] the physical world is augmented with digital information . . . AR is where, for example, video images of real scenes are overlaid with 3D graphics.' Basically, a picture (known as a trigger image) is used to generate an 'aura', for example a video or other graphics, which appears over the top of the image. Like the NFC device, an app is needed to use the iPad's camera to generate and display this additional information. Perhaps the most common augmented reality app used in primary schools is Aurasma – currently free for a basic account. You create the auras on the website and then log into the same account on the device (a class account might be best so you do not need to share any login details). One basic example could be a picture of a child's piece of writing; when you look at it through the app, you see a video of the child reading it or a picture of the pupil who wrote it. Or, a map of the area can be put on a display board in the classroom and pictures of local landmarks can be added as an aura. It is hard to do the effect justice in words, so it is best to experience it by downloading an app and searching for examples. But, to give you some ideas to start with, in his blog on primary education and ICT, Parkinson (2013) suggests the following:

- Making a truly interactive display, rather than putting up work with explanations from teachers, examples of work could be used to trigger video explanations from the children.
- Cross curricular opportunities can be used to link writing with art or drama by using a picture of a story to reveal artwork linking to that story.
- When looking at an example of a particular text type children can scan it to reveal the features used or more of an in depth analysis.
- In Numeracy, teachers can make an aura showing a particular method for solving a calculation that children can scan to remind them.
- Science/History/Geography topics can be truly brought to life. Rather than just using a book children can scan an image to reveal videos and images packed with much more interesting facts and information . . .
- Lower down the school, to help children with initial words for reading, auras can be created to associate a word with a particular picture. They could scan numbers to reveal pictures of the number – for example – the number 3, scanned reveals 3 apples. Making learning much more visual and engaging.
- Assessment – AR could reduce so much paperwork if an aura was made for a child to show a recording of them reading, or working on a particular maths objective. You would be able to demonstrate that children can meet certain objectives. Imagine scanning a picture of a child with a leveling sheet to then reveal examples that back up your judgement as a teacher.
- I have also seen Christmas cards used to make Auras to attach a personal message from the children.

Many of these examples are teacher-led, but it is quite possible that pupils will think of their own use of auras in their own work.

Having identified some of the features of tablets (especially the iPad), we now need to examine the process of introducing them into the primary school in more detail, based on guidance from Beauchamp and Hillier (2014).

Introducing iPads into the primary school

Primary schools may wish to consider the issues below prior to purchase and during the early stages of use. This list is not exhaustive, and to support these recommendations we have added a checklist in Table 5.1 below for those considering purchasing iPads (or indeed any other tablets).

Prior to purchase

Prior to purchasing iPads, schools should plan carefully how they will be stored, charged, loaded with software and timetabled and their impact monitored.

When iPads are introduced

Perhaps most importantly, consider if the iPad is actually the best resource to use to achieve the learning outcome, and whether it should be used for all or part of the taught session or activity. Both Beauchamp and Hiller (2014) and Beauchamp, Burden and Abbinett (2015) suggest that the following are vital for successful implementation:

- Master the generic features of the iPad such as camera (still and video), internet, searching the iPad and so on before loading it with apps.
- Allow teachers to take home iPads and 'play' – particularly at its early stages of use (for instance, purchase them just before a school half-term or holiday).
- Allow pupils (of all ages) to train teachers and other pupils. Many schools use this as an opportunity to recognise higher levels of achievement (more able and talented) in ICT in the same way as they do for other areas of the curriculum and call these pupils 'digital leaders' or similar titles.
- Consider how teachers can be provided with opportunities to witness the use of iPads in other classes (school-based observation), as this type of training is highly valued.

When iPads are being used

- Encourage pupils to move beyond 'research' in independent work and use all of the features of the iPad.
- Introduce apps slowly and choose them carefully to match the age group and learning outcomes.
- Plan how work will be organised, saved and named: for example, using a folder hierarchy to group apps and work according to subject and/or age group or class.
- Explore how the features of iPads (such as sound, pictures, video and particular apps) can be used for teacher assessment and pupil self-assessment.

- Investigate the use of mirroring systems (such as Apple TV) to allow pupils and teachers to share work with the whole class.
- Consider ways in which parents can learn more about how iPads (or other technology) are being used in school.

The use of iPads will never replace effective teaching, or indeed other forms of technology. The iPad has particular strengths and these should be identified and exploited, but it should complement rather than replace other forms of technology and teaching styles – iPads should be built in, not bolted on. In addition, although iPads can help facilitate independent learning, pupils will still need to be supported (by an adult or another pupil) in using them to their full potential.

A particular feature of iPads highlighted in research is that, although the pedagogic skills and imagination of the teacher remain central to their effective use, they also provide an opportunity to develop a classroom practice in which pupils not only learn *from* teachers but also learn *with* teachers.

Checklist of things to consider before investing in iPads

My own experience as a governor of primary schools for many years suggests that all members of the school community need to be fully involved in any investment in iPads. With this in mind, the following questions may be appropriate for both staff and governors, and indeed school councils, to ask when considering an investment in iPads, or in any other mobile technologies – but note that this is just a starting point, not an exhaustive list.

Having successfully introduced iPads within the school, the next step is to work with them outside the classroom and further afield.

Working outside the classroom – authentic learning contexts

In our discussion on green screen use above, we noted its ability to create a variety of authentic settings. Burden and Maher (2015, p176) remind us, however, that 'one of the liberating features of mobile technologies is their portability, which allows them to be taken into the field to support pupils' gathering of data that can then be used back in the classroom to further their understanding of the focus of the investigation. In this way the devices support pupils' learning in authentic settings.' Although discussing geography field trips, Medzini, Meishar-Tal and Sneh (2015) suggest that the major uses of mobile technology outside the classroom are: consumption of information; creation of information; and communication. We will consider each of these to examine their potential uses in primary teaching.

Information consumption

Medzini, Meishar-Tal and Sneh (2015) highlight three potential uses of mobile technology outside the classroom: accessing information from the internet, augmented

Table 5.1 Checklist for iPads

Who	What	Where	When	How
Who is going to use them (staff, pupils, in what order)?	What areas of learning, subjects and age groups will we focus on – if any – when they are first introduced or when more iPads are bought?	Where are they going to be used (in what years and locations – on-site and off-site)?	When are they going to be used (timetabled or ad hoc)?	How are they going to be used?
	What other resources will you/we need (e.g. infrastructure or hardware, such as covers or leads)?		When will you/we need additional infrastructure (e.g. Apple TV or charging trolleys)? [Budget planning cycle]	How does this relate to our school improvement plan (SIP)?
	What do iPads do better than our existing resources?			How will they improve our provision?
Who will monitor the use of iPads?	What difference do you/we feel/ they will make?	Where shall we look for impact?	When do we get feedback or check if we need more iPads?	How will we get feedback on effectiveness?
Who is going to provide training (local authority, outside agency, members of staff or pupils)?				How will we measure the impact (e.g. by teachers, pupils and parent survey, governor visits)?
Who will charge, store and book out iPads if needed?	What equipment will we need to add apps and charge the iPads?	Where are they going to be charged and stored?	When are they going to be charged?	

(continued)

Table 5.1 (continued)

Who	What	Where	When	How
Who will add apps?	What budget are we going to use? (Is it devolved to a certain amount?)			How are we going to pay for apps?
Who is going to provide training, feedback and support to parents?	What training are we going to provide and what feedback or support to parents?	Where are going to provide training, feedback and support to parents?	When are we going to provide training, feedback and support to parents?	How are we going to inform and involve parents?
Who will formulate 'rules' of use (including safe use online and around the school)?	What (positive) rules, if any, will we introduce?	Where will 'rules' be displayed, if at all?	When will we introduce 'rules'?	How will rules be formulated (bottom up or top down)?
Who will amend relevant policies and home–school agreements?				How will this impact on other ICT resources (such as ICT suites or fixed PCs)?

1. It should be remembered that studies to date have found no robust evidence of iPads raising attainment. Nevertheless, it is suggested that the increased motivation on the part of both teachers and pupils found in research to date is unlikely to lessen attainment, so staff and pupil *opinions* are important measures.

reality and location-based information. The first of these is self-explanatory and we have already discussed augmented reality. However, we have not yet considered the use of location-based opportunities facilitated by the GPS (Global Positioning System) and mapping facilities of mobile devices with an internet connection. As well as providing access to maps of locations, the technology also allows you to 'tag' where you are, for instance to record the locations of specific places visited on a trip. With some apps you can take a picture, 'geo-tag' it (to record the location) and even record a memo about the location – all of which can be used later in the classroom. Although this type of activity may be better suited to older pupils in the primary school, even young pupils need to be aware that many phones automatically geo-tag the places where pictures were taken – with obvious e-safety considerations. Some primary schools produce guidance on this for parents and pupils (for example http://engayne.co.uk/wp-content/uploads/2015/12/geotagging.pdf), and you may want to consider when pupils should be introduced to these ideas.

Creating information

In general terms, creating information could include documentation, measurement and information sharing. If pupils are learning outdoors or in other informal settings, documentation can use many modes, such as using a mobile device to record text, images (moving and still) and voices. Measurement can take many forms, using both built-in capabilities, apps and other forms of technology, such as handheld sensors in science. All of these will allow measurements to be taken of distance, temperature, sound levels, altitude and so on. As well as investigations, data can be collected for a range of other areas of the curriculum, such as interviewing older members of the community for a history topic, or outside the formal curriculum, such as recording highlights of a class trip to a residential centre or museum – as we will also see with social media in Chapter 6. We have already discussed the many ways in which the information created can be shared and used later in the classroom once it has been collected.

Communication

Medzini, Meishar-Tal and Sneh (2015, p17) suggest that mobile devices serve 'as means of communication that offer the possibility of reporting by actual voice conversations, by text messaging or by video conferences . . . [They] also can be used in the learning context as a means of communication between various groups of learners at different locations outside the classroom.' So if pupils have a wireless connection in the school grounds, they are also able to communicate both in real time (for example, through videoconferencing) or by uploading to the school's servers or other cloud storage systems.

Whatever way a mobile device is used, however, the pedagogic challenge for teachers 'is to avoid diverting the learner's attention from the learning environment to the mobile devices, while at the same time making use of these tools to extend the learner's capabilities and contribute to active learning' (Medzini, Meishar-Tal and Sneh, 2015, p18). Although we have discussed the iPad a lot so far, even this is not a panacea for ICT in primary education (Beauchamp, Burden and Abbinett, 2015). Indeed, it may be that other mobile devices are better suited, particularly to younger pupils. Or, it may be that a clipboard, paper and pencil would be better still. This reinforces a key message about the selective use of technology that appears throughout this book: 'the use of M-Learning tools themselves does not guarantee their potential being realised. The key to success is the ability of educators to design and develop pedagogically sound opportunities and environments that enhance learning' (Duncan-Howell and Lee, 2007, p223).

Assessment with mobile technology

In this chapter we have considered the ways in which mobile technology can be used in teaching and learning, but we have not fully considered how it can be used in both peer and teacher assessment. The principle we will outline here also applies across the curriculum, at all ages, and reflects the fact that assessment can take many forms. We are concerned here with why we should use mobile technologies rather than other forms of ICT. Perhaps the most important reason is that 'in the primary school, pupils' achievements can often be spontaneous and transitory, and it is only through the use of technology that some of these can be captured and shared' (Beauchamp, 2015, p222). In addition, if we are making learning mobile, assessment also needs to be mobile – even if it is linked to more 'wired' and fixed systems in due course – such as a school assessment package that can also be accessed by fixed PC. Mobile technologies are useful because they present

> a large number of new opportunities to set up, mark, feedback and share these assessments in a wide range of settings, both inside and especially outside of the classroom – which can be particularly useful in early years settings. While primary teachers have had the opportunity to use digital cameras (both still and moving image), sound recorders (which can now nearly all be plugged easily straight into a computer), as well as laptops and fixed PCs, in the past these were often separate devices. In addition, material from these devices needed to be transferred to a laptop or PC to be shared. Recent advances in mobile technology mean that not only are all of these facilities available in one device, but results can now be shared instantly both within the classroom and beyond. The ability to mirror these devices on other classroom technologies such as the interactive whiteboard, opens up opportunities for peer assessment, as well as discussion of ideas, which we will return to below. This also allows opportunities to use the features of other ICT resources, such as the ability to annotate assessment work undertaken outside of the classroom on the interactive whiteboard as a means of feedback by the class teacher.
>
> (Beauchamp, 2015, pp218–19)

As well as the IWB, mobile devices allow assessment information captured by peers and teachers to be stored easily on devices and also on networked or secure cloud systems through the use of e-portfolios. As these are web-based, they can store data in many forms, including text, image and sound, so they are ideally suited to saving assessment data (including data created by pupils).

SUMMARY

In this chapter we have defined mobile technology and mobile learning (m-learning). We have identified how pupils can learn both *with* and *from* mobile devices, exploiting the unique opportunities they provide using both current and emerging technologies. In addition, we have seen that mobile technologies provide singular opportunities for teachers (and indeed pupils) to assess learning. Finally, we have seen that the portability and functionality of mobile technologies also allows learning to move beyond the classroom, both within the school grounds and beyond.

References

Al Hamdani, D.S. (2014) 'A constructivist approach to a mobile learning environment', *International Journal of Computer Applications*, 93(4), pp41–6.

Bauman, Z. (2005) 'Education in liquid modernity', *Review of Education, Pedagogy, and Cultural Studies*, 27(4), pp303–17.

Beauchamp, G. (2015) 'ICT and assessment' in Younie, S., Leask, M. and Burden, K. (eds) *Teaching and Learning with ICT in the Primary School*, 2nd edition, London: Routledge, pp210–24.

Beauchamp, G. and Hillier, E. (2014) *An Evaluation of iPad Implementation across a Network of Primary Schools in Cardiff*, Cardiff: Cardiff Metropolitan University.

Beauchamp, G., Burden, K. and Abbinett, E. (2015) 'Teachers learning to use the iPad in Scotland and Wales: a new model of professional development', *Journal of Education for Teaching: International Research and Pedagogy*, 41(2), pp161–79.

Burden, T. and Maher, D. (2015) 'Mobile technologies and authentic learning in the primary school classroom', in Younie, S., Leask, M. and Burden, K. (eds) *Teaching and Learning with ICT in the Primary School*, 2nd edition, Abingdon: Routledge, pp171–82.

Ciampa, K. (2014) 'Learning in a mobile age: an investigation of student motivation',

Journal of Computer Assisted Learning, 30(1), pp82–96.

Ciampa, K. and Gallagher, T.L. (2013) 'Getting in touch: use of mobile devices in the elementary classroom', *Computers in the Schools*, 30(4), pp309–28.

Clary, D., Kigotho, M. and Barros-Torning, M. (2013) 'Harnessing mobile technologies to enrich adolescents' multimodal literacy practices in middle years classrooms', *Literacy Learning: The Middle Years*, 21(3), pp49–60.

Couse, L.J. and Chen, D.W. (2010) 'A tablet computer for young children? Exploring its viability for early childhood education', *Journal of Research on Technology in Education*, 43(1), pp75–96.

Domingo, M.G. and Garganté, A.B. (2016) 'Exploring the use of educational technology in primary education: teachers' perception of mobile technology learning impacts and applications' use in the classroom', *Computers in Human Behavior*, 56, pp21–8.

Duncan-Howell, J. and Lee, K.T. (2007) 'M-learning: finding a place for mobile technologies within tertiary educational settings', Singapore: Ascilite, http://www.ascilite.org/conferences/singapore07/procs/duncan-howell.pdf (accessed 10 December 2015).

Fox, S. (2012) 'Using green screening to enhance the curriculum (and beyond!)', http://www.ictopus.org.uk/downloader.php?f=sgp%7C143 (accessed 1 February 2016).

Hassler, B., Major, L. and Hennessy, S. (2016) 'Tablet use in schools: a critical review of the evidence for learning outcomes', *Journal of Computer Assisted Learning*, 32(2), pp139–56.

Kearney, M., Schuck, S., Burden, K. and Aubusson, P. (2012) 'Viewing mobile learning from a pedagogical perspective', *Research in Learning and Technology*, 20(1), http://researchinlearningtechnology.net/index.php/rlt/article/view/14406 (accessed 16 December 2015).

Keengwe, J. and Bhargava, M. (2014) 'Mobile learning and integration of mobile technologies in education', *Education and Information Technologies*, 19, pp737–46.

Kress, G. and Pachler, N. (2007) 'Thinking about the "m" in m-learning', in Pachler, N. (ed.) *Mobile Learning: Towards a Research Agenda*, London: WLE Centre, Institute of Education, pp7–32.

Kukulska-Hulme, A. (2009) 'Will mobile learning change language learning?', *ReCALL* 21(2), pp157–65.

McNaughton, D. and Light, J. (2013) 'The iPad and mobile technology revolution: benefits and challenges for individuals who require augmentative and alternative communication', *Augmentative and Alternative Communication*, 29(2), pp107–16.

Medzini, A., Meishar-Tal, H. and Sneh, Y. (2015) 'Use of mobile technologies as support tools for geography field trips', *International Research in Geographical and Environmental Education*, 24(1), pp13–23.

Naismith, L., Lonsdale, P., Vavoula, G. and Sharples, M. (2004) *Literature Review in Mobile Technologies and Learning*, Bristol: Futurelab.

O'Malley, C. and Fraser, D. (2006) *Literature Review in Learning with Tangible Technologies*, London: Futurelab.

Parkinson, L. (2013) 'Augmented reality in the classroom', http://mrparkinsonict.blogspot.co.uk/2013/01/augmented-reality-in-classroom.html (accessed 1 February 2016).

Price, S. (2007) 'Ubiquitous computing: digital augmentation and learning', in Pachler, N. (ed.) *Mobile Learning: Towards a Research Agenda*, London: WLE Centre, Institute of Education, pp33–54.

Roschelle, J., Sharples, M. and Chan, T.W. (2005) 'Introduction to the special issue on wireless and mobile technologies in education', *Journal of Computer Assisted Learning*, 21(3), pp159–61.

Sharples, M. (2002) 'Disruptive devices: mobile technology for conversational learning', *International Journal of Continuing Engineering Education and Life Long Learning*, 12(5/6), pp504–20.

Traxler, J. (2007) 'Defining, discussing and evaluating mobile learning: the moving finger writes and having writ . . . ', *International Review of Research in Open and Distributed Learning*, 8(2), http://www.irrodl.org/index.php/irrodl/article/view/346/875 (accessed 16 December 2015).

Traxler, J. (2010) 'Students and mobile devices', *ALT-J: Research in Learning Technology*, 18(2), pp149–60.

Turvey, K., Potter, J., Allen, J. and Sharp, J. (2014) *Primary Computing and ICT: Knowledge, Understanding and Practice*, 6th edition, London: Sage.

Webb, M. (2014) 'Pedagogy with information and communications technologies in transition', *Education and Information Technologies*, 19, pp275–94.

Further reading

Scottish Government (2013) *Guidance on Developing Policies to Promote the Safe and Responsible Use of Mobile Technology in Schools*, http://www.gov.scot/resource/0043/00438214.pdf (accessed 3 January 2016).

Useful websites

Augmented reality

Mr P's blog: http://mrparkinsonict.blogspot.co.uk/2013/01/augmented-reality-in-classroom.html

Free online teleprompter: http://www.cueprompter.com/

QR code construction: http://www.qrstuff.com/

Social media in the primary school

In this chapter we will define what social media is and consider how the different categories of social media can provide unique teaching and learning opportunities for both pupils and teachers. We will identify both positive and negative features of social media use for schools, teachers and pupils. We will also consider how social media can provide personalised CPD (continuing professional development) for teachers beyond that provided by their school, as well as connecting them to networks of other primary teachers around the world.

Ofcom, in its *Adults' Media Use and Attitudes Report 2015,* provides evidence that 'over the last ten years internet use has increased substantially, both at home and elsewhere' and that 'nine in ten adults now go online in any location' (Ofcom, 2015, p8). Allied to this increased use of the internet, both at home and beyond, adults' use of social media has risen substantially over the years:

> *Nearly three quarters (72%) of internet users have a social media profile, compared to 22% in 2007. Furthermore, four fifths (81%) of these people use social media at least once a day; an increase from 30% in 2007.*
>
> *Although 16–24s have always shown the highest levels of social media use compared to older ages, the most marked increase over the last eight years has been among the 35–44s – a 68 percentage point increase from 12% to 80%.*
>
> (Ofcom, 2015, p9)

Therefore, whatever age you are, it is highly likely that most of you reading this will already use social media in a personal capacity. Increasingly, primary teachers are also using social media in a professional capacity in teaching and learning and to communicate with parents and a wider global audience. In addition, although most primary schools have had a website for many years, they are also gradually using different social media to support teaching and learning and to communicate with a range of stakeholders. Before looking at both teacher and school use of social media in more detail, we must briefly consider what we mean by 'social media' and how it differs from more traditional media.

What is social media?

Like many terms, social media can mean different things to different people, but, like mobile technologies, it relies on the use of the internet to create, upload and share a variety of modes of communication. The Oxford Dictionary defines social media as 'websites and applications that enable users to create and share content or to participate in social networking'. As such, social media does not refer to a particular program or website, but the activity of sharing or networking with others using the internet and a variety of ever-changing and developing tools and apps. Like most activities, people have always used writing and other modes to communicate and form networks, but the difference now is the use of the features of ICT (see Chapter 1). In addition, the increased use of mobile devices means that things can be shared anywhere there is an internet connection, both in and out of school.

It is important that all staff share a common understanding of what 'social media' actually means; this is often found in the relevant school policy. For instance, here is one example:

> *For the purpose of this policy, Social Media is the term commonly used for websites which allow people to interact with each other in some way – by sharing information, opinions, knowledge and interests. Social networking websites such as Facebook, Bebo and MySpace are perhaps the most well-known examples of Social Media, but the term also covers other web-based services such as blogs, video and audio podcasts, wikis, message boards, photo documents and video sharing websites (such as YouTube) and micro blogging services (such as Twitter). This definition of social media is not exhaustive as technology develops with new ways of communicating advances every day.*
>
> (http://www.sacredheartgateshead.org/wp-content/uploads/
> 2015/02/Social-Media-Policy.pdf)

This final point is essential, but also means that primary school social media policies need to be revisited regularly, and may be better if they refer to a type of technology (such as a tablet) rather than a specific device (such as an iPad) or program. However, in this definition particular apps and sites are named which will inevitably become obsolete.

ACTIVITY

On your own, or with a group, discuss how you would revise the above definition to future-proof it as much as possible. Or, do you think it is adequate as it stands? If so, why? To do this you might want to compare existing school policies that you have seen or used.

An alternative definition, which avoids mentioning individual programs, is provided by Davis et al. (2012, p1), who suggest that social media refers to 'web-based and mobile applications that allow individuals and organizations to create, engage, and share new user-generated or existing content, in digital environments through multi-way communication'. We will use this definition for the remainder of the chapter and we will now consider the broad categories, or types, of social media covered by this.

How is social media different from other media?

Earlier in the book we examined the features of ICT (see Chapter 1) – in other words, the things it could potentially do better than other, more traditional tools. In essence, these are the things that make social media different from other media, where 'media refers to the vehicle through which information is conveyed, such as television, a book or website' (Twiner et al., 2010, p212). As social media uses a range of internet-capable devices, in most cases this means things are done quicker than with traditional media, in terms of both construction and distribution. We could suggest, therefore, that effective use of social media needs to take advantage of all these features. Examples include the following:

- *Quality* – there have always been good-quality paper and books, for instance, but here we mean the ability of technology to enhance input: for example, untidy handwriting on old paper is transformed into high-quality text on blogs.
- *Speed.*
- *Reach* – again, books have always had a potential global reach, but technology allows this to be instant (as with 'Speed' above).
- *Accessibility* – text can be read online and offline, often on very small devices.
- *Access* to many things in one place – there is access to the outputs of many people in many forms on one device – even on very small devices, such as phones.
- *Mobile* – media can be constructed anywhere and then shared anywhere with internet access.
- *Usability* – this includes, for instance, the ability to translate between languages on web pages, or change the size of pages and text, or read text aloud to help with accessibility.
- *Permanence* – some forms of media, such a paper, have a limited lifespan during which they can be used.
- *Edibility/provisionality* – traditional media can be hard to change quickly or even at all. For example, this is the second edition of this book, but it will not be available until the whole editing and printing process is complete. If I were posting online, it would be done instantly. This is also true of online work done by primary school pupils.

This last point is perhaps one of the most significant changes from traditional media and has both advantages and disadvantages, and teachers need to make primary pupils aware of these. This is the move away from 'filter then publish' to 'publish then filter' by creators of digital content (Shirky, 2008, cited in Hellen, 2011, p108). Hellen (ibid., p108) explains the significance of this both in school and beyond, for both adults – such as teachers – and pupils, when stating that:

This represents the difference between the circumstances of today's primary school children and that of most adults when they were in school. It has more far-reaching consequences than may seem apparent to most at present. The filtering role, previously carried out by specialist gatekeepers such as teachers, editors, authors themselves and publishers now has to be carried out, in most instances, by individuals. This is of particular significance for children. Even with the best monitoring systems in place, whether adults insisting on being present when their children are accessing the internet, or having internet filtering programs in operation, none of these are foolproof and children have increasing opportunities for unsupervised use of the internet. Even if a child has very computer-literate and conscientious parents the likelihood is that not all their friends' parents will.

There are obvious e-safety considerations you need to think about here (which we will return to later in this chapter), but the key idea may be that 'publish then filter' is perhaps the default approach for primary pupils as it is all they have ever known. There are obvious benefits, which we have considered, but there are also many potential problems with this.

ACTIVITY

On your own, or with a group, identify the implications (both positive and negative) of the move from 'filter then publish' to 'publish then filter' across the curriculum and then decide how you can pass these on to your pupils in lessons.

Categories of social media

Perhaps the broadest definition is that all social media facilitate 'communicating, collaborating and self-publication/broadcast' (Turvey et al., 2014, p235). Within these broad uses we can further subdivide social media into categories, each of which has a range of different sites and apps, although there is much overlap between them. I have given some examples for each but only to help you identify each category, as these may wain and others may rise over time:

- blogs (e.g. Wordpress or Blogger) and micro-blogs (e.g. Twitter)
- wikis (e.g. Wikipedia)
- discussion forums (e.g. TES community)
- social networking (e.g. Facebook, LinkedIn or Google Plus)
- bookmarking and curating sites (e.g. Pinterest or Scoop.it) – personal and public
- content sharing and media sharing (e.g. YouTube, Flickr or Instagram).

Blogs and micro-blogs

Originating from the term 'weblog', a blog is personal or group webpage consisting of frequently updated entries (posts) arranged chronologically, with the most recent first. It is distinct from a more traditional written (text) log as it also uses features of online technology – including hyperlinks, images, movies and podcasts – and is accessible anywhere with internet via many devices and apps. Yang and Chang (2012, p126) state that: 'Most blog platforms provide a personal writing space, which is easy to publish, sharable, and automatically archived, empowering users to form learning communities through inter-linkages.' This enables the blogger to provide very current information sharing and to encourage interaction from readers, wherever they may be in the world. Indeed, one of the great benefits of education blogs for teachers is how they can provide insights into different educational systems and alternative perspectives on common problems.

It could be argued that knowing the audience you are writing for, their concerns and daily realities will encourage the reader to react, and respond, to the blog. This is impor-tant, as Richardson (2010) suggests that blogs should 'demand' interaction by engaging readers in ideas, as well as posing questions and providing links to challenge and stimulate thinking. A good blog should combine the best of solitary reflection (by the author or blogger) and social interaction with readers. For this to be the case, the blogger needs to avoid what Richardson (ibid.) calls 'journaling' (that is, 'This is what I did today . . . '), as, although it might be interesting to a few people who know the blogger, it does not engage the wider readership with ideas. In addition, just providing links and describing a resource for teaching might engage the reader, but might not necessarily challenge their thinking. A good educational blog should 'be a medium for reflective writing which in turn can promote learning' (Robertson, 2011, p1631). In other words, the blogger should, among other things (which you can add yourself after you have read some blogs):

- understand their audience – provide user-centred content;
- do their research – do not, for example, perpetuate educational 'myths' such as VAK (visual–audio–kinaesthetic);
- tell others about ideas in an interesting and engaging way using language their audience will understand;
- use images, videos, podcasts, and so on;
- pose challenges or invite responses;
- provide links to interesting resources;
- post regularly and respond to comments from readers.

Finally, most primary teachers are very busy, so it is important that they are prompted to return to the blog. The same applies to parents reading a school or class blog, or a student teacher reading a blog by their lecturer or a teaching union. All these people are not likely to remember to check the blog to 'pull' the information from the site, particu-larly if they read more than one blog. Instead, with the use of RSS (rich site summary or really simple syndication), a notification of any new content or changes in the blog can be 'pushed' to the reader if they subscribe (just like a magazine that was delivered to your house in the past) and use an RSS reader – which can be a standalone program or part of some email programs. Whatever RSS reader you use, it will collate live notifications of changes to any of the blogs you subscribe to in one place and you can decide whether to read or not – just like email! Although it can be annoying to get lots of updates, one feature of a good blog is that it is regularly updated both in terms of new content and also in replying to comments made by readers to previous posts, so be prepared for this and make choices about which blogs to continue to follow.

In primary schools, it is not just teachers who write blogs – there is an increasing range of blogs written by, and for, primary school pupils. Just like any other form of writing, pupils need to consider their audience and adopt an appropriate style, but blogging can provide a real global audience and purpose for their writing.

ACTIVITY

On your own, or with a group, use a search engine to search 'primary school blogs' or search 'Edublog Awards'. You will find many examples of school and class blogs. Read and evaluate some of these to identify best practice and to see how you could use blogs with your class.

While you are doing this, check any 'rules' or guidance they provide, so that you can use them in your class, and make a list of any new skills you may need to learn.

Wikis

A wiki is also a webpage, but, unlike a blog, it is not arranged chronologically – although changes are date stamped. In essence, wikis are

> *websites that allow their users to create and edit content. Different wiki services offer*
> *different levels of functionality, although they all include functionality for editing by more*
> *than one person, either restricted to members or open to a wider public. They commonly*
> *also include the ability to compare previous versions of a page, a separate page for*
> *discussion and a user history that tracks the time and content of contributions and edits.*
>
> (Grant, 2006, p105)

In addition, a wiki is not really 'owned' by one person or organisation, but allows users to collaborate in forming the content of a website. The best known example is probably Wikipedia, but wikis can be much smaller and even focus on only one thing, like a class topic. As they are web-based they can also be constructed and accessed from anywhere with an internet connection. This means that work can be done both in school and at home – with necessary permissions and access or privacy controls – with the potential to engage parents as well as pupils.

Wikis 'provide users with both author and editor privileges; the overall organization of contributions can be edited as well as the content itself. Wikis are able to incorporate sounds, movies, and pictures; they may prove to be a simple tool to create multimedia presentations and simple digital stories' (https://net.educause.edu/ir/library/pdf/ELI7004.pdf). Wilson (n.d.) suggests that what sets a wiki apart from other websites and blogs is that 'a wiki provides the facility for creation and editing of an online space by multiple users, with a transparent trail of edits for all who visit, making changes (and who made them) visible to all, and providing the facility to set alerts to changes made on the wiki so that anyone can be notified of changes as soon as they are made'.

What you use to construct a class or school wiki will depend on the software you have available, but they can be standalone or part of your school website or virtual learning environment (VLE), if you have one. Whatever platform you choose, it is not necessary to use coding or complex formatting, making them easy to use. The values of a class wiki are outlined by one American elementary (primary) school, which says that a wiki encourages pupils to:

- contribute ideas and knowledge;
- collaborate with others;
- co-operate by 'listening' to others' ideas – and being willing to change their own ideas;
- care enough to contribute;
- celebrate learning – their own and that of others (https://desbuffalo.wikispaces. com/).

The ideas of collaboration and co-operation are important, and wikis allow contributors to both add and delete content (although it does keep a record of deleted content).

Examples of primary school wikis in Falkirk primary schools in Scotland (Wilson n.d.) include:

- Outdoor learning or class trip observations, individually or jointly with others.
- Science experiment planning, the process and record of observations – you can add video, pictures and audio descriptions.
- Historical project – bringing together different pages perhaps by different learners on their chosen area of a local study, or a combined research topic on a historical theme.
- Creative writing – individuals can use the revision feature of the tool to demonstrate to their teacher and others how their writing has developed. Other learners can be invited to add comments to encourage and offer suggestions.
- A teacher can collate all resources on a single topic into one online space, bringing together documents in different formats, video, audio, images and links to related resources elsewhere.
- Set tasks for learners, and the wiki can also be the space for them to submit their work – the wiki can be set to only be viewable by those in the class, or each pupil can have a space private to them and their teacher, with only the teacher's main wiki space able to be seen by the whole class.

ACTIVITY

On your own, or with a group, consider the value of pupils constructing a wiki on a topic they are studying in school.

If you feel it is valuable for your class, consider the following questions:

- How would you do this? For instance, does your school already have a VLE that allows you to do this?
- What new skills will you need to learn?
- Who would you need to consult about implementing this?
- What school policies do you need to consult?
- What privacy settings would you need to use?

Discussion forums

Discussion forums (sometimes called online forums, bulletin boards, message boards or discussion groups) are basically websites where users (who often have to register with the provider before being allowed to contribute) can leave questions and expect readers to respond. They are normally organised around specific themes. One example in education is the TES Community (https://community.tes.com/), which has over 4 million members at the time of writing. Although much of the site may be of interest, there is one section devoted specifically to primary education (https://community.tes.com/forums/primary.36/). I have suggested elsewhere that 'this type of online peer-to-peer support has many advantages for teachers, especially the fact that they can personalise not only the content of their professional development, but also who provides it and when and where to take part in development activities' (Beauchamp with Purcell, 2016). We will return to the benefits of social media in continuing professional development (CPD) in more detail below.

Social networking

This is perhaps the most well-known and widely used form of social media. In addition, there is a lot of guidance available (see 'Useful websites' below), but we will examine some key issues. Essentially, social networking can have two target networks: professional (for example using LinkedIn) and personal (for example Facebook). There are certain benefits and concerns about both, but perhaps the main common factor is that they both create a globally available image of you as a person and as a teacher. Perhaps the key idea is to be aware of the 'digital footprint' you leave with both. It may be that you have used social media for many years, and your younger self may have been less aware of the permanency and visibility of posts. Essentially you need to consider that anything you post on a social media site, at any age, could remain available – even if you do not know it is there. We therefore need to make the distinction, which primary pupils need to be aware of, between *active* (where a user shares personal data online deliberately) and *passive* (where data is collected without the user knowing) digital footprints.

Digital footprints

We cannot assume that primary pupils, or even teachers, fully understand this issue. Kligienė (2012, p67) describes users' varying understanding about their digital footprint in that

> some of them know and take care of collected and accumulated their data [sic], while others have not got the slightest idea about data collection and their possible handing over to the companies having interest in them, still others are aware and think that it is worth giving data in exchange for better and innovative products, services; and, finally, some users are aware of that only partly, but underestimate the risk emerging due to a large amount of the data accumulated.

The information and images of yourself you share can have a significant impact on your professional life, both positively and negatively. For instance, I know of head teachers who will do an internet search for potential teachers (students and in-service) and see what they find. I am sure that all of you reading this book will be far too sensible, but imagine a colleague who may have thought it was a good idea to post a picture of him- or herself drinking wine and standing on a table in fancy dress (I am not making this up!) at the time (perhaps 2am?). If you forget to check your privacy settings, it may not create the best impression in advance of an interview for a classroom teacher job. In addition, your new class may find it very entertaining when their older brother or parents find it as well! As Moore (2012, p87) points out, such posts can be 'problematic . . . when a parent, school official, employer or other authority views reputation-damaging information'. On the other hand, finding more positive images and information about you and what you do and have done may be a good starting point for an interview. JISC provides an important reminder when it states that: 'Educators are role models in the digital space' (https://www.jisc.ac.uk/news/why-educators-need-social-media-07-jul-2015).

It is important to remember that once an image has appeared on the internet, it may still be there even if you change your settings later – particularly if you were 'tagged' in it. You need also to remember that you might appear, or be tagged, in other people's photos and may not even be aware of them! For many people, the privacy setting guides for Facebook Basic (at the time of writing https://en-gb.facebook.com/help/325807937506242/) and Advanced (currently https://en-gb.facebook.com/help/466544860022370/) might not be top of their reading lists, but for student teachers, teachers and schools perhaps they ought to be.

Most of these concerns about safe social networking are summed up simply in advice for children from the Australian Government's Office of the Children's eSafety Commissioner (https://www.esafety.gov.au/esafety-information/esafety-issues/social-networking). This suggests that children should be aware of the following (although this is equally applicable to teachers):

- Limit your friend list – don't 'friend' random people.
- Protect your privacy – don't share your password and set your profile to private.
- Your personal details are valuable –don't share them.
- Protect your reputation – keep it clean and ask yourself: would you want others to see what you upload?
- Be careful who you trust – a person can pretend to be someone they are not.
- Don't use a webcam with people you do not know.
- Think before you post, chat, upload or download.

In Wales, SWGfL (2016) considers 'Digital footprint and reputation' and suggests that:

It is important for children and young people (and adults) to understand that:

- most information posted online can be searched and seen by potentially huge, invisible audiences
- can be copied, altered, and sent to others, and is persistent – it's almost impossible to take down as it can start to spread the minute it is posted
- Information that people post can get out of their control fast, so it is important to consider the consequences beforehand.

Therefore, it is important that children and young people have opportunities to:

- identify some of the benefits of sharing information online
- reflect on the risks of sharing inappropriate information online
- think critically about what they choose to post and share about themselves online.

At primary level pupils learn a simple message that the information they put online leaves a digital footprint or 'trail'. This trail can be big or small, helpful or hurtful, depending on how they manage it.

Having considered some potential problems, there are also many benefits for teachers and schools in using carefully managed and regularly updated social networking to connect both pupils and teachers with parents, and with others in their local community and around the world. It provides a forum for promoting pupils and their work, as well as encouraging interaction.

ACTIVITY

On your own, or with a group, see what schools you know have Facebook accounts and compare how they use them to identify good practice that you can apply yourself.

Bookmarking or curating sites and content sharing or media sharing

In reality, there are many similarities and overlaps between bookmarking and content sharing, so we will consider them together. The key features of both are that they allow you easily to collect a wide variety of resources in one place, for your own use or to share with a wider audience. These resources link back to the site where they were found, allowing users to access them, often simply by clicking on an image. As many of these sites are graphics-based platforms, they are also suitable for use with younger pupils for whom reading text-based sites may be a challenge – although images also encourage adult users!

To begin with, let us consider the personal benefits for you as a teacher. It would not be unusual for a teacher browsing the internet to find many sites that interest them. In the past, these could have been added as favourites to an internet browser, but they would therefore be restricted to the device you were using when you found them. The key difference with a bookmarking site is that you can 'clip' this site to a program that is installed on all of your computers and mobile devices. These can be tagged and put in different categories, such as areas of the curriculum, and as soon as your device connects to the internet the sites are synchronised between all your devices. Bookmarking, however, is only part of some programs – for example, Evernote and OneNote – that also allow you to synchronise photographs, movies, spoken notes and so on. This is particularly useful if you see something and take a picture using the app rather than your camera, as it will then be available on all your devices – and via the internet, if you login to your account.

Although it is possible to share your bookmarks and other resources, perhaps the main purpose of this type of activity is to collect resources that will be useful to you as an individual teacher, rather than to a wider audience. Many teachers, however, are happy to share things they find with a wider audience, but they should have this audience in mind when they bookmark or curate their site – in the same way that pupils are encouraged to be aware of the audience they are writing for. Current examples of bookmarking, curating and content-sharing sites include Pinterest and Scoop.it, but these may have gone out of fashion or been replaced by the time you read this!

CASE STUDY

A teacher's use of Pinterest with their class and wider audience – including parents

Although this case study uses a specific website, the principles are the same for any similar type of website or app.

A class teacher was starting a new topic. After setting up a Pinterest account, the privacy settings were adjusted (as the default on most social media is 'public') to keep them secret – for example, links to other social media such as Facebook were disabled, hiding the profile from Google searches and making the boards 'secret'. A board was set up for each group in the class, where, along with the teacher, they were invited to 'pin' materials based on their topic work. Another board was set up for parents to give them news of what the class was doing and also to provide homework or other materials. Finally, another board was set up for the teacher to share 'pins' with the whole class. The group boards were used to collect contributions for each group activity and the whole-class board was used by the teacher

to host topic-related resources such as examples of persuasive writing, creative writing prompts and examples of pupils' work from the teacher's own school and others.

After consulting the school's social media policy (which had to be updated based on this activity), the teacher set up an after-school meeting with parents. At this meeting, login details of the site were shared (so that they were all 'authors' of the same site rather than linking from their own sites), 'acceptable use' was discussed and an agreed 'policy' was recorded to share on the site with anyone not present. Training was provided by the teacher, some of the pupils in the class and the school's 'digital leaders' on how to use the site. The importance of not sharing details was stressed, so that only pupils and parents could gain access to the site. (The current link to guidance on this for Pinterest is https://help.pinterest.com/en/articles/edit-your-account-privacy.) The teacher also

(continued)

(continued)

produced a short guide (which was shared on the site) for parents who could not attend. One challenge for the teacher was that some pupils did not have internet access at home, so a time was arranged when they could stay for a short time after school, with their parents if necessary, to access and use the site, or they could access it during lunchtime or playtime on their own.

During the term, the pupils, with engagement from their parents, contributed 'pins' to their group sites, and these were used and reviewed in lessons. In addition, the class teacher used the class board in a range of teaching activities and communicated with parents on the shared board.

As other teachers found out about the site, they also began to use their own sites. The school even began its own Pinterest site, linking to other schools around the world. In addition, the success of the training session with parents encouraged other such activities relating to ICT and computing,

which proved very beneficial in increasing parental engagement in these areas. In addition, the teacher was asked to do a presentation to the school's governors, who were very interested in how social media could be used. Some were very sceptical to start with, but the talk convinced most that, with a proper pedagogic focus and taking account of school policies, social media could be a very valuable tool for teaching and learning. It also provided them with practical examples of why the school e-safety policy needed updating.

To see how this could work, have a look at these Pinterest sites:

'Primary teaching resources and ideas': https://uk.pinterest.com/tesResources/primary-teaching-resources-and-ideas/

'Teaching tools for the primary school classroom': https://uk.pinterest.com/mapofcali/teaching-tools-for-the-primary-school-classroom/

'Primary classroom': https://www.pinterest.com/explore/primary-classroom/

E-safety and social media: protecting children from radicalisation (Prevent)

In the case study above, a key concern of parents was e-safety – see also Chapter 4. Although there are wider e-safety concerns with using ICT, there are specific issues with the growth of social media use by young children in general and in primary education in particular. As the Scottish Government (2013, p3) points out: 'For children and young people, the internet is a place, not a thing. It's a social space where they can hang out and meet friends. Like any place that children and young people go, there are benefits and risks. We wouldn't expect children and young people to behave appropriately without guidance from adults in any other context.' In a report on e-safety in the primary school, Shipton (2011, p1) states that:

*The development and use of digital technology has grown quickly, and advancements
in social networking sites, web-cams, portable media devices, and online gaming have
been particularly appealing to children and young people. Whilst these technological
developments bring benefits and opportunities to children and young people in terms of
their learning and development, they also bring about safeguarding implications.*

Changes in government policy in all countries have acknowledged this, with a growing
emphasis on preventing radicalisation – which we will return to later. In addition, these
concerns are also reflected in inspection frameworks across the UK. There is therefore
a growing need to have a specific focus on the e-safety implications of social media in
primary schools. Even though many social media sites have a lower age limit, we cannot
ignore the fact that many young children either join themselves or access social media
via their parents or elder siblings. Indeed, it may be that primary pupils are influenced
by what is seen as acceptable behaviour by these groups. This is important, as Moore
(2012), although researching with young mothers, identifies many issues that primary
teachers need to be aware of when teaching social media use. Moore (ibid., p87) reports
that: 'Young people often post provocative photos of themselves and each other, reveal
private thoughts and vulnerabilities, and seem to spend much time making themselves
transparent to the world'.

Even if primary pupils do not actually do these things themselves, it does not mean
that they do not witness them. This can apply to all types of material, but there is a current focus on ideas that can lead to extremism and radicalisation of parents and children.
As we have already seen, 'Social media has become an essential and exciting part of how
we live. Millions of young people use these platforms daily to share content. But there
are a small minority of users who exploit social media to radicalise and recruit vulner-
able people' (DfE, n.d.). We cannot ignore the potential impact in primary schools, as a
recent BBC report in the UK (http://www.bbc.co.uk/news/uk-35360375) asserted that 'A
total of 415 children aged 10 and under have been referred to the government's deradi-
calisation programme in England and Wales over the last four years'.

Advice from the National Union of Teachers (NUT, 2016, p1) states: 'The introduction
of Part 5 of the Counter-Terrorism and Security Act 2015 gives the Prevent strategy legal
status in schools and colleges in England and Wales which are now obliged by statute
"to have due regard" to the need to prevent people from being drawn into terrorism.'
The *Prevent Strategy* helps us understand 'due regard' when it states that 'schools can help
to protect children from extremist and violent views in the same ways that they help to
safeguard children from drugs, gang violence or alcohol. Schools' work on *Prevent* needs
to be seen in this context' (HM Government, 2011, p69). This is a challenging area for all
teachers, and if you are not sure about your role it is essential that you seek further advice.
Some further information can be found in 'Useful websites' at the end of this chapter.

School use of social media

There are perhaps two main uses of social media by a primary school: teaching and
learning (which we will consider in later chapters); and promotion of the school and its
pupils. In the same way in which student teachers, serving teachers and prospective parents check school websites to find out about the school, they will also now check their

social media presence. Even just having a social media presence tells them something about the school, but if the social media is current and vibrant, presenting a positive identity and ethos, it makes the school even more appealing to those who want to work or send their children there.

In addition, although looking at American high school principals (head teachers) rather than primary schools, Cox and McLeod (2014) explored why they used social media and found four main reasons:

1. Social media tools allow for greater interactions between school principals and their stakeholders.
2. Social media tools provide stronger connections to local stakeholders, to fellow educators, and to the world.
3. Social media use can have a significant impact on a school principal's personal and professional growth.
4. Social media use is an expectation; it is no longer optional.

The first two reasons demonstrate the ability of social media to spread the word about you and your school and encourage interactions with a range of 'stakeholders'. These may include (and you can add to this list):

- existing parents and extended family (around world)
- potential parents
- potential sponsors
- other schools
- inspectorates.

We will return later to the value of social media in professional growth (for *all* teachers, not just school leaders), but the fourth reason (social media is an expectation and is no longer optional) is perhaps the most important and shows that primary schools cannot ignore the rise of social media – any more than some may have initially ignored the rise of school websites in previous years. Given the large number of adults who use social media, as outlined at the start of this chapter, it is highly likely that the majority of parents at the school will use social media and expect the school to do the same.

This can have many benefits. For instance, Britland (2012) suggests '[u]sing Facebook as a "broadcast" account. This is a one-way communication from the school to parents, an information portal if you like. This is a great use of social media for many reasons including: quick, easy, cheap, most parents will have an account, saves on "lost" letters on the way home and also saves on printing costs.' In addition, other school partners, such as Parent Teacher Associations (PTAs), also have Facebook and Twitter accounts that they use to help promote the school and events they are organising – although, as the school name is often on the account, it is worth someone keeping an eye on the tone and content. Indeed, in a small-scale study of Twitter use in ten primary schools in England and Wales, Langford and Beauchamp (2015, p4) found that schools 'tended to use Twitter predominantly as an informative tool for parents and the local community, rather than an education and learning platform for the pupils'. The study identified nine clearly defined categories, as shown in Table 6.1.

Table 6.1	Definitions of categories	
Out of school	**Definition**	**Example tweet**
Admin	Information which facilitates the smooth running of the organisation.	'School dinner money is due next Wednesday'
Specific projects	Projects in which the school is involved, internally or externally.	'Our school council have placed drop-in boxes around the community. Please help us recycle!'
Celebrations Religious Achievements	A tweet that marks an important event or occasion related to the school, an individual or the wider society.	'Year 1 & 2 enjoying taking part in the school nativity' 'Congratulations to Joe Blogs who has just passed his Cycling Proficiency test'
Live Updates In School Out of School	A tweet bringing something or someone up to date, or an updated version of something.	'Year 2 are enjoying playing in the arts and crafts corner this morning' 'Year 6 are thoroughly enjoying their trip to Sherborne Castle today'
Curriculum Numeracy Literacy Other	A tweet that refers to any academic, curriculum-based activity.	'Year 5 had a Warburton's workshop and created healthy sandwiches this afternoon' 'Nursery have been writing their sounds in shaving foam. We had lots of fun and it was nice and messy' 'Nursery are using iPads to count and sort this morning'

These categories reflect the everyday activities of a primary educational setting, but the study found that 'admin' was the most popular use of Twitter by the primary schools, as shown in Table 6.2.

ACTIVITY

On your own, or with others, look at a school Twitter site and see if it reflects the same pattern of use, or if there are other categories of use that you can see. Decide what your own priorities would be in the list of categories and how you would ensure that the school used its Twitter account to focus more on this issue.

Table 6.2	Most frequently used categories	
Popularity ranking	**Category**	**Total no. of tweets**
1st	Admin	1,543
2nd	Live updates in school	1,282
3rd	Live updates out of school	972
4th	Curriculum Other	857
5th	Specific Projects	504
6th	Celebrations Achievement	315
7th	Curriculum Literature	313
8th	Curriculum Numeracy	160
9th	Celebrations Religious	139

CASE STUDY

Using Facebook and Twitter on school trips to communicate with parents

A primary school was taking its Year 5 classes on their first residential trip for one week. As the bus was pulling away, the use of social media began to keep parents, siblings and other classes informed of their progress and activities. As the pupils were not allowed to take mobile phones, social media (mainly Twitter) served as an important, real-time newsfeed. Obviously, the school was aware that it had followers other than the parents, so it was careful not to name pupils in any tweets, but photos showed parents how their child was getting involved in activities. When the coach arrived, tweets and posts showed the residential centre and rooms within it so everyone at home could visualise the setting. At various times throughout each day, pictures were posted of pupils completing climbing and canoeing activities and so on. The teachers were careful to ensure that all the pupils were included as often as possible, and often used group photos. They were also careful to include pictures of other parts of the day, such as meal times, so that those at home had a complete picture of what had been happening. All of these photos could be downloaded by parents to have a record of what their child had done. On the way back, the coach was

> delayed and the Facebook and Twitter feeds were used to keep parents up to date. Throughout the week, parents responded to or commented on the social media postings so teachers and pupils knew that they were following what was going on. Parents also posted messages of thanks to the teachers after the pupils returned home.

In addition, one primary school highlighted other uses on their Twitter site. These included (http://gorseybank.net/page/twitter/10787):

1. celebrating achievement – of individuals, teams and the school as a whole;
2. collaborating with pupils and teachers in other schools;
3. updating people about school events and news (including links to new posts on the school website);
4. engaging pupils by connecting with people all over the world, including industry experts, scientists, sports people and musicians;
5. engaging the whole school community in discussion about what matters in the school;
6. giving pupils an insight into, and stimulating conversation about, events and issues around the world that matter to them.

Implications of social media use for school policy

Many of the activities above are already covered under existing school policies. But there may be a need to develop a specific social media policy (you can find many examples simply by searching for 'primary school social media policy') that might also link to other policies, such as bullying or behaviour management. Like all policies, these will need to be updated as technology and associated programs and apps develop. These policies normally include guidance for both teachers *and* pupils and it is very important that student teachers in particular are aware of them.

Teacher use of social media – CPD

Having discussed personal and school use of social media, we now need to consider how teachers can use social media as a form of personalised continuing professional development (CPD). Trust (2012, p133) suggests that 'many teachers are joining online communities of likeminded individuals and are subscribing to various blogs and Web sites to continue learning and improve their professional practice'. These online communities are very useful for busy teachers as they 'support teachers to cooperate across regions and countries, without the need for physical travel. As such, they provide opportunities for cooperation that may not exist locally or may be inhibited by institutional barriers' (Holmes, 2013, p107). McCulloch, McIntosh and Barrett (2011, p4) suggest that 'using emerging technologies and social media tools, teachers are beginning to take control of their own professional development, finding new ways to learn from each other, to reflect on their own practice, and to develop learning and support networks of like-minded professionals all over the world'. They conclude (ibid., p18) that social media can help teachers to:

- keep up to date with current debates in a way and at a time that suits them;
- draw on ideas from around the world, challenging their own perspectives and inspiring new ways of thinking;
- reflect on their own practice and shape ideas through discussion of this practice;
- connect with others in similar positions in order to share plans and approaches, and for support and reassurance.

We have already seen that discussion forums can be helpful in this respect, but Twitter and Facebook can be very helpful for finding out about local events and networks you may otherwise have missed.

As with many forms of CPD, you will need to make a decision about whether using social media contributes in a meaningful way. Some of the key advantages are that ideas are 'pushed' to you and can be accessed on a range of devices at any time of the day. On the other hand, some of you may find this a distinct disadvantage. Perhaps the key message is that using social media as part of your CPD is something that cannot be ignored. Try it; you might like it!

ACTIVITY

Having looked at the use of social media in the primary school from many viewpoints, on your own, or with a group, discuss and then complete the table below, summing up how you feel social media can best be used in the primary school by the whole school, teachers, pupils, parents and other stakeholders, such as governors. A start has been provided for you but please add to this and even add new column headings.

Table 6.3   The uses of social media

Learning	Pupil support	Community building	Expanding connections
Links to materials connected to topics (e.g. Pinterest)	Homework support – links and prompts	Clusters of schools (around the world)	Connect school with other schools
		Local area – e.g. community groups, police, etc.	Connect teachers with other teachers
		Showcase work and pupil achievement	Connect school with parents

SUMMARY

In this chapter we identified a range of different categories of social media, including social networking, blogging, book-marking and content-sharing. Each of these presents unique opportunities for teaching and learning. We also considered the potential benefits of using social media for schools, pupils and for teachers. We also noted the potential benefits for teachers of using social media in terms of developing networks beyond their school and even their country, leading to increased opportunities for professional development. To balance these positive features we highlighted that social media needs to be used with care, by both pupils and teachers. Pupils need to be aware from a young age that they are leaving a digital footprint which they may not even be aware of or even have total control over. We also noted possible concerns about the negative influence of some social media. These negative features do not mean, however, that social media should be avoided. Like all ICT resources, social media should be used when it is the best resource to achieve the intended outcomes, not just because it is there.

References

Beauchamp G. with Purcell, N. (2016) 'Current developments in education' in Wyse, D. and Rogers, S. (eds) *A Guide to Early Years and Primary Teaching*, London: Sage, pp45–66.

Britland, M. (2012) *Social Media for Schools: A Guide to Twitter, Facebook and Pinterest*, *The Guardian*, 26 July, http://www.the guardian.com/teacher-network/2012/jul/26/social-media-teacher-guide (accessed 11 June 2016).

Cox, D. and McLeod, S. (2014) 'Social media strategies for school principals', *NASSP Bulletin*, 98(1), pp5–25.

Davis, C.H.F. III, Deil-Amen, R., Rios-Aguilar, C. and Canche, M.S.G. (2012) 'Social media in higher education: a literature review and research directions', unpublished paper, http://works.bepress.com/hfdavis/2/ (accessed 18 January 2016).

DfE (n.d.) 'How social media is used to encourage travel to Syria and Iraq: briefing note for schools', London: Home Office and Department for Education (DfE), https://www.gov.uk/government/uploads/system/uploads/attachment_data/file/440450/How_social_media_is_used_to_encourage_

travel_to_Syria_and_Iraq.pdf (accessed 3 January 2016).

Grant, L. (2009) 'I DON'T CARE DO UR OWN PAGE!' A case study of using wikis for collaborative work in a UK secondary school', *Learning, Media and Technology*, 34(2), pp105–17.

Hellen, M. (2011) 'Information handling and adaptive expertise', *Education and Information Technologies*, 16(2), pp107–22.

HM Government (2011) *Prevent Strategy*, London: HMSO.

Holmes, B. (2013) 'School teachers' continuous professional development in an online learning community: lessons from a case study of an eTwinning learning event', *European Journal of Education*, 48(1), pp97–112.

Kligienė, S.N. (2012) 'Digital footprints in the context of professional ethics', *Informatics in Education*, 11(1), pp65–79.

Langford, E. and Beauchamp, G. (2015) 'The use of Twitter by primary schools in England and Wales: a multiple case study', *Cardiff School of Education Research Papers*, pp4–22.

McCulloch, J., McIntosh, E. and Barrett, T. (2011) *Tweeting for Teachers: How Can Social Media Support Teacher Professional Development?*, London: Pearson Centre for Policy and Learning, http://www.itte.org.uk/sites/default/files/Tweetingforteachers.pdf (accessed 29 December 2015).

Moore, S.C. (2012) 'Digital footprints on the internet', *International Journal of Childbirth Education*, 27(3), pp86–91.

NUT (2016) *Education and Extremism: Advice for Members in England and Wales*, London: National Union of Teachers (NUT), http://www.mta-uk.org/wp-content/uploads/2015/06/prevent-strategy.pdf (accessed 11 June 2016).

Ofcom (2015) *Adults' Media Use and Attitudes*, London: Ofcom.

Richardson, W. (2010) *Blogs, Wikis, Podcasts and Other Powerful Web Tools for Classrooms*, London: Sage.

Robertson, J. (2011) 'The educational affordances of blogs for self-directed learning', *Computers & Education*, 57, pp1628–44.

Scottish Government (2013) *Guidance on Developing Policies to Promote the Safe and Responsible Use of Mobile Technology in Schools*, Edinburgh: Scottish Government, http://www.gov.scot/resource/0043/00438214.pdf (accessed 3 January 2015).

Shipton, L. (2011) *Improving E-safety in Primary Schools: Guidance Document. Final Report*, Sheffield: Sheffield Hallam University, Centre for Education and Inclusion Research.

SWGfL (2016) 'Digital footprint and reputation', Exeter: South West Grid for Learning (SWGfL), http://hwb.wales.gov.uk/Resources/resource/536929bd-a274-4d30-b933-b6903b7787e8 (accessed 1 February 2016).

Trust, T. (2012) 'Professional learning networks designed for teacher learning', *Journal of Digital Learning in Teacher Education (International Society for Technology in Education)*, 28(4), pp133–8.

Turvey, K., Potter, J., Allen, J. and Sharp, J. (2014) *Primary Computing and ICT: Knowledge, Understanding and Practice*, 6th edition, London: Sage.

Twiner, A., Coffin, C., Littleton, K. and Whitelock, D. (2010) 'Multimodality, orchestration and participation in the context of classroom use of the interactive white-board: a discussion', *Technology, Pedagogy and Education*, 19(2), pp211–23.

Wilson, M. (n.d.) 'Why Wikis – the wonderful world of wikis in the classroom', http://tinyurl.com/h83nxa6 (accessed 17 June 2016).

Yang, C. and Chang, Y.-S. (2012) 'Assessing the effects of interactive blogging on student attitudes towards peer interaction, learning motivation, and academic achievements', *Journal of Computer Assisted Learning*, 28, pp126–35.

Further reading

Childnet International and TDA (2011) 'Social networking: a guide for trainee teachers and NQTs', London: Childnet International, http://www.childnet.com/ufiles/Social-networking.pdf (accessed 19 June 2016).

Gunuc, S., Misirli, O. and Odabasi, H. (2013) 'Primary school children's communication experiences with Twitter: a case study from Turkey', *Cyberpsychology, Behavior & Social Networking*, 16(6), pp448–53.

ICO (n.d.) *Social Networking and Online Forums: When Does the DPA Apply?* Wilmslow: Information Commissioner's Office (ICO), https://ico.org.uk/media/for-organisations/documents/1600/social-networking-and-online-forums-dpa-guidance.pdf (accessed 3 January 2016).

McCulloch, J., McIntosh, E. and Barrett, T. (2011) *Tweeting for Teachers: How Can*

Social Media Support Teacher Professional Development?, London: Pearson Centre for Policy and Learning, http://www.itte.org.uk/sites/default/files/Tweetingforteachers.pdf (accessed 29 December 2015).

Monks, C.P., Robinson, S. and Worlidge, P. (2012) 'The emergence of cyberbullying: a survey of primary school pupils' perceptions and experiences', *School Psychology International*, 33(5), pp477–91.

Scottish Government (2013) *Guidance on Developing Policies to Promote the Safe and Responsible Use of Mobile Technology in Schools*, Edinburgh: Scottish Government, http://www.gov.scot/

resource/0043/00438214.pdf (accessed 3 January 2015).

Tangen, D. and Campbell, M. (2010) 'Cyberbullying prevention: one primary school's approach', *Australian Journal of Guidance and Counselling*, 20(2), pp225–34.

Victoria State Government (2013) *Activity Guide for Teachers of Primary School Students. Module: Social Media*, Melbourne: Victoria State Government, Department of Education and Training, http://www.education.vic.gov.au/Documents/about/programs/bullystoppers/teacherguideprimarysm.pdf (accessed 19 June 2016).

Useful websites

E-safety

Child Exploitation and Online Protection Centre: https://www.ceop.police.uk/

UK Safer Internet Centre: http://www.saferinternet.org.uk/advice-and-resources/young-people/3-11s Resources for children aged 3–11.

Government guidance

Australian Government: https://www.esafety.gov.au/esafety-information/games-apps-and-social-networking A guide to using games, apps and social media. Explains and gives advice on many social media apps.

Department for Education (England) – 'Protecting children from radicalisation: the prevent duty': https://www.gov.uk/government/publications/protecting-children-from-radicalisation-the-prevent-duty

Department for Education and Home Office (England) – 'The use of social media for online radicalisation': https://www.gov.uk/government/publications/the-use-of-social-media-for-online-radicalisation

Department for Education and Home Office (England) – 'How social media is used to encourage travel to Syria and Iraq: briefing note for schools': https://www.gov.uk/government/uploads/system/uploads/attachment_data/file/440450/How_social_media_is_used_to_encourage_travel_to_Syria_and_Iraq.pdf

Teaching union advice

NASUWT – 'Social networking: guidelines for members': http://www.nasuwt.org.uk/InformationandAdvice/Professionalissues/SocialNetworking/NASUWT_007513 Advice from the NASUWT teachers' union.

Advice from other organisations

Childnet International and TDA: http://www.childnet.com/ufiles/Social-networking.pdf A leaflet entitled 'Social networking: a guide for trainee teachers and NQTs'.

Activities for pupils

Victoria State Government, Australia: http://www.education.vic.gov.au/Documents/about/programs/bullystoppers/teacherguideprimarysm.pdf The module *Activity Guide for Teachers of Primary School Students. Module: Social Media* is designed for primary school students, who work through six scenarios that deal with social media.

ICT in the early years

In this chapter we will examine the place of ICT in the particular context of early years teaching. We will consider how the unique pedagogy of this age range can influence the use of ICT and we provide examples of what this may look like in action.

The early years context

In recent years, early years education and pedagogy have received 'unprecedented global attention' (Gourd, 2014, p56). This attention has also coincided with devolved education across the UK resulting in distinctive and sometimes innovative practice (Taylor, Joshi and Wright, 2015). Some countries have developed their own unique early years policies, such as *Te Whāriki* in New Zealand, which are cited around the world – although Blaiklock (2010, p201) suggests that, in *Te Whāriki*, the 'holistic and integrated nature of curriculum means that subject content areas (e.g., art, music, science, literacy) can be overlooked'.

Within these approaches, play is a key component, and play should be 'given status when it is valued, assessed and used to assess learning' (Fisher, 2013, p44). In the UK, play is a central part of provision: for example, the Early Years Foundation Stage (EYFS) in England states that 'each area of learning and development must be implemented through planned, purposeful play and through a mix of adult-led and child-initiated activity' (DfE, 2014, p9). Also, in the current Foundation Phase in Wales, 'Children learn through first-hand experiential activities with the serious business of "play" providing the vehicle' (DCELLS, 2008, p4) – although we have noted earlier that there will be a new curriculum in Wales in the near future. In countries such as Norway, Sweden and Japan, variations on a pedagogy of play in the early years can be identified (Synodi, 2010), and, in Australia, the Early Years Learning Framework (EYLF) also has a play-based model (Leggett and Ford, 2013). Within these international developments, play is the dominant discourse, but we need to be aware that there is a danger that it has been idealised in some discussions (Kingdon, 2014).

A key part of early years pedagogy has been the growth in outdoor learning, 'which is central to effective early years education and indeed across the primary school' (Beauchamp with Purcell, 2016, p57). This centrality is acknowledged in Scotland's *Curriculum for Excellence through Outdoor Learning*, which states that: 'The journey through education for any child in Scotland must include opportunities for a series of planned, quality outdoor learning experiences' (Learning and Teaching Scotland, 2010, p5). In Northern Ireland, guidance in *Learning Outdoors in the Early Years* (Bratton et al., 2005, p11) suggests that: 'Outdoors is an equal player to indoors and should receive planning, management, evaluation, resourcing, staffing and adult interaction on a par with indoors.' Play is an essential part of this outdoor provision, and Haughton and Ellis (2013, p83) suggest that this provides 'a rich setting for children's imagination and fantasy'. They do, however, add the caveat that 'for outdoor play to be at its most effective it should not be seen as an opportunity to take indoor activities outdoors. Rather it should be viewed as an opportunity for children to play in a context that allows them to combine play with sensorial experiences, talk and movement' (ibid., p83). At the same time, advances in technology have allowed mobile devices to become part of this play beyond the classroom, although Edwards (2013, p199) suggests that 'in many countries technologies are still not fully integrated with perspectives on play-based learning in early childhood education'.

This is unfortunate, because pupils arrive at primary school with experience of an increasingly sophisticated array of technology (Marsh et al., 2015) to use in work and, more importantly for this chapter, play. There is little doubt that there has been a growth in what we can call ICT, or digital, play. One study in Greece (Nikolopoulou and Gialamas, 2015) even suggests that ICT play has replaced traditional childhood play. Whatever the extent of ICT play in the early years,

> Digital play and technologies are increasingly recognised as significant aspects of young children's experiences and participation in contemporary, post-industrialised communities. As a consequence, many countries have begun to grapple with the pedagogical and curriculum implications associated with integrating digital play and technologies into early years provision.
>
> (Stephen and Edwards, 2015, p227)

One of the challenges in integrating digital play into early years provision is that young children are very likely to arrive at school with some understanding of technology and some 'tacit knowledge' of computers and electronic toys (Hayes, 2006). Marsh et al. (2005, p5) undertook a large study of parents, carers and early years practitioners and concluded that 'young children are immersed in practices relating to popular culture, media and new technologies from birth. They are growing up in a digital world and develop a wide range of skills, knowledge and understanding of this world from birth.' More recently, in a review of research into ICT in the early years, Aubrey and Dahl (2008, p4) found evidence that

> most young children aged from birth to five years are growing up in media-rich digital environments in which they engage actively from a very early age. Family members are positive about this and actively promote the use of new technologies through on-going social-cultural practices of the home. They welcome ICT education outside the home and believe that it should be included in the curriculum from the earliest days. Young children are confident with new technologies and are very willing to explore new gadgets that they have not encountered before.

This openness to explore, or play with, new technologies is something that teachers need to both embrace and facilitate, and there is some evidence of this in primary schools when teachers are learning to use the iPad (Beauchamp, Burden and Abbinett, 2015), although it is not yet evident in other technologies.

Although teachers may be worried by new technologies, or about damaging expensive equipment, we need to be sure that this is not transmitted to young children, or that other obstacles are not put in the way of their natural curiosity or willingness to explore new technologies. Having said this, there are potential obstacles to using ICT resources in the early years that need to be considered when planning learning experiences. These could include:

- robustness of hardware – little hands can cause big damage!;
- size of hardware – especially if intended to be held in small hands;
- degree of fine motor skills needed to use or control equipment;
- use of language (spoken instructions on websites) or writing (or other symbols, including letters) that are not developmentally appropriate.

ACTIVITY

Consider ICT equipment in a classroom you know well and consider how these potential obstacles can be overcome for early years pupils so that they do not prevent use, both pragmatically (such as buying protective cases for iPads) and in the way you plan your lessons (such as where the activity takes place and what support is provided).

Within an early years setting there is a wide range of levels of development, and by considering these factors you are also thinking about issues of differentiation with learners of the same age. How would you apply this in your lessons with ICT resources?

In addition to functioning ICT equipment, Morgan and Siraj-Blatchford (2009) point out the importance of also having 'pretend' technological devices to use alongside other play equipment. They suggest that:

> ICT education may be supported through the inclusion of ICT props such as 'point of sale' cash registers and bar code scanners, pretend (or working) telephones and computer equipment. Often the props can be made in collaboration with the children developing a play area for a particular topic such as 'At the Vets', 'Going to the Dentist', 'At the Travel Agency' or a 'Supermarket' etc. Role projects of this kind are often supported by visits to the appropriate veterinary surgery, travel agents or supermarket.
>
> (Morgan and Siraj-Blatchford, 2009, p15)

As part of these visits, pupils will also see functioning ICT versions of their own play equipment; indeed, this could be part of an ICT walk below. But, back in the classroom, ICT equipment is part of pupils' everyday life, so should be part of their everyday play.

ACTIVITY

ICT walk

ICT equipment: digital voice recorders, video cameras, and digital camera

Features of ICT

Speed

Automation

Interactivity

Take children on a walk, first of all around the classroom, then around the school and even beyond – such as a visit as noted above. Make a list of all the ICT that you see. *Why not use ICT (iPad, digital voice recorders, video cameras, digital cameras) to make the list?* The discussion about what is ICT and what is not is a central part of this activity. Also, reviewing the list(s) afterwards (using an interactive whiteboard (IWB), a PC/laptop or paper) can be useful in highlighting the wide range of both ICT equipment we rely on and also other things that depend on them (street lights, traffic lights, and so on). This could be done as a group activity, with each group reporting back to the class or other groups. This can also link to displays and setting up activity areas and so on.

In using ICT in the early years, the Developmentally Appropriate Technology in Early Childhood Education (DATEC) project suggested that there are seven general principles for

determining the effectiveness of ICT applications – or uses of ICT – in the early years, to help practitioners provide the best possible experiences. They are:

1. ensure an educational purpose
2. encourage collaboration
3. integrate with other aspects of curriculum
4. ensure the child is in control
5. choose applications that are transparent – their functions should be clearly defined and intuitive
6. avoid applications containing violence or stereotyping
7. be aware of health and safety issues

Parental involvement should also go hand-in-hand with these.

(http://www.datec.org.uk/guidance/DATEC7.pdf)

Since these principles were developed, it has become necessary to amend the latter to include e-safety – see Chapter 4.

In addressing the first of these, we should not neglect ICT equipment and software not specifically aimed at the education market; however, their use 'should be educational in nature and this effectively excludes all those applications where clear learning aims cannot be identified' (Siraj-Blatchford and Whitebread, 2003, p8).

We have already considered the importance of collaboration (dialogic and interactive teaching), the child being in control (co-constructor of knowledge) and health and safety issues and e-safety. But, the third principle is vital in the context of early years education, where developing the whole child is considered to be important and 'learning is holistic and interconnected. The young child does not separate experiences into different compartments' (Fisher, 2013, p55). In this context, ICT is not a separate 'subject', but contributes to all areas of learning. Having said this, the EYFS in England does outline a progression in ICT use and skills which requires that, from birth, pupils are expected to show an interest in 'toys and resources that incorporate technology', progressing through to 'showing interest in toys with buttons and flaps', before gaining 'basic skills in turning on and operating some ICT equipment', completing a 'simple program on a computer' and using ICT 'to perform simple functions' (DCFS, 2008, pp83–4).

ACTIVITY

Our talking book – our class

ICT equipment: digital cameras, IWB, computer, software package to create pages (e.g. ActivStudio or Notebook, even PowerPoint), imagination and voice recorder (e.g. built in to computer, digital voice recorder or mobile phone)

Features of ICT

Speed

Automation

Capacity

Range

Provisionality

Interactivity

Children take digital photographs of each other. They could be wearing their own clothes or fancy dress, depending on the story. For instance, one picture could be 'My name is . . . ' and show the child in normal clothes and the next could be 'I want to be a . . . ' with them dressed up in the relevant clothes. Make pages by inserting pictures, then make voice recordings of the children saying the text above (or whatever else they want to say!). When complete, show the 'talking book' to the class but also share it with other classes – and even keep it for next year to show as an example, for staff training sessions, or for parents' evening. A green screen could make this more exciting or authentic.

Extension: Text can be added with children helping, as their ICT skill level allows. You could use a keyboard or scan in their writing (e.g. their name) if appropriate.

This type of activity can also work with different titles, such as 'We can count' or 'We speak Welsh or French'.

While curricula do vary, we can use examples from some to explore how ICT should be used in early years settings. For instance, the current guidance in Wales for the Foundation Phase echoes the child-centred learning ethos discussed above when it states that:

> *ICT should be holistic and integral across the curriculum. Children's ICT skills, knowledge and understanding should be developed through a range of experiences that involve them (i) finding and developing information and ideas, (ii) creating and presenting information and ideas.*
>
> *Children's progression in ICT capability should be observed with an understanding of child development and the stages children move through. Children should be given opportunities to develop their skills using a wide range of equipment and software.*
>
> (DCELLS, 2008, p11)

The Scottish curriculum provides a helpful, and child-centred, categorisation, which can also help us identify what skills and resources we need to provide for young children. For example:

- I explore software and use what I learn to solve problems and present my ideas, thoughts, or information.
- I enjoy exploring and using technologies to communicate with others within and beyond my place of learning.
- I enjoy taking photographs or recording sound and images to represent my experiences and the world around me.

(http://tinyurl.com/3ebp88e)

From this we can see that we need a range of ICT equipment, functioning and not functioning (for role-play situations). As well as a laptop and handheld computers (and touch screen devices such as iPads) and age-specific software, early years settings also need a variety of ICT resources that could include:

- PCs
- tablets
- digital cameras or video recorders (still images and movies)
- good internet and Wi-Fi connection – access to email
- microphones (or digital recorders – including on portable devices)
- programmable toys
- remote control toys
- walkie-talkies
- electronic microscopes
- musical devices (e.g. keyboards)
- overhead projector
- IWBs.

As technology advances, so will the length of this list. In fact, by the time you read this you may be thinking, 'Why is . . . not included?' For all of these pieces of equipment, young children will need some explicit ICT skills to use them effectively, but these can be taught as required within the context of topics. With support from classroom assistants or other children who can work with them, *all* young children can be supported to gain the necessary 'technical' or IT skills. Indeed, young children will pick up many skills informally from observing others, as they do in their homes by watching older siblings or parents. You should not underestimate what children are able to achieve by taking part in activities with others or without formal guidance.

ACTIVITY

Bear hunt (or any suitable story involving moving from place to place)

ICT equipment: floor robot and 'maps'

Features of ICT

Automation

Interactivity

After hearing a story (such as the 'Bear Hunt'), children develop a map on large pieces of paper of the places in the story using pens, paint or any other suitable medium (creative development). When they are ready, children can work in pairs or small groups to control the programmable toy or floor robot as it moves from place to place on the map.

There is an obvious link here to the early stages of programming, and this can be explored specifically in developing basic algorithms based on directions and distance travelled (for example with basic arrows and then words).

Extension: Children can develop new maps and then make the story to go with them. These can be developed as stories, short plays (videoed) or even podcasts, as well as for use with floor robots or programmable toys. Alternatively, children could build a physical maze using outdoor equipment that the robots have to navigate.

Problem solving, creativity and the 'playful' use of ICT

We have already established that young children are not afraid to 'play' and be creative with ICT in general. Some types of ICT aim to specifically exploit this by using the unique features of ICT we have examined in earlier chapters. This is particularly true of games and simulations. Whitebread (2006) outlines three characteristics of these which research suggests are good for helping young children understand and mentally 'represent' problems they are trying to solve:

1. Problems are embedded in 'meaningful contexts' – e.g. adventure stories where the child helps the characters overcome a series of challenges rather than being faced with these same challenges in isolation and without a context – the latter being what Whitebread (ibid., p87) labels 'arid and obviously artificial problems of the "if two men can dig a hole in three days" variety'.
2. Problems are simplified or 'cleaned up' to help young children see the significant features – in the same way we simplify the way we talk to younger children.
3. The same kinds of problems are posed in a variety of different contexts.

Whitebread (2006, p93) concludes that 'well constructed adventure games and simulations provide a wealth of opportunities for children to practise the skills of reasoning, hypothesis testing and decision making'. These games and simulations can be found on CD-ROMs, in specific software programs and increasingly on websites. Although not all of the latter are aimed at the education market specifically, they can have a valid use in educational settings if carefully used and monitored. Indeed, some 'collaborative' internet games can actually allow children to join forces in problem solving with others in different classes, schools or even countries.

ACTIVITY

Our outdoor play area

ICT equipment: video or sound recorders, IWB or computer with sound capability

Features of ICT

Speed

Automation

Range

Provisionality

Interactivity

Provisionality: As well as using features such as undo and redo on the IWB, provisionality also applies to other ICT equipment, through the taking and deleting of photographs, and the iPad or digital camera – see below.

Although this is about the outdoor area, the activity can be repeated in other contexts, such as 'My favourite place' (in school). The focus of the activity is to produce material for a new page on the school website. (If you search the internet for 'Our outdoor play area' you will find some examples but few contain materials by pupils – the vocabulary is a giveaway – and they show limited use of ICT except for digital pictures.) The pupils are asked to take pictures of their favourite part of the outdoor play area and record their thoughts (using a variety of media) on why they like it and what they do there. The activity takes place in small groups as part of a rotation of activities and the group is supported by an adult helper – but only in using equipment if they choose to use it. After material is collected, the class discusses what they would like to use by viewing it on the IWB or other suitable medium. The end product is uploaded to the school website.

Research tip: Mosaic approach

As many teachers undertake research of some kind, even if not for an academic qualification, we will briefly consider the advantages of using ICT in the Mosaic approach, as the activity outlined above could form part of such a piece of research. Clark (2010) provides more details of the Mosaic approach, but in essence it uses a mixture of traditional (observation and interview) and other techniques (or pieces) to build a picture from a variety of sources and individuals. It is particularly useful for finding the views of pupils in early years settings – but it could be used with all ages, including adults. The 'pieces' of the mosaic are:

- observation
- interviews
- book making
- tours
- slide shows
- map making.

Each technique, or 'piece', is intended to contribute to the whole picture or mosaic, but there is no reason why each should not be used separately – as in 'Our outdoor play area'. Of particular interest to us is how ICT can contribute. In the context of traditional techniques such as observations and interviews, there is an obvious role for video and audio recording. What is perhaps of more interest is how ICT can contribute to the other 'pieces'.

Book making provides pupils with an opportunity to use photography to take photos of important things in their environment and to compile them into a book, using either a computer or iPad (for instance, with the Book Creator app). Only one child at a time uses the camera or iPad, but others can accompany the photographer – including the adult in a passive role (in other words, making sure not to suggest what is to be photographed). Any device can be used to take the pictures, but it may be best to use digital cameras designed for use with early years pupils or an iPod/iPad with grips fitted if necessary to help them hold it steady. The aspect of provisionality we have discussed above means that children can take, retake and delete as many photographs as the capacity of the camera will allow. (This is a great advantage over disposable cameras, which contain a finite amount of film.) The digital nature of these photographs also means that compiling a book, or indeed adding them to a slide show, is an easy task. When compiling the book, it is also easy to view the pictures using a variety of tools.

(continued)

(continued)

Tours encourage pupils to show adults around their environment, indicating what is important to them. Individuals, pairs or small groups can conduct these tours. The role of the 'researcher' in the process is as an interested adult. Clark (2010, p37) suggests that 'the use of child-led tours privileges the way that young children communicate in active, visual ways. This method does not rely on verbal communication as children can point out features, but rich conversations may be triggered by children walking through their environment'. Although Clark suggests that the researcher takes field notes, it may also be possible, with the advent of very small cameras, to also use video recordings to capture gesture, emotion and vocabulary.

Slide shows can be used to show not only pictures taken by the pupils, but also those of other settings. Early work in this area used slide projectors, but the ability of an IWB to allow a number of pupils to view the same image, or to show images on suitable television screens, has changed the nature of this work, if not the name. The role of the researcher is to monitor the actions of the children as they interact with the images and record any resulting conversations.

Map making can range in sophistication from young children's interpretations of their environment in any form, through to more sophisticated versions using ICT tools. The intention of creating the maps, which can hold information about both the past and the present, is to record both remembered events and geographical locations. ICT also has a role in recording (for example, by scanning work) and sharing the work of others. The main function of the map is to enable the children to record significant places: 'this is not map making in order to gain accurate topographical records' (Clark, 2010, p40).

As already stated, although the intention is to create an overall picture made up of many pieces, each technique may also be valuable to teachers as a separate activity in gaining evidence of how children feel about their environment and about each other. Even if not used for research purposes, such information is valid in records of achievement or pupil profiles.

When to use ICT in the early years

With such a wealth of resources available, it is important to consider *when* they can be used. All such decisions need to be focused, as usual, on exploiting the features of ICT to best effect and on how ICT contributes to achieving the desired learning outcome. Many of these uses of ICT will take the form of interactions between pupil and ICT, or between pupils through ICT. Based on a small-scale case study of literacy activities in an American kindergarten, Labbo et al. (2000) suggest three kinds of interactions with ICT that could be effective in early years settings:

1. *Brief targeted moments* – these consist of activities that take 5 to 10 minutes to complete.
2. *Spur-of-the-moment ideas* – these usually consist of child-initiated, spontaneous activities that can be accomplished with little prior planning and that make use of available materials.
3. *Thematically linked activities* – these are carefully planned, multi-layered activities that involve multiple opportunities to learn key concepts in various ways.

Within these interactions, and others besides, teachers need to make decisions about what equipment to use, but Kennington and Meaton (2009) remind us that the most important factor is not the equipment, but the way it is used. They also rightly suggest that it is not always the most expensive piece of equipment that is the best. They give the example of 'talking tins', which are small plastic 'discs' (8cm diameter and 2cm deep) that can record sound (from 10 seconds to 40 seconds and costing from about £3 to £8 at the time of writing) and play it back at the press of a button. They also have a built-in magnet, which means they can be attached to suitable metal objects or surfaces – although there are also straps to attach them to other things. There are many variations of this, some of which even trigger sound by motion detection, so that when a child enters a 'zone' the sound (instructions, clues and so on, recorded by teachers or pupils) are played automatically. (See for example, http://tinyurl.com/q2fxvz.)

These simple devices, and whatever replaces them as technology advances (including augmented reality – see Chapter 5), have many uses for both pupils and teachers. Like other ICT resources that do similar things, these devices do not get bored of saying the same thing time and again. They can be re-recorded easily (but can also be locked to prevent loss of recording), and are easy to carry and operate. A few examples of their use are given below, all with educational purposes, but you could easily think of more:

- Pupils draw pictures of themselves and put them on the wall. They record their name and something about themselves on the 'tin' and stick this to the wall with a 'press me' or similar pictorial label.
- The teacher places the tins around the outdoor play area with instructions of where to go next on a treasure trail.
- The teacher places tins around the school hall with instructions for activities (e.g. jump in the air three times).
- The teacher places the tin next to an activity with no adult support as a reminder of what to do.
- The teacher puts tins next to objects with recordings of a language being learned (e.g. Welsh) or English for learners.

ACTIVITY

Message in a (electronic) bottle

ICT equipment: video or sound recorders, IWB or computer with sound capability, clip art of bottles or digital pictures, suitable background

Features of ICT

According to your ICT confidence, you can start this activity in any way but the key idea is that the message has washed up on shore. One easy way is to use an image similar to the first picture above on a PowerPoint slide with wave sound effects. You can then have another image on the next slide and include your own message and picture, for example a picture of a teddy and a message asking for help finding it – you can also record the speech and click on it (or auto play)

to read the text for those who may find it hard to read. Many activities could follow this model – e.g. find a hidden teddy, plan a journey to find him . . . Alternatively, you could just use the first slide (using the features of ICT – sound, automation, and so on) and then produce 'the actual bottle' and open it with the children.

ICT and personal confidence

In addition to the confidence that ICT can give to pupils by presenting their written work in a highly professional manner, instead of in their emerging handwriting, it can also be used to give pupils a voice. This 'voice' can be through a variety of formats, such as photography or music, but can also encourage pupils to use their real voice in new ways. James and Cane (2009) report a range of instances, including:

- using a remote-controlled car to encourage a pupil to extend his sentences;
- using a karaoke machine to encourage a withdrawn three-year-old to sing, and then continue to talk to the class through the system;
- using a voice changer device to encourage a pupil who was self-conscious about his accent to talk to peers.

From this we can see that ICT can help young children to find a variety of voices that can encourage communication, not only with other pupils but also with teachers.

SUMMARY

From all of the above, we can conclude that ICT use should form part of a heuristic learning experience, with play being central to learning using both functioning and non-functioning ICT resources. In this sense, ICT can be the subject of play, a tool for play or a method of stimulating play. Although some explicit teaching of skills will be required, pupils are also able to learn from each other, by observing the teacher and by using ICT resources to gain access to a range of different voices to facilitate and encourage communication.

References

Aubrey, C. and Dahl, S. (2008) *A Review of the Evidence on the Use of ICT in the Early Years Foundation Stage*, Coventry: Becta.

Beauchamp, G., Burden, K. and Abbinett, E. (2015) 'Teachers learning to use the iPad in Scotland and Wales: a new model of professional development', *Journal of Education for Teaching: International Research and Pedagogy*, 41(2), pp161–79.

Beauchamp, G. with Purcell, N. (2016) 'Current developments in education', in Wyse, D. and Rogers, S. (eds) *A Guide to Early Years and Primary Teaching*, London: Sage, pp45–66.

Blaiklock, K. (2010) 'Te Whāriki, the New Zealand early childhood curriculum: is it effective?', *International Journal of Early Years Education*, 18(3), pp201–12.

Bratton, C., Crossey, U., Crosby, D. and McKeown, W. (2005) *Learning Outdoors in the Early Years*, http://ccea.org.uk/sites/default/files/docs/curriculum/area_of_learning/fs_learning_outdoors_resource_book.pdf (accessed 17 February 2016).

Clark, A. (2010) *Transforming Children's Spaces: Children and Adult's Participation in Designing Learning Environments*, London: Routledge.

DCELLS (2008) *Framework for Children's Learning for 3 to 7-year-olds in Wales*, Cardiff: WAG.

DCFS (2008) *Practice Guidance for the Early Years Foundation Stage*, Annesley: DCFS Publications.

DfE (2014) *Statutory Framework for the Early Years Foundation Stage: Setting the Standards for Learning, Development and Care for Children from Birth to Five*, London: Department for Education (DfE).

Edwards, S. (2013) 'Digital play in the early years: a contextual response to the problem of integrating technologies and play-based pedagogies in the early childhood curriculum', *European Early Childhood Education Research Journal*, 21(2), pp199–212.

Fisher, J. (2013) *Starting from the Child: Teaching and Learning in the Foundation Stage*, 4th edition, Maidenhead: McGraw-Hill Education.

Gourd, J. (2014) 'The influence of international policy', in Kingdon, Z. and Gourd, J. (eds) *Early Years Policy: The Impact on Practice*, London: Routledge, pp56–74.

Haughton, C. and Ellis, C. (2013) 'Play in the Early Years Foundation Stage', in Palaiologou, I. (ed.) *The Early Years Foundation Stage: Theory and Practice*, 2nd edition, London: Sage, pp73–87.

Hayes, M. (2006) 'What do the children have to say?', in Hayes, M. and Whitebread, D. (eds) *ICT in the Early Years*, Maidenhead: Open University Press.

James. K. and Cane, C. (2009) 'Giving, children a voice by using ICT', in Price, H. (ed.) *The Really Useful Book of ICT in the Early Years*, London: Routledge, pp53–68.

Kennington, L. and Meaton, J. (2009) 'Integrating ICT into the Early Years curriculum', in Price, H. (ed.) *The Really Useful Book of ICT in the Early Years*, London: Routledge, pp4–24.

Kingdon, Z. (2014) 'Policy and the change in the early years learning environment', in Kingdon, Z. and Gourd, J. (eds) *Early Years Policy: The Impact on Practice*, London: Routledge, pp152–72.

Labbo, L.D., Sprague, L., Montero, M.K. and Font, G. (2000) 'Connecting a computer centre to theme's literature and kindergarteners' literacy needs', *Reading Online* 4(1).

Learning and Teaching Scotland (2010) *Curriculum for Excellence through Outdoor Learning*, Glasgow: Learning and Teaching Scotland, https://www.educationscotland.gov.uk/Images/cfeoutdoorlearningfinal_tcm4-596061.pdf (accessed 30 November 2015).

Leggett, N. and Ford, M. (2013) 'A fine balance: understanding the roles educators and children play as intentional teachers and intentional learners within the Early Years Learning Framework', *Australasian Journal of Early Childhood*, 38(4), pp42–50.

Marsh, J., Brooks, G., Hughes, J., Ritchie, L., Roberts, S. and Wright, K. (2005) *Digital Beginnings: Young Children's Use of Popular Culture, Media and New Technologies*, Sheffield: Literacy Research Centre, University of Sheffield.

Marsh, J., Plowman, L., Yamada-Rice, D., Bishop, J.C., Lahmar, J., Scott, F., Davenport, A., Davis, S., French, K., Piras, M., Thornhill, S., Robinson, P. and Winter, P. (2015) *Exploring Play and Creativity in Pre-Schoolers' Use of Apps: Final Project Report*, http://www.techandplay.org (accessed on 22 February 2016).

Morgan, A.I. and Siraj-Blatchford, I. (2009) *Using ICT in the Early Years: Parents and Practitioners in Partnership*, London: Practical Pre-School Books.

Nikolopoulou, K. and Gialamas, V. (2015) 'ICT and play in preschool: early childhood teachers' beliefs and confidence', *International Journal of Early Years Education*, 23(4), pp409–25.

Siraj-Blatchford, I. and Whitebread, D. (2003) *Supporting ICT in the Early Years*, Maidenhead: Open University Press.

Stephen, C. and Edwards, S. (2015) 'Digital play and technologies in the early years', *Early Years*, 35(2), p227.

Synodi, E. (2010) 'Play in the kindergarten: the case of Norway, Sweden, New Zealand and Japan', *International Journal of Early Years Education*, 18(3), pp185–200.

Taylor, C., Joshi, H. and Wright, C. (2015) 'Evaluating the impact of early years educational reform in Wales to age seven: the potential use of the UK Millennium Cohort Study', *Journal of Education Policy*, 30(5), pp688–712.

Whitebread, D. (2006) 'Creativity, problem-solving and playful uses of technology: games and simulations in the early years', in Hayes, M. and Whitebread, D. (eds) *ICT in the Early Years*, Maidenhead: Open University Press, pp86–106.

Further reading

Palaiologou, I., Walsh, G., MacQuarrie, S., Waters, J. and Dunphy, E. (2013) 'The national picture', in Palaiologou, I. (ed.) *The Early Years Foundation Stage: Theory and Practice*, 2nd edition, London: Sage, pp37–54.

Useful websites

Homerton Early Years Centre: http://homerton.cambs.sch.uk/information-for-practioners/ict-in-the-early-years/ Website with resources for exploring how ICT can be used in the EYFS. The site has areas covering planning and resources and a gallery of images showing ICT in action. It also has links to the Centre's previous website with many other resources.

ICT, English and digital literacy in Key Stages 1 and 2

In this chapter we will examine how ICT has changed the conventional notion of literacy, as well as the emerging field of digital literacy, and consider the impact of this in the classroom. The potential use of ICT in the areas of speaking and listening, reading and writing is analysed, taking account of a range of new literacies. Ideas in this chapter, and the next, will not be tied to age-related progression, such as Key Stages 1 and 2, but rather will consider the progression in, and of, ideas. This is important because, as we saw in Chapter 3, ideas do not develop in strict accordance with age.

Literacy

As we have seen in earlier chapters, advances in ICT both inside the classroom and beyond have led to a situation where new skills are needed by both teachers and learners across the curriculum. This is particularly true in the area of literacy, and Haggerty (2010, p177) asserts that 'calls to broaden notions of "literacy" from a focus on print-based and verbal literacies to the incorporation of a range of modes of communication and representation are increasing'. Such a change of focus means that learners are required to move beyond traditional printed texts and even the use of text itself. As Clary, Kigotho and Barros-Torning (2013, p49) point out: 'In today's world, a literate person must be able to read and create a range of paper-based and online texts (e.g., newspapers, pamphlets, websites, books, Kindle), participate in and create virtual settings (e.g., classrooms, Second Life, Facebook, Elluminate, blogs, wikis) that use interactive and dynamic Web 2.0 tools, and critically analyse multimodal texts and integrate visual, musical, dramatic, digital, and new literacies.' Since this was written, we could also add being able to code using a range of programming languages. We arrive at a situation where, 'In the 21st century the ability to understand digital, visual and audio media is a form of literacy which is as basic as reading and writing skills' (Duchak, 2014, p41).

It could be argued that, of all these potential new forms of literacies, 'digital literacy' has emerged as the most common in educational discourse, particularly in recent times. It is, however, situated in a complex set of other literacies, both old and new. Figure 8.1 below shows some that a child will encounter in the primary school, starting with the focus in most current curricula on traditional print literacy.

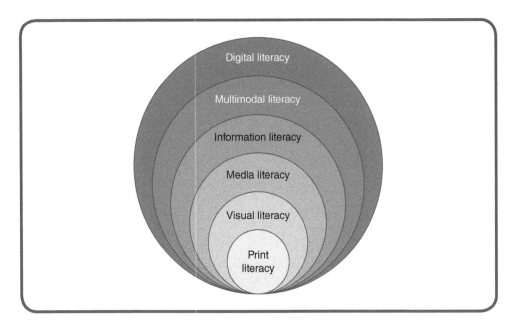

Figure 8.1   Traditional versus new literacies

This model is not hierarchical, but does show the current centrality of print literacy in primary schools, which may change as years go by. It also necessarily simplifies the relationship between these literacies (and omits others), but even these are often inter-connected and overlapping. For instance, many pieces of hardware and software do not rely on text or reading, but rather convey information and meaning using a range of modes (such as icons or images, both moving and still), sometimes displayed through a range of media. Thus, from an early age, pupils have to move beyond their print literacy and use, for instance, their visual and multimodal literacies to interpret meaning.

The result of this – and of other factors, such as the growth of the internet and mobile access to it – is that new key skills are needed in relation to ICT and English, which will help in both accessing materials and constructing content. In this context, we could con-sider that literacy 'is the broader canvas. ICT is the medium of access and construction' (Brindley, 2000, p14). Using this 'medium' can, however, present both technical and phil-osophical challenges. Technical challenges can come from new techniques to be mastered (such as hyperlinks and coding), but some also come from the attitudes of those who contribute to the fast-growing amount of information available to pupils – and indeed teachers. One of the most significant is the move away from 'filter then publish' to 'publish then filter' by creators of digital content (Shirky, 2008, cited in Hellen, 2011, p108).

To accommodate such changes, Rudd and Tyldesley (2006) suggest new skills are needed. These include the following:

- *The ability to find information* – learners no longer have a conventional index, table of contents or page numbers. Instead they have to learn to navigate electronic texts, and teachers need to equip them to recognise signposts and clues.
- *The ability to develop critical thinking and evaluate* – when we pick up a book or a letter, we have learned to make some judgements about reliability and authority.

Electronic media do not always give the same clues. The validity of a text from a respectable publisher offers some assurance of quality, whereas a website can be published by anybody.

- *The ability to re-present information in different ways for different audiences* – new media literacy relies heavily on the skill of reading. It is important, however, that children are taught to produce text as authors, web designers or multimedia creators.
- *The ability to use new media as a creative space* – we have already seen some examples of how new media can lead to creativity in a way that is simply not possible without ICT. Indeed, there is evidence from primary schools in Hong Kong and other countries that media education, as a discrete area of learning, can be beneficial in enabling primary pupils to construct and interpret a range of media (Cheung, 2005).

In order to learn these across the curriculum, there is often a need to teach specific skills in advance of them being required, and it could be argued that this need will be greater in the earlier years of the primary school. Bennett, Hamill and Pickford (2007) provide a model of ICT capability (see Figure 8.2) that shows how pupils develop growing independence based on increasing acquisition of skill, routines, techniques and key ideas of ICT. They suggest that the shape of the cone represents 'both the progression of activities . . . [and] the numerical relationships between the elements of capability, e.g. the key ideas of ICT are relatively few in number compared to the number of basic skills that must be learned' (ibid., p21). Considering where pupils start in the spiral is important to ensure challenge. In addition, however, considering such a model also reminds us that for each lesson or topic you teach you cannot assume that pupils have the necessary expertise and you may have to start at the bottom, teaching new skills, before pupils can work independently. This applies even in Year 6 if the pupils are mastering a new piece of equipment or software. In planning lessons, an easy mistake is to equate older children automatically with independence in one area, just because they have it in another. If you get this wrong it can easily wreck your lesson timings as you have to spend time teaching an ICT skill and then have limited time left to do the activity you have planned. This applies both within ICT as a subject and in applying it in other areas of the curriculum.

This model, however, may not apply to all new technologies. For instance, Beauchamp, Burden and Abbinett (2015) suggest that, with the iPad, there may be no need to teach any skills at all as pupils either arrive at school knowing them or they are so intuitive that they (and teachers) pick them up from 'playing' with devices.

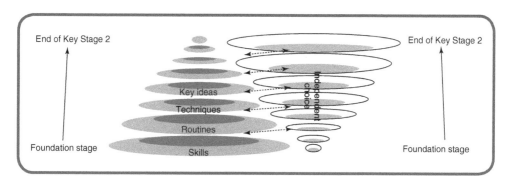

Figure 8.2   **A model of ICT capability – the global level**

Digital literacy

As Bjørgen and Erstad (2015, p115) point out: 'During the last decade, digital literacy has emerged as a key term in policy, practice and research. Still it is often unclear what this term implies.' Lankshear and Knobel (2006) suggest that definitions fall into two categories: conceptual and operationalisation or procedural – which define tasks and skills, and so on, which will be adopted into a curriculum. The latter accords with Buckingham's view that, with the introduction of multiple 'literacies' (such as visual, emotional, multimedia and even multi-literacies) over the last 20 years, the original meaning of literacy (relating to the medium of writing) has been lost to the extent that it now is used as a 'vague synonym for competence, or even skill' (2015, p22). Sefton-Green, Nixon and Erstad (2009, p108), however, assert that: 'It is clearly far too superficial simply to equate digital literacy with *using* digital technologies, because the notion of *literacy* evokes a multiplicity of competencies, skills and knowledges.'

Despite this, 'traditional' skills such as reading and writing remain important, but they

are not restricted to the mere coding and decoding of text, rather they are being used to describe the processes of extracting meaning from, and recording and presenting your own meaning through, the full range of media. This would include the ability to manipulate the basic tools required to create and access these media, just as holding a pen, forming letters and turning pages are part of text-based literacy. The end-products of literacy can range from a note to the milkman, to a hypertext on the Romans to a feature film. The common thread is that an author or group of authors have an idea or set of ideas which they wish to present to an audience.

(McFarlane, 2000, p19)

Such an approach would use many modes of communication (see 'Multimodal and multimedia capability' in Chapter 1), including visual representation, sound, movement, gesture and language, although the value of individual modes made vary between countries and cultures. What does not vary, however, is that in any single communicational event, different modes will be combined, with one or more becoming more prominent depending on the person communicating, the message they are trying to give, and their intended audience. In this situation, 'meaning is made through complex interactions between the different modes' (Sutherland, Robertson and John, 2009, p118), and Kress and Jewitt (2008) assert that no communication is 'monomodal'.

One implication of such views is that we must challenge 'the implicit assumption that speech and writing are always central and sufficient for learning' (Kress and Jewitt, 2008, p2). Such an assertion does not in any way imply that speech and writing are not vital for education, but it does suggest that we should consider carefully their position in a constantly evolving world of technology. Following this consideration, we may conclude that pupils need to be equipped to view language as a 'metamode' (Matthewman, 2009) that enables them to access the meanings of a wide variety of texts, images, sounds and information within their cultural context, in terms of both the school setting and wider society. ICT is the source of some of these modes, but it also provides access to others, as well as a means of raising and answering questions through shared endeavour – more on this to follow below. Unfortunately, in educational terms, we have to frame this argument in the slightly less esoteric context of the requirements of a national curriculum, which at present focuses on spoken language, reading and writing. We will now consider these in turn, as they would be important even without a national curriculum.

Spoken language

There has been much research in recent years in the United Kingdom (UK) that explores how ICT contributes to developing talk in the classroom. This is particularly true when using the interactive whiteboard (IWB), especially in the context of whole-class teaching. We have already briefly discussed dialogic teaching (see Chapter 2), but it is now possible to explore this and other concepts in relation to ICT in more detail. Central to this exploration are three components of the dialogic approach outlined by Warwick, Hennessy and Mercer (2011):

- Dialogue should support the co-construction of knowledge and understanding.
- Dialogue should make reasoning explicit.
- Dialogue should be cumulative.

The authors report that 'cumulative' talk can be interpreted in different ways, but conclude that 'whole-class dialogue should allow the participants to orientate themselves to other perspectives and to evaluate their own ideas and solutions against others' statements and propositions' (Warwick, Hennessy and Mercer, 2011, p307). In this context, it is important to note that 'dialogue' can include spoken language, but also includes other modes of communication facilitated by the IWB, such as annotating, drawing, sorting and manipulating images. This is important, as it allows pupils who may not normally join in spoken conversation, or find this difficult for any reason, to join in dialogue with others. In the remainder of this chapter, 'talk' will be used as a generic term, to include dialogue and other forms of talk, as outlined above, so that talk 'is both the medium of learning and a tool for learning' (Myhill, Jones and Hopper, 2006, p7).

Central to facilitating effective talk is the language teachers use, particularly when questioning. This is important because, in the past, some studies have claimed that 70 per cent of talk in the classroom is done by the teacher (Baumfield and Mroz, 2002) and that it 'is now well recognized that this is a variable that impacts on students' learning and achievement' (Geoghegan, O'Neill and Petersen, 2013, p120). This is supported by Mercer, Dawes and Staarman (2009, p355) who report that:

There is much support from research for teachers giving attention to how they use talk to guide pupils' understanding, and for actively involving pupils in that process. However, research also shows that this seems to have had relatively little impact on the quality of classroom talk, which is still commonly dominated by closed questions, short pupil response and little direct attention being given to the use of talk for teaching-and-learning.

Unfortunately, other studies have supported this. For instance, in a study of primary school classes, Myhill, Jones and Hopper (2006) found, in common with earlier studies (e.g. Hargreaves, Hislam and English, 2002), that 60 per cent of primary teacher's questions required a factual answer: that is, questions that require a predetermined response. In addition, Tanner and Jones (2007, p323) report that, in whole-class teaching, 'although teachers now ask more questions, most pupil responses remain very short, just five seconds on average, and involve three or fewer words'. This is perhaps not unexpected when much talk, especially in whole-class teaching, is dominated by a 'recitation script' (Tharp and Gallimore, 1988) in which the IRF (initiation, response, follow-on) model still dominates. Smith, Hardman and Higgins (2006, p444) report that this is

> particularly prevalent in directive forms of teaching and often consists of closed teacher questions, brief pupil answers which teachers do not build upon, superficial praise rather than diagnostic feedback, and an emphasis on recalling information rather than genuine exploration of a topic. Recitation questioning therefore seeks predictable correct answers and only rarely are teachers' questions used to assist pupils to more complete or elaborated ideas.

The dominance of teacher questions also has an impact on the number of questions that pupils ask within the school setting. Evidence from earlier studies highlights how few questions pupils ask when they enter school compared with the many they ask their parents before entering school – from 50 per cent at home to 5 per cent upon entering nursery according to one study (Tizard and Hughes, 1984, cited in Baumfield and Mroz, 2002).

Such a situation is hardly likely to encourage effective learning, so we need to consider how ICT, especially the IWB (and now potentially the iPad), can encourage a use of higher order skills in talk and can encourage pupils to ask and respond to questions. However, teachers still need to ask more open questions and allow pupils the chance to think about their responses before answering. No amount of ICT can help this to happen, and the focus must remain primarily on developing effective pedagogy and only then using ICT. There remains, however, a tension between the need for extended responses (and critical engagement) and the requirements for 'pace' in lessons – the latter is something that ICT can be good at and even encourage.

Despite concerns about pace, ICT does provide a powerful tool for developing all aspects of talk. Using the full range of ICT (or ICTs, if you prefer), you have a variety of options that can provide a stimulus to start dialogue and to facilitate extended dialogue using a variety of modes and media, and also a means of saving the 'dialogue' (in spoken and other modes, as discussed above) in a variety of formats that can be shared as necessary. As the person in control of access to ICT resources (at least in the first instance), the teacher is crucial in terms of facilitating dialogue through effective generic planning and classroom practice, but also in planning and facilitating the use of ICT for this purpose if it is the best option. We will now consider how ICT(s) can help to start, enable or extend, save and share 'talk'.

Stimulating or initiating 'talk'

Perhaps the most common use of ICT to initiate talk is as a whole-class activity at the start of lessons. As a 'digital hub' (Cutrim Schmid, 2010), the IWB provides a range of options that can provoke classroom talk in this context. The use of the IWB should, however, always be considered alongside other non-ICT options, as sometimes they may provide something ICT cannot. It is very difficult for a video to compete with a student teacher (or other adult) rushing into the classroom dressed as an explorer wanting to tell the children about their adventures and asking the class to help save a colleague left behind – as witnessed in one Key Stage 1 lesson recently, along with background jungle noises playing over the classroom speakers triggered through the IWB by the classroom assistant just before the teacher entered the room. (I should perhaps mention that this student teacher was a drama specialist, which helps!) What ICT *can* do is to then show the children high-quality pictures of the jungle and videos of some of the animals that live there, as well as a map that allows you to zoom in from above down to ground level, not to mention opening and replying to an email from the explorer who was left behind (using a solar-powered computer, in case they ask!) – which you sent in a fit of creativity the night before while preparing your costume! Remember, all of this (except the dressing up) can be done in one place on the IWB, hence the digital hub. What is suggested here, as elsewhere, is that you use ICT for what it can do better than anything else. (If you can't face dressing up, then a video sent via email may be the next best thing – although more preparation is required, as well as technical skill in recording and editing the video and then sending, saving and accessing it.) Although this starts as a whole-class activity, the next step could be to discuss with talk partners or small groups depending on the outcomes you wish to achieve.

Much recent research has focused on how the IWB can create a 'dialogic classroom' (Warwick, Hennessy and Mercer, 2011) or encourage 'dialogic space' (Mercer et al., 2010) using a variety of multimodal interactions (Hennessy, 2011). In all of these approaches, the IWB allows children to undertake collaborative learning with dialogue at the centre of the activity. This dialogue, and the use of the IWB, is set within a classroom pedagogy that allows for the development of the necessary talk skills and interactive skills to ensure that children can work together effectively. In other words, we cannot assume that children will use talk or co-operate effectively without explicit teaching of relevant skills – see, for example, 'Talk Lessons' (Wegerif and Dawes, 2004). Interactive technologies (such as the IWB) have a role in helping to initiate, define, undertake and record tasks (Mercer et al., 2010). Table 8.1 (**http://dialogue iwb.educ.cam.ac.uk/resources/**) provides a useful framework for you as a teacher to both develop and observe how a class may interact and the associated behaviours to make this interaction effective.

Tools to enable or extend 'talk'

It is important to reiterate here that ICT on its own will not facilitate an environment where talk will flourish. The talk needs to be situated in a wider pedagogic practice where pupils have opportunities to contribute ideas that both you and other children take seriously, and to ask and answer questions to build shared understanding. This is true at all ages, from reception to the end of the primary phase – and hopefully beyond. Central to this dialogic pedagogy (Alexander, 2008) is the posing of open-ended higher-order questions, contributing ideas, reflecting on what has been said and interpreting as necessary to help develop ideas. To aid in this process, Mercer et al. (2010, pp381–2) suggest that the IWB allows children easily to:

• access relevant material prepared by the teacher, which is relevant to the task, and move backward and forward through it according to their needs;
• annotate that material to take account of the developing discussions;

Table 8.1	Using the IWB to support the development of dialogue in the classroom	
In my classroom, we . . .	**You will see us . . .**	**So that we can . . .**
• respect, trust and listen to each other • take risks and experiment by trying out new teaching approaches • encourage children to be responsible for their own learning • use good subject knowledge and awareness of our children's needs to help us use children's contributions to advance the dialogue taking place • support children in a range of ways to enable them to share their views and ideas • value talk in our lessons and plan for it to take place • are willing to sometimes change our minds • continue a dialogue over time, from lesson to lesson • use a wide range of IWB features and resources to stimulate, enhance and record aspects of our learning	• sharing, discussing, commenting on and exploring our views and ideas • asking each other questions • showing that we consider other people's views • sometimes trying to reach a shared understanding by building on what people say • giving feedback and responding in a helpful way – being a 'critical friend' • realising what we need or would like to learn and doing something about it! • using what we already know to help us • reasoning and thinking aloud • telling each other what we have learnt when we have been thinking by ourselves • using classroom resources, including the IWB, in different ways to help us in our learning • saying why we agree or disagree with an idea	• realise what we still need or want to learn and how we might like to do it • extend and refine what we already know • explain our reasoning clearly • help each other to understand things in a new way • come to agreement • express a range of views

- remove and modify what they have written to take account of each other's views and their changing shared ideas;
- ensure that all members of the group can see what is being discussed, and what any member has contributed as annotations to the material;
- offer advice to each other about their annotations or other treatment of the material (e.g. the selection of specific slides or searches for relevant information).

While the above is true of the IWB, it may also be increasingly true that mobile devices (such as the iPad) can also offer the potential to do the same thing, which can be useful in encouraging and extending talk in groups. In the above use of the IWB, we can see that ICT is allowing pupils to make their thinking explicit and open to all, which is another important feature of enabling and extending talk. This is a central feature of using the IWB in this context and one that can only take place in a supportive classroom atmosphere, where mistakes are seen as acceptable and a step to further knowledge. It is suggested that, to be effective, such an approach needs to be introduced at an early age and be part of a whole-school strategy. At the very least, it needs to be consistent when *you* are teaching a class. This is not always straightforward due to pressures of time, but, if time is given in planning to providing opportunities for such discussion, it is more likely to happen.

WHAT DO YOU THINK?

You are teaching a lesson using an IWB. You use the wrong feature and the work you have prepared disappears. You have reassured pupils that it is all right to make mistakes in your class, but what do you do next?

Saving and recording 'talk'

Once the talk has been generated, it is also useful to be able to save or record it. Each different mode or media used may require specific knowledge of how to save and share, depending on the hardware and software involved, but generic principles can be applied to all. Central to acquiring the necessary skills is the belief that talk has merit and is worth sharing. As in much written work, and in accordance with many curriculum expectations, we need to consider the target audience for the talk both in terms of style and in taking account of their developmental capabilities – with young children who cannot read, it would be inappropriate to use text but video may be suitable. The options for sharing are many and include:

- email
- website, blog or wiki
- intranet
- pen drive
- secure online storage, such as Dropbox or similar – which can also be synchronised with home and school computers or other devices (e.g. iPads).

The whole process, not just the end result, of constructing, saving and sharing work should be part of the educational process and can reflect the belief that pupils are actively involved in their learning. With mobile devices, the saving (and sharing) does not even have to be done by you, as many mobile devices allow easy uploading facilities that can be operated by very young children. In this case, the role of the teacher is really to lead the process (for instance, initiate a discussion about the options and ensure that the right questions are asked – about online security, for example) rather than complete the steps in the process – although you need to be familiar with the process to help if required. In saving work on networks, or in online storage facilities, you are also creating digital portfolios. In this case the audience is twofold: the first is the pupils themselves, to aid in reflecting on their work; the second is others in school and beyond – including parents.

As work is stored, and added to over time, there is evidence that compiling and then using digital portfolios (that is, the electronic storage of work) in primary schools is an effective stimulus for talk (Wall et al., 2006), as well as an enjoyable and valuable activity that encourages pupils to think not only about their work, but also about themselves as learners (McLeod and Vasinda, 2009).

Sharing 'talk'

As 'talk' becomes available in real time and online, we need to consider potential audiences beyond those immediately involved. Beyond the confines of the classroom, Dawes, Mercer and Wegerif (2000) remind us that the 'C' in ICT refers to communication, both sharing information and jointly constructing knowledge. They suggest further that, with advances in ICT, this should be communication both within the classroom and at a distance. As such, we can consider how ICT can contribute to sharing talk between:

- individuals
- groups
- the whole class
- classrooms within a school
- schools.

Podcasts

One way of sharing talk is to use podcasts. In simple terms, a podcast is an audio recording that is hosted on a website, such as your school website, and can be listened to anywhere in the world with an internet connection. As such, 'A podcast is like a radio show. However, instead of being broadcast live, a podcast is recorded and then distributed over the internet' (http://www.teachingideas.co.uk/multimedia/podcasting-0). Deal (2007, p2) suggests that podcasts are normally linked thematically and 'are accompanied by a file called a "feed" that allows listeners to subscribe to the series and receive new episodes automatically'. In creating the finished sound file, it is unlikely that a complete file can be recorded in one 'take', so it is likely that a sound editing program will be needed. There are many options available commercially as well as free programs such as Audacity (http://audacity.sourceforge.net/), all of which allow you to edit and save sound in a variety of formats. Using this type of program, or other free programs such as Garage Band on Apple computers, it is possible to add musical introductions and other features. In addition to these slightly more complicated programs, it is also possible to create and upload podcasts on mobile devices such as iPhones or android-based phones – although they may not allow the creation of different tracks, so everything may have to be done in real time as a live event. It may be, however, that less sophisticated types of software could allow you to create and upload podcasts in a variety of settings outside the classroom, such as on a school trip. This can also be useful in relating to work across the curriculum (see Chapter 10), as some apps are also linked to mapping services that show the location where the podcast was recorded. The caveat to using any sites other than your school website to host your podcasts is that ultimately you have less control – you need to read the host site's terms and conditions carefully.

To create a podcast, the basic requirements are a microphone (built into many computers and mobile devices), a computer and an internet connection. Beyond these basics, however, we need to understand the purpose of a podcast before proceeding. In the context of this chapter, the purpose is to share 'talk', but this talk should have a purpose. To be effective, a podcast should be more than a recording of the lesson or an event (such as a class assembly) that takes place in real time – although there is no reason why extracts from such recordings should not be included in a podcast. Such events are 'of the moment' and there may be better ways (such as video) of recording them, and the recording would have a different purpose. This distinction is important, because, as Middleton (2009, p144) points out, when discussing the use of podcasts in higher education, 'disappointingly, the term is synonymous in some quarters with the transmission of the teacher's knowledge through the distribution of recorded lectures'. We have seen throughout this book that, although ICT is good at transmitting knowledge, we need to use it more imaginatively. In this case, we need to see how podcasts can be used with primary pupils to help them work collaboratively to co-construct knowledge and understanding. To do this, they need to be actively involved in both the design and construction of podcasts.

CASE STUDY

Examples of primary school podcasts are increasingly common. One is provided by The Downs CE primary school, whose website gives detailed notes on how the pupils produce their podcasts. In summary:

We begin each week by deciding what we're going to put into each show, and organising who is going to make the different parts of it. Some of us might find and record jokes, others might research and record a news article, whilst another group might prepare and record an interview with a member of staff, or with a special guest . . . It's really difficult trying to make The Downs FM in our usual lesson time because there are so many children in the class, and it's not very easy giving them all a job to do. So, we usually prepare for our shows during our lunchtimes. Sometimes we record the show in front of our class, as this gives us an audience (who can also get involved in the show), but that makes things a little more nerve-wracking!

In this case, uploading of the finished file and setting up the relevant feed to allow subscribers to receive the broadcast are done by the class teacher. Many schools, however, will have an ICT co-ordinator who could do this, but the process is not complicated and can be done from within a variety of programs. Before starting to produce your own podcasts, it would be best to listen to the work of other primary schools –for example, see http://www.longshawprimaryschool.com/podcast-page

Although it may seem from the above that the process of creating podcasts is complicated, they have some advantages, in common with all material posted on a virtual learning environment (VLE) or website. These include that they:

- are produced specifically for the pupils in the class for school;
- are available 'on demand' at any time of the day and from anywhere with an internet connection;
- have the potential to help pupils with special needs;
- are useful if pupils miss lessons;
- can help with communication with parents, who can listen to podcasts with their children;
- can be helpful for pupils with English as an additional language (EAL);
- can motivate pupils if they are involved in the production of materials;
- can help develop teamwork if groups of children are involved in production;
- can help develop literacy skills (such as writing scripts or interview questions, or writing for a particular audience) and they can also allow pupils to develop and practise their speaking and listening skills;
- add another 'layer' to the text as it can be easier to recognise, or add, emotion in the spoken word – it also personalises the experience for the children if they hear other children of their own age;
- are portable, as they can be downloaded onto any MP3 player, computer or iPod, or even burned onto CDs – all of this means that podcasts can be listened to anywhere, from the pupil's bedroom to in a car on a journey.

To balance this list of advantages, we also need to consider the disadvantages of podcasting compared with other forms of communication. These include the following:

- It is difficult to include links to websites in podcasts compared with text-based material, where these can be included as clickable links.
- It may take a longer time to refine the finished product compared with a piece of writing, as they are more difficult to edit.
- There is a degree of technical knowledge required.
- As above, it may be difficult to involve the whole class actively in producing the podcasts.

As well as creating your own podcasts, there are also others available that can be used in lessons. These can normally be listened to directly from the website by clicking on the relevant file name – although the IWB, or computer, will have to have speakers attached and the sound turned up. An added bonus of podcasts, which does not relate directly to your pupils, is that they can also be used as part of staff training and continuing professional development (CPD) work, with the same advantages as above.

Reading

We have already seen that the reading of text alone (one mode of communication) is not sufficient on its own. An added complication is that, as a 'situated social practice' (Moss,

2008, p73), reading can have different interpretations, motivations and expectations, on the part of both teachers and pupils. In addition, these may be at variance with social practice in another setting, such as at home. In the context of the school, reading often has a highly prescribed interpretation and purpose as defined in a curriculum.

In a curriculum, success in reading can be limited to, for example, the successful reading aloud (or just 'decoding') of words from the text (script) without any deviation, the successful retrieval of specified information from a (non-fiction) book, or answering questions about the text which show an agreement with the views of the examiner or teacher (Moss, 2008). Such an interpretation may, however, be at odds with other, more idiosyncratic views on the nature and purpose of reading on the part of the pupil. In addition, the emphasis on text-based resources may not reflect children's experience of reading other multimodal sources, such as games or web pages.

We have already considered the use of computer games in Chapter 1, but there is some evidence that 'appropriately designed computer games can play a useful role in helping some struggling readers at home' (Holmes, 2011, p15). As we have seen earlier, however, although commercial off-the-shelf software (COTS) provides authentic gaming experiences that children will be familiar with from home, it does not mean that the reading skills required, or developed, will be helpful in the school context. Again, we see the tension between the demands of the school curriculum and the real-life experience of many children.

WHAT DO YOU THINK?

Should equipping pupils with the reading ability to meet the prescribed needs of a national curriculum be more important than preparing them to read material of their own choosing in a range of formats?

While it could be argued that meeting the curriculum requirements is enough, in an ever-changing world of technology, is using traditional paper-based texts a suitable first choice of approach? Should digital books or reading from a screen in a games-style format or from a mobile device be the first choice of medium? When will technology replace books – or will it?

Despite this, some ICT resources are helpful in developing reading, but, as with 'real' books, the resources need to be used with care as they are not enough on their own. For example, e-books may be useful in the classroom, particularly with an IWB for whole-class work or on an iPad for individual or group reading, but there is evidence that adult support is vital for progress to be made with young children in phonological awareness and emergent word writing (Korat, Shamir and Arbiv, 2011). This is in line with other research that suggests that, when using ICT, the role of the teacher as guide is still just as important as it is in other teaching situations without ICT (Postholm, 2006).

Beyond specific ICT reading resources (such as talking books), there is also a role for ICT in the recording of more conventional reading practice, such as reading to an adult. We have already seen that such work can be recorded and used for evidence or as record of achievement files, or as part of a digital portfolio.

Writing

There are many pragmatic uses of ICT in the teaching of writing, such as direct teaching of phonics using the IWB or 'drilling' of spellings, followed by reinforcement using computer programs. These use the features of ICT effectively, but are by necessity largely teacher-centred (the teacher at the IWB) or teacher-directed (the teacher chooses the programs to be used and when to use them). In order to make effective use of ICT, however, we need to consider how we can also become pupil-centred, which can be just as, or even more, effective in terms of developing writing. This can work with groups and even in whole-class teaching. For instance, Maher (2010) gives an example from two primary school classes in a school in Australia where the IWB was used to facilitate group sharing of texts and the construction of a whole-class text with either the teacher or a pupil at the front of the class. In this instance, the IWB facilitated writing with 'student-centred whole-class interactions that are dialogic in nature' (ibid., p149).

One of the key features of ICT that helps in this is the fact that pupils can use provisionality (see Chapter 1) to experiment and interact with text (Davies and O'Sullivan, 2002). This can only take place, however, within the confines of the curriculum – unless ICT is used more creatively in extracurricular activities such as clubs. As with reading, there remains a possible tension about the nature and purpose of writing between what a curriculum demands and the views of the pupils themselves.

As we have discussed, pupils have many modes of writing available to them in schools, as well as a potential worldwide audience for their writing, and we will explore some of these below. Perhaps the most obvious, and earliest, use of ICT in writing is as what Papert (1993) called a 'writing instrument'. It is a sign of the speed of advances in this area that, even in the second edition of his seminal work, Papert still retained the paragraph which claimed that 'most newspapers now provide their staff with "word processing" computer systems. Many writers who work at home are acquiring their own computers, and the computer terminal is steadily displacing the typewriter as the secretary's basic tool' (ibid., p30). The ubiquitous nature of PCs in homes, offices and schools today, and the power and sophistication of the 'word processing' packages, signal the speed of progress – let alone being able to word process with voice recognition, or use touch screen technology.

When using ICT in writing, Wegerif and Dawes (2004, p106) suggest that, 'for children in primary schools, developing the capacity to interact effectively with computers requires the teaching of a classic literacy and ICT literacy' – to which we can now add digital literacy. They further suggest that 'classic literacy, ICT literacy and oracy are interlinked. Ways of writing begin as ways of talking' (ibid., p107). Just as we have seen above that ICT, especially the IWB, has the potential to be very effective at encouraging talk, we can see that such activities are also contributing to the development of writing. These activities could not take place without specific ICT skills (ICT literacy) on the part of the teacher and the pupil, and planning when to teach these in advance of when they are required is, as we saw earlier, central to effective lessons. If such planning takes place, however:

Digital technologies have opened up new opportunities to children to learn about how texts are constructed. Whereas in the past, producing printed texts, animations and films required specialist technology and skills, new digital technologies have made it possible for people to produce all kinds of texts from their own homes. Using new technologies it should be possible to encourage children to acquire their own experience of being producers of texts, becoming involved in choosing how to assemble resources to generate meanings.

(Eagle et al., 2008, p12)

An important challenge for primary teachers is ensuring that all these possibilities are exploited, but there are obvious implications for their own knowledge of ICT. If these opportunities are exploited, and once writing begins, another feature of ICT comes into play: the ability to communicate with others quickly.

Collaborative writing

Collaborative writing, within and between classes and schools, is possible with many online websites (such as PrimaryPad: http://primarypad.com/, MeetingWords: http://meetingwords.com/, or Google Docs), although these are not always free and you need to ensure that any projects you create are open to members only. It is also important to check that your projects are not going to be deleted after a certain period of time, particularly if they provide evidence for assessment or records of work. (The ability to have these features may be one of the differences between free and subscriptions services.) Despite these caveats, the ability to collaborate in real time, with each pupil's text being highlighted in a different colour, can provide a real stimulus for writing activities.

Another platform for collaborative writing is a wiki (see Chapter 6 for more details). There is currently little research evidence examining how wikis are used with primary children in the UK, but some evidence from primary pupils in Hong Kong suggests that wikis help to develop teamwork, encourage peer-to-peer interaction and facilitate online group work. If teachers also join in and post feedback, this helps in the process of constructing group writing (Woo et al., 2011). Some caveats for the use of wikis will be familiar from earlier chapters, but they include the need for adequate training for both pupils and staff, as well as factors such as class size and instructional design (Engstrom and Jewett, 2005). In particular, the wiki model is difficult with whole-class use at the same time as a page cannot be edited by more than one person at a time, although this would not apply if groups or individuals were working on different pages one at a time.

Creative writing

One of the most significant changes brought about with advances in ICT is the potential for primary pupils to write for a large range of new and different audiences and purposes. Bennett (2004, p47) suggests that these could include:

* communicating with real and fictional people via fax, email, webchat, and so on;
* reading and contributing to online stories;
* creating web pages to communicate information and ideas.

The fictional characters in the first bullet could include those from traditional written texts, or from talking books or even from ICT-based games. The latter have also been used as a stimulus for creative writing in terms of 'what happened next?', composing new scenarios or challenges and new endings, or writing character sketches for individuals within the games – see, for instance, Sandford et al. (2006).

Another important feature of ICT is that it can produce high-quality presentations of work in a variety of formats, regardless of the ability of the pupils concerned. This is not to suggest that presentation is more important than content, but it can encourage pupils to take pride in their work and may also help those who may be discouraged if their handwriting is not a strong point. In addition, modern word processing programs can help pupils of all ages to be creative in how the writing is presented (think 'Charlie and Lola'!), or to achieve effects of characterisation (for example, a different font for each character to reflect their speech), or, for instance, to make a text (or part of it, such as a treasure map found in the story) appear old to reflect its setting.

ACTIVITY

On your own or in a group, make a list of positive and negative points of using ICT devices to present written work for two contrasting age groups within the primary school. If working with others, discuss why you have made these decisions. If working on your own or with others, see if there are common features in each age group or if there are different and distinct reasons for your choices.

Another way of using ICT in creative writing is demonstrated by resources such as Teachers TV (now archived under different websites, such as the TES, due to funding cuts), which provide a series of 'short but dramatic' video clips to serve as 'story starts'. These are aimed at children from Year 1 to Year 6 and can be played on the IWB and classroom speakers to provide a very effective stimulus to creative writing. For example, one set of story starts provides seven different clips for use on the IWB, aimed at Y1–Y6, including 'an alluring jewellery shop, a ghostly graveyard and a tunnel with a warning' (https://www.youtube.com/watch?v=ac7I6UDSuOQ). The main activity can remain traditional story writing with pen and paper, but ICT is used for something that it is good at and cannot be done easily another way. A follow-up activity for this could be for children themselves to use ICT to create their own story starts, both for other classes in the school and for the same year group next year. Other examples include clips aimed specifically at Year 1 and Year 2 that use a variety of puppetry techniques to begin the story of traditional tales such as Red Riding Hood, the Miserly Farmer, the Key in the Sea, the Raja's Secret and Aladdin (http://tinyurl.com/3ma7rom). Pupils could also construct their own versions of this using an app such as Puppet Pals on the iPad.

The IWB can also be used effectively both to collect vocabulary and to plot storylines (by dragging and dropping ideas) as a whole class or group. Remember that the IWB is not just for the teacher, but can be used as a tool for pupils in group work while others work on other resources or activities. In addition, by connecting a wireless keyboard to the computer attached to the IWB, it is easy to pass this around to achieve group or class word banks, stories or poetry. In this activity, pupils are again working collaboratively (they can choose who has the keyboard next) and need to take account of the work of others that has preceded theirs. You can also easily step in (by reclaiming the keyboard) to add your own contributions to extend or refocus the activity without having to stop the flow of the lesson and give verbal instructions.

As we have seen above, the IWB in particular offers many affordances for literacy activities. However, effective planning is the key to making best use of the technology and making full use of its features. To help with this planning, Table 8.2 below (adapted from Kennewell and Beauchamp, 2007) provides some examples of how the IWB, laptop or tablet device can provide both potential for, and structure in, literacy activities – but, as we will see later, the examples in the table can be adapted for other areas of the curriculum or indeed for cross-curricular activities.

Table 8.2	Possible actions for which ICT provides potential and structure	
Action	**Meaning**	**Example**
Composing	Ideas can be recorded accurately as they arise	Students record vocabulary for a class poem – exemplar for individual work
Editing	The data stored and displayed can be changed easily with no trace of the original	Individual students revising their poems on a laptop or iPad after group or whole-class discussion using the IWB
Selecting	Choice of pre-existing resource or procedure can be made (e.g. from a list)	Students select the appropriate words from a list of vocabulary in a language exercise – drag and drop on the IWB
Comparing	Features of the same object from different views or different items displayed can be compared	The teacher displays pictures of a flower taken from different angles or different flowers, or uses the iPad mirrored on the IWB, looking for common features and discussing vocabulary for writing in science
Retrieving	Stored resources can easily be retrieved for use	Teacher retrieves examples of the same work (e.g. creative writing or a pupil's presentation) from different classes or students retrieve files to complete their work or demonstrate it to peers
Apprehending	The display (text, images, sound, diagrams) makes it easier for students to see or interpret	An image or sound effect can be added to illustrate the meaning of an unfamiliar word on the IWB, or the IWB can be used to read a 'big book' or a talking book
Focusing	Attention can be drawn to particular aspects of a process or representation	The teacher uses the 'reveal' tool to focus attention or uses zoom/magnify to look closer at a seed to identify how it becomes attached to an animal for dispersal

(continued)

Table 8.2	(continued)	
Action	**Meaning**	**Example**
Transforming	The way that the data is displayed can be changed	Students and/or the teacher discuss the effect of changing the font on the appearance of a newspaper article they have written about the school fair
Role playing	Activities can be carried out in a way that is similar to activities in the 'real world'	Students use the IWB to write a menu for a café in the 'play corner'
Collating	A variety of items from different sources can be brought together into a single resource	Students collect ideas (e.g. pictures, words or artefacts) using digital cameras and laptops (or iPads) from around the school grounds and review them by mirroring the iPad on the IWB for class project work
Sharing	It is easy to communicate and interchange resources and ideas with others	The teacher retrieves a PowerPoint presentation on grammar compiled by colleagues from the school network
Annotating	Notes can be added to a process or representation at the time of use	The teacher annotates the PowerPoint presentation or students annotate a picture for work in history
Repeating	An automated or stored process can be repeated at will	Students can replay an animation of the flow of blood through a heart when discussing or writing an explanation
Modelling	A process can be simulated by representing relationships between variables	Students enter different food quantities into a spreadsheet and watch the effect on graphs representing high-energy foods and food for growth – this can accompany discussion and cumulative talk
Cumulating	Building up a representation of knowledge in a progressive manner	Students compile a group presentation (using a variety of media) over the course of a term or topic before presenting it to their peers
Revisiting	Repeating an activity or returning with a different focus	A list of ideas generated by the class at the start of the lesson is reviewed following an internet search and discussion
Undoing	Reversing an action	A tentative idea or solution to a problem is removed without trace

Questioning	A piece of dialogue requiring a response	'What other adjectives could we use there?'
Prompting	An action or piece of dialogue that suggests what someone should do	'Try to find another word that means the same thing there'
Responding	Action that is contingent on a previous question or prompt	Change 'big' to 'enormous' in an example of text on the IWB when prompted

There could be many more examples and we could go on considering ways in which ICT is beneficial in literacy, but in reality the potential is limited only by the pedagogic vision of the teacher.

SUMMARY

In this chapter we have explored how new literacies are needed in all areas of English to help make sense of, and explore, an increasing range of modes of communication. ICT enables a wide range of 'talk' to take place and be shared, both within the school and beyond. As part of this sharing, we have seen how ICT can encourage collaboration, for instance in writing in a range of forms. This does not, however, mean that traditional talk is neglected. It is suggested that pupil talk can in fact be enhanced and enriched, as ICT provides a powerful set of tools for developing all aspects of talk. Using the full range of ICT, you have a variety of options that can provide a stimulus to start dialogue and to facilitate or extended dialogue using a variety of modes and media, and also a means of saving the 'dialogue' (in spoken and other modes, as discussed above) in a variety of formats that can be shared as necessary. We have also seen how some ICT resources can be helpful in reading, but, as with 'real' books, the resources need to be used with care, as on their own they are not enough. In fact, this same caveat applies to all uses of ICT in English, and indeed in other subjects. Your skills as a teacher remain vital in ensuring that ICT is used only when it enhances learning and teaching, and not just because it is there.

References

Alexander, R.J. (2008) *Towards Dialogic Teaching: Rethinking Classroom Talk*, 4th edition, Thirsk: Dialogos.

Baumfield, V. and Mroz, M. (2002) 'Investigating pupils' questions in the primary classroom', *Educational Research*, 44(2), pp129–40.

Beauchamp, G., Burden, K. and Abbinett, E. (2015) 'Teachers learning to use the iPad in Scotland and Wales: a new model of professional development', *Journal of Education for Teaching: International Research and Pedagogy*, 41(2), pp161–79.

Bennett, R. (2004) *Using ICT in Primary English Teaching*, Exeter: Learning Matters.

Bennett, R., Hamill, A. and Pickford, T. (2007) *Progression in Primary ICT*, Oxford: David Fulton

Bjørgen, A.M. and Erstad, O. (2015) 'The connected child: tracing digital literacy from school to leisure', *Pedagogies: An International Journal*, 10(2), pp113–27.

Brindley, S. (2000) 'ICT and literacy', in Gamble, N. and Easingwood, N. (eds) *ICT and Literacy*, London: Continuum, pp11–18.

Buckingham, D. (2015) 'Defining digital literacy: what do young people need to know about digital media?', *Nordic Journal of Digital Literacy*, Jubileumsnummer, pp21–35.

Cheung, C.K. (2005) 'The relevance of media education in primary schools in Hong Kong in the age of new media: a case study', *Educational Studies*, 31(4), pp361–74.

Clary, D., Kigotho, M. and Barros-Torning, M. (2013) 'Harnessing mobile technologies to enrich adolescents' multimodal literacy practices in middle years classrooms', *Literacy Learning: The Middle Years*, 21(3), pp49–60.

Cutrim Schmid, E. (2010) 'Using the interactive whiteboard as a "digital hub"', *Praxis Fremdsprachenunterricht*, 4(10), pp12–15.

Davies, H. and O'Sullivan, O. (2002) 'Literacy and ICT in the primary classroom: the role of the teacher', in Loveless, A. and Dore, B. (eds) *ICT in the Primary School*, Buckingham: Open University Press.

Dawes, L., Mercer, N. and Wegerif, R. (2000) 'Extending talking and reasoning skills using ICT', in Leask, M. and Meadows, J. (eds) *Teaching and Learning with ICT in the Primary School*, London: Routledge.

Deal, A. (2007) *Podcasting: A Teaching with Technology White Paper*, Pittsburgh, PA: Carnegie Mellon University.

Duchak, O. (2014) 'Visual literacy in educational practice', *Czech-Polish Historical and Pedagogical Journal*, 6(2), pp41–8.

Eagle, S., Manches, A., O'Malley, C., Plowman, L. and Sutherland, R. (2008) *From Research to Design: Perspectives on Early Years and Digital Technologies*, Bristol: Futurelab.

Engstrom, M.E. and Jewett, D. (2005) 'Collaborative learning the wiki way', *TechTrends*, 49(6), p12.

Geoghegan, D., O'Neill, S. and Petersen, S. (2013) 'Metalanguage: the "teacher talk" of explicit literacy teaching in practice', *Improving Schools*, 16(2), pp119–29.

Haggerty, M. (2010) 'Exploring curriculum implications of multimodal literacy in a New Zealand early childhood setting', *European Early Childhood Education Research Journal*, 18(3), pp177–89.

[illegible], E. (2002)
[illegible] al Literacy
[illegible] ns,
[illegible]
[illegible] 1),
[illegible]

[illegible] ng
[illegible] d
[illegible] 7–22.

Hennessy, S. (2011) 'The role of digital artefacts on the interactive whiteboard in supporting classroom dialogue', *Journal of Computer Assisted Learning*, 27(6), pp463–89.

Holmes, W. (2011) 'Using game-based learning to support struggling readers at home', *Learning, Media and Technology*, 36(1), pp5–19.

Kennewell, S. and Beauchamp, G. (2007) 'The features of interactive whiteboards and their influence on learning', *Learning, Media and Technology*, 32(3), pp227–41.

Korat, O., Shamir, A. and Arbiv, L. (2011) 'E-books as support for emergent writing with and without adult assistance', *Education and Information Technologies*, 16, pp301–18.

Kress, G. and Jewitt, C. (2008) 'Introduction', in Kress, G. and Jewitt, C. (eds) *Multimodal Literacy*, New York: Peter Lang Publishing, pp1–18.

Lankshear, C. and Knobel, M. (2006) 'Digital literacy and digital literacies: policy, pedagogy and research considerations for education', *Nordic Journal of Digital Literacy*, 1(1), pp12–24.

Maher, D. (2012) 'Teaching literacy in primary schools using an interactive whole-class technology: facilitating student-to-student whole-class dialogic interactions', *Technology, Pedagogy and Education*, 21(1), pp137–52.

Matthewman, S. (2009) 'Discerning literacy', in Sutherland, R., Robertson, S. and John, P. (eds) *Improving Classroom Learning with ICT*, London: Routledge, pp115–37.

McFarlane, A. (2000) 'Communicating meaning: reading and writing in a multimedia world', in Gamble, N. and Easingwood, N. (eds) *ICT and Literacy*, London: Continuum, pp19–24.

McLeod, J.K. and Vasinda, S. (2009) 'Electronic portfolios: perspectives of students, teachers and parents', *Education and Information Technologies*, 14, pp29–38.

Mercer, N., Dawes, L. and Staarman, J.K. (2009) 'Dialogic teaching in the primary science classroom', *Language and Education*, 23(4), pp353–69.

Mercer, N., Kershner, R., Warwick, P. and Kleine Staarman, J. (2010) 'Can the interactive whiteboard help to provide "dialogic space" for children's collaborative activity?', *Language and Education*, 24(5), pp367–84.

Middleton, A. (2009) 'Beyond podcasting: creative approaches to designing educational audio', *ALT-J: Research in Learning Technology*, 17(2), pp143–55.

Moss, G. (2008) 'Putting the text back into practice: junior-age non-fiction as objects of design', in Kress, G. and Jewitt, C. (eds) *Multimodal Literacy*, New York: Peter Lang Publishing, pp73–87.

Myhill, D., Jones, S. and Hopper, R. (2006) *Talking, Listening, Learning*, Maidenhead: Open University Press.

Papert, S. (1993) *Mindstorms: Children, Computers, and Powerful Ideas*, New York: Basic Books.

Postholm, M.B. (2006) 'The teacher's role when pupils work on task using ICT in project work', *Educational Research*, 48(2), pp155–75.

Rudd, A. and Tyldesley, A. (2006) *Literacy and ICT in the Primary School: A Creative Approach to English*, London: David Fulton.

Sandford, R., Ulicsak, M., Facer, K. and Rudd, T. (2006) *Teaching with Games: Using Commercial Off-the-Shelf Computer Games in Formal Education*, Bristol: Futurelab.

Sefton-Green, J., Nixon, H. and Erstad, O. (2009) 'Reviewing approaches and perspectives on "digital literacy"', *Pedagogies: An International Journal*, 4(2), pp107–25.

Smith, F., Hardman, F. and Higgins, S. (2006) 'The impact of interactive whiteboards on teacher–student interaction in the National Literacy and Numeracy Strategies', *British Educational Research Journal*, 32(3), pp443–57.

Sutherland, R., Robertson, S. and John, P. (2009) *Improving Classroom Learning with ICT*, Milton Park, Abingdon and New York: Routledge.

Tanner, H. and Jones, S. (2007) 'Using video-stimulated reflective dialogue to learn from children about their learning with and without ICT', *Technology, Pedagogy and Education*, 16(3), pp321–35.

Tharp, R. and Gallimore, R. (1988) *Rousing Minds to Life*, New York: Cambridge University Press.

Wall, K., Higgins, S., Miller, J. and Packard, N. (2006) 'Developing digital portfolios: investigating how digital portfolios can facilitate pupil talk about learning', *Technology, Pedagogy and Education*, 15(3), pp261–73.

Warwick, P., Hennessy, S. and Mercer, N. (2011) 'Promoting teacher and school development through co-enquiry: developing interactive whiteboard use in a "dialogic classroom"', *Teachers and Teaching*, 17(3), pp303–24.

Wegerif, R. and Dawes, L. (2004) *Thinking and Learning with ICT: Raising Achievement in Primary Classrooms*, London: Routledge.

Woo, M., Chu, S., Ho, A. and Li, X. (2011) 'Using a wiki to scaffold primary school students' collaborative writing', *Educational Technology & Society*, 14(1), pp43–54.

Further reading

Janssen, J., Stoyanov, S., Ferrari, A., Punie, Y., Pannekeet, K. and Sloep, P. (2013) 'Experts' views on digital competence: commonalities and differences', *Computers & Education*, 68, pp473–81.

Owen, M., Grant, L., Sayers, S. and Facer, K. (2006) *Social Software and Learning*, Bristol: Futurelab.

Useful websites

Using the IWB to Support Classroom Dialogue: http://dialogueiwb.educ.cam.ac.uk/ Project based at the University of Cambridge (UK) that includes a range of professional development resources, videos and further reading.

Hertfordshire Grid for Learning Podcasting: http://www.thegrid.org.uk/learning/ict/technologies/web2.0/podcast/ Provides guidance and examples of school podcasts.

ICT and mathematics in Key Stages 1 and 2

In this chapter we will consider the important role that talk also plays in teaching mathematics. We will explore how the use of signs and symbols in mathematical language makes this process potentially challenging and can lead to misconceptions. We will also examine how ICT can help to address these misconceptions, as well as how it can be used in the areas of number, shape, space and measure, and handling data.

In mathematics in the primary school, language is central to effective teaching and learning. It is particularly important that you and your pupils have a shared understanding of the language you use in mathematics and how this may vary from the use of the same words or phrases in other contexts – both in the curriculum and outside school. An additional complication is that, as well as words, the mathematical language 'uses symbols to represent numbers and number operations (such as the word "nine" to represent this quantity or the written sign "+" to represent combining quantities)' (Manches, 2006, p18). Turner and McCullouch (2004, pp2–3) suggest that the resultant ambiguity can be identified in the following ways:

1. Meaning that differs according to whether the word is used as a noun or a verb – for example, the word 'note' can mean an instruction (verb), a form of currency (noun) and a musical symbol (noun).
2. Words that are derived from the same root, but that have a different meaning in an everyday context – for example, the net of a shape and a fishing net. Some words in this category have two or more mathematical meanings that are used in a mathematical context (e.g. 'left' denotes direction and also identifies a numerical remainder).
3. Homophones and homonyms – for example, one/won or count/Count Ferdinand.

If pupils do not understand that language is being used in a mathematical context, it is possible that they will develop misconceptions (see below) through misunderstanding the context in which the word is used (hence perhaps adopting an inappropriate strategy), or not understanding what they are required to do. It is important to note that this applies both to spoken language and to words that appear in other forms, such as work you have prepared on the interactive whiteboard (IWB), a worksheet or text book. Perhaps the key idea here is that, if necessary, you need to identify potential confusing language at the planning stage, plan how to address this or introduce the term, and continue to make it explicit throughout the lesson that you are using words in a mathematical context. This should be continued in subsequent lessons in mathematics and reinforced in other areas of the curriculum – questions could include: 'What did this word mean when we used it in maths?', 'What else can it mean?' and 'What does it mean in our science/music/etc. lesson today?' – to ensure that pupils fully understand words before using and applying them. (A useful summary of vocabulary and possible misunderstandings in mathematics can be found in Turner and McCullouch, 2004, pp7–10.)

TIP

Although we have discussed the use of language in mathematics, the same concerns and processes apply in any area of the curriculum that uses specialist language which has more than one meaning, such as computing, music, science and geography.

Decide on appropriate mathematical language for your class (both written and spoken), and make clear any misunderstandings about its use, before considering the use of ICT.

Misconceptions

Hollins and Whitby (2001, p2) provide a useful summary of how misconceptions apply to science – and this has resonance in other areas of the curriculum – when they state:

> concepts will always be rooted in our own previous experience, which will influence our attempts at understanding. There is a sense in which our concepts can never be 'wrong', as they are a reflection of our level of understanding at that time. They may not, however, concur with accepted scientific ideas and may therefore be 'misconceptions'. For us to be able to alter our conceptual understanding, new experiences must be encountered which challenge the existing concept. If this challenge involves too big a leap from currently held ideas, the new ideas will be dismissed out of hand, or lip-service will be paid to them while the original concept remains intact. If the challenge involves a sufficiently different rethink of the currently held concept, then the concept may be adapted or changed to fit the new experience; learning will therefore take place. A major part of our role as teachers must therefore be to ascertain children's current understanding and then structure new experiences to bring about this learning.

The ability of ICT to present ideas in a variety of ways can help structure new experiences, but only if you as the teacher have sufficient understanding of the area yourself. If this is not the case, you are in danger of perpetuating the misconceptions of pupils or introducing new ones of your own! As Murphy (2006, p229) states, 'teachers' knowledge of mathematics should be of sufficient depth to enable them to represent it in a variety of ways and to be flexible enough to enable them to interpret students' ideas and address misconceptions'.

It is important, however, to state clearly that misconceptions are not always a bad thing. In fact, quite the opposite may be true at times. In mathematics, misconceptions can 'often reveal much about children's thinking and how they acquire – or not, is the case may be – an understanding of complex mathematical concepts' (Cockburn and Littler, 2008, p3). Exploring how children acquire their ideas is perhaps the most fundamental part of finding suitable teaching methods to address a misconception – and to inform your future teaching to ensure that you do not either introduce new misconceptions or reinforce others. In addition, discussing ideas with pupils can also allow you to make the important distinction between an error and a misconception. Hansen et al. (2014, p11) states that errors in mathematics (but this is equally applicable to other areas) can be made for many reasons, including 'carelessness; misinterpretation of symbols or text; lack of relevant experience or knowledge related to that mathematical topic/learning objective/concept; a lack of awareness or inability to check the answer given; or the result of a misconception'. In addition, don't forget to consider the more obvious explanations, such as you made the task too hard!

TIP

Have you checked that other adults in the classroom are aware of possible misconceptions before the lesson starts?

Unless we know how the problem is formed, it is very difficult to 'transform' (see Shulman in Chapter 2) your own understanding of a topic into something that children may understand. It could also be argued that by guiding children back through the same process by which they acquired the knowledge in the first place, but 'correcting' where it went wrong (by new experiences, explanation and so on), may be the most effective way of arriving at an alternative conception. (This does make the assumption that it was not you who caused the misconception in the first place – in which case, you should know how it was formed!) This can only be done if you know how pupils' views were formed. So, how can ICT help in establishing this?

In earlier chapters, we have seen that ICT can allow pupils to record their thoughts in a wide variety of ways. They are able to write, draw, and record both sound and video, or any combination of these depending on their age and ability. All of these activities can be done as an individual or as a group and, of course, they can be saved to be shared with others in the classroom or elsewhere. In the latter instance, asking your pupils to explain their understanding of something to another group of pupils in another school can be a very good pretext for an assessment activity – but is hopefully equally valid as a teaching activity for the pupils in the other school. It is very important in this instance to realise the transformative and empowering nature of ICT in enabling someone who may, for instance, find writing difficult but can happily make a voice recording of their thoughts. This may be especially true of children with particular needs that make expressing their thoughts difficult in more conventional ways. Central to this discussion is the realisation that voice recordings or digital images have equal worth to some more traditional methods of assessment.

Examples of misconceptions

Let us consider how ICT help address a misconception in both Key Stages 1 and 2, in this instance in mathematics. Before doing so, however, we should be clear about the distinction in mathematics between 'procedural' and 'conceptual' knowledge – that is, knowing how and when to use computations (Nunes, 2001). In the examples that follow, we are concerned with conceptual knowledge, but ICT can also help with procedural knowledge – but in a more straightforward way, such as using the IWB for explicit teaching, modelling and practice of relevant procedures.

Key Stage 1: A new animal house for the zoo

In a reception class the pupils are learning mathematical language relating to size. The scenario is that they have been asked (by email) to design a new house for some of the animals in the local zoo. It becomes obvious that many children think giraffes are very small – smaller than hippos. After discussion it emerges that the toy hippo and giraffe the children play with in the classroom are the source of the misconception. Obviously, it would be ideal to let the children see the real animals, but, as this may not be possible, movies of the real animals are a useful substitute – you decide not to use cartoons as they may reinforce the same or different misconceptions (such as that animals can talk!). You find a suitable video on a zoo website and show it to the whole class on the IWB – you have made sure that the video contains suitable reference points (like a human adult) the pupils may be familiar with (in the absence of real animals or life-size models!) to help them realise the relative size. During and after the video the children are able to use suitable language, such as 'They are taller than a teacher', which would help them design the new homes. The same exercise is then repeated with a hippo. After this is completed, you must then ensure that the relative size to each other is discussed. Do not assume that, just because they can make correct relative size statements about each animal compared with humans, they will automatically make the relative judgement between the animals. Remember that the objective was to realise that giraffes are taller than hippos and hence would need different houses; the humans are just a familiar comparator to aid this concept – in the absence of a trip to the zoo!

ACTIVITY

Discuss with others whether you would accept it if children stated that the giraffe is 'bigger than an adult'? If not, why not?

You may find the example below of good practice from Ofsted of interest in this context.

CASE STUDY

Good practice: language development	Learning mathematical language in a Reception class. The children's language and conceptual understanding were developed securely through a range of well planned activities that provided plenty of opportunity for them to use new words, make comparisons and reason.

The teacher was working outside with a group of five children. They were wearing hard hats and were 'working' on a construction site, designing and building a house for the Three Billy Goats Gruff. They had a superb range of equipment from which to choose, including planks of various lengths and wooden blocks of different shapes and sizes. The teacher participated in their play, asking well phrased questions to develop and assess their understanding of shape, weight and length, such as 'Can you find a shorter plank than that one?' and 'Is it heavier than the other one or lighter?' She recorded the children's responses on a prepared sheet.

The activity was followed up well, using the interactive whiteboard and a program that showed pictures of different sized houses with three creatures of varying sizes alongside. The children were asked whether they thought the house would be better for the caterpillar, the dog or the giraffe, and were asked to explain why. All could offer good reasons: 'The giraffe's too tall, he wouldn't fit in'. 'It's a middle-sized house and the dog's middle-sized'. The children thoroughly enjoyed the activities, which also developed their gross motor skills, language, creative and social skills.

Other child-initiated activities included role play in the toy shop where children were pricing items and buying and selling them. They had the idea of using coins and giving change even though they did not fully understand the mathematics: 'Here's 1p'; 'Thank you – you need 1p back'.

From Ofsted, 2009, p11

Key Stage 2: Area of a shape

An example of a misconception in primary school mathematics, provided by Hansen et al. (2014), is that when you double the size of a shape, the area will double. They point out that this is based on the idea that in mathematics whatever happens on one side of an operation also happens on the other, but it could also just be that the pupils may regard it as 'common sense'. In order to address this misconception, the IWB and associated software can be very useful. For instance, by opening a page of squared paper and drawing a square 2x2, the whole class – this can even be demonstrated to a group or individual – can count both the length of the sides and the number of squares within the shape. (They can also do this by writing numbers on the board, shading in squares using IWB pens or measuring with a rule from the software tools.) If this process is repeated with a shape of 4x4 squares, it is easy to count again both the length of the sides and the number of squares within the shape – provided, of course, that the pupils understand the concept of area. With the IWB, this process can be repeated as necessary with different-sized rectilinear shapes. Due to the features of ICT, this can be done quickly and accurately and any results can be saved, printed or shared.

You may find the example below of weaker practice from Ofsted of interest in this context.

CASE STUDY

Weaker factors: gaps in subject knowledge	A Year 6 lesson on interior angles of polygons in which a teacher's weak subject knowledge led to pupils' incorrect understanding.

A Year 6 class was investigating the interior angles of regular polygons. Many found this difficult, but higher-attaining pupils had found that a pentagon has interior angles of 108 degrees. The teacher said that this was not correct and encouraged them to divide 360 degrees by 5 to get the answer, stating 'the angles in any polygon add up to 360 degrees'. This gave the answer of 72 degrees, which puzzled the most able pupils as the interior angles were clearly bigger than right angles. Other pupils appeared to just accept the rule which they then incorrectly applied to other polygons.

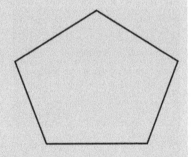

How might it be improved?	The teacher had not realised that this was a gap in her knowledge. Possibly, she had confused previous knowledge about external angles which do sum to 360. If she had had the confidence to ask the able pupils to explain their answer, she might have recognised her error. She returned to the pupils' answer of 108 degrees in the next day's lesson.

From Ofsted, 2009, p12

ACTIVITY

Discus how the IWB and its tools, or other forms of technology, could have helped to avoid this scenario.

Breadth of study

Hughes, Desforges and Mitchell (1999, p76) assert that 'children need to be taught from an early age how to apply their mathematical knowledge in a range of contexts and settings'. Like science in the next chapter, mathematics is a conceptual subject where learners need to progress from the observable to something much less tangible. Even apparently simple ideas such as zero are in fact very difficult to understand (Cockburn and Littler, 2008). We have seen in earlier chapters that ICT can help to visualise, or model, ideas by using a variety of modes and media. In mathematics in the primary school, this is likely to become more useful as pupils progress from 'hands-on' practical work with real objects (manipulatives) to activities that cannot be solved by the manipulation of tangible objects. Manches (2006, p18) points out that there is a need to evaluate 'the potential for digital technologies to support learning in this area by enhancing such physical learning materials'. The advantages of doing this are outlined by Samara and Clements (2009), who explore the benefits of using what they label 'computer manipulatives' – for instance, manipulating base-ten units on a computer or IWB compared with using 'real' versions. A key idea here is that, although 'physical concrete materials' may be needed to build meaning in the first instance, pupils then need to be able to reflect on their actions. ICT provides the potential for pupils to do this, for example by allowing them 'to explore geometric figures in ways that they cannot with physical shape sets. For example, children can change the size of the computer shapes, altering all shapes or only some' (ibid., p148).

WHAT DO YOU THINK?

A junior class was studying three-dimensional shapes. The teacher put a collection of shapes on the tables of each group. The teacher introduced the lesson using a PowerPoint on the IWB. This gave the lesson objectives and then moved to a discussion about the properties of the shapes that the teacher showed on the IWB on successive slides. The shapes on the table remained untouched throughout this discussion. The teacher then used the IWB to show a scan of the actual worksheet, which the pupils then completed. The pupils were allowed to use the shapes if they required them when completing the sheet, but very few did as they had gained the information they needed from the IWB. The work was collected in for marking

(continued)

(continued)

and the lesson ended with a whole-class activity using a game from a website that covered the properties of shapes.

As most of the pupils successfully completed the worksheet, it could be argued that this was an effective use of technology. What do you think? What were the strengths and weaknesses of this approach?

Progression in mathematical thinking

Inherent in the discussion above is the ability of ICT to help with progression in mathematical thinking. For example, progression, perhaps over a period of years, might involve moving from counting the numbers of toy ducks, pigs and chickens (tangible objects), to drawing a pictogram (a representation of the real object) as a class activity (on the IWB using software with data input by the teacher), then children constructing pictograms on a laptop, then a bar chart (using abstract data input by the pupils in a more complicated program such as Excel), through to the manipulation of data in dynamic graphing software to explore the effect of changing variables (done by pupils on the IWB to explore their own ideas with the whole class). The time taken for this progression will vary and be guided by the developmental stage of members of the class rather than their age. While you may be planning each part of this progression, it is necessary to remember that the 'baseline' (an assessment of the starting point of knowledge or experience) will be different for individual pupils and one extreme would be that all of these stages may be represented by levels of development in one class!

Another example could be of progression in understanding fractions. Early work on fractions may include practical work with real objects, such as cutting up fruit or a cake. In developing this concept the IWB can be useful in moving to annotating representations of the fruit or cake, through to symbolic representation and dragging and dropping activities using matching symbolic and pictorial representations. (There is another dimension here – or lack of it! – as we move from 3D shapes to 2D representations, you need to be sure that pupils understand this conceptual step.)

Although not all stages of progression in maths will use ICT, the IWB in particular – and perhaps some of the growing number of apps on tablet devices – does allow you to model what is required in subsequent activities: for instance, by using the ruler or protractor built into most IWB software for demonstrating how to measure. Although pupils could undertake similar work on the IWB, it is really a tool for the teacher to use to ensure that pupils understand the task before they use real measuring equipment in practical work.

Number

We will now consider how ICT can contribute to the development of understanding number. Central to this process is the exploration of what ICT can offer that will enhance the existing learning environment. Such an approach is based on an acceptance of Yelland and Kilderry's (2010, p95) belief that 'new technologies or ICT can provide different opportunities for thinking about and extending the teaching and learning of mathematical skills and processes'. They go on to assert that ICT is most likely to be used effectively in multidimensional mathematical tasks that 'are characterised by the students having greater autonomy in terms of the amount of input that they have into the direction of their learning' (ibid., p101). This is in contrast to a unidimensional mathematical task, which 'is characterised by simple sequences of activity that often have a single outcome, minimal opportunities for exploration and where mathematical concepts and processes are introduced via structured tasks' (ibid., p97). ICT can be used in both of these approaches, but the multidimensional approach reflects the interactive and dialogic strategies discussed in earlier chapters and is more likely to result in the creative use of technology, and hence new opportunities for learning. It is necessary to point out that such an approach does not mean the exclusive use of ICT, but rather its selective use (by the pupils). In reality, it is suggested that the mastery of 'basic' skills is likely to be achieved by unidimensional tasks, but this should not be at the expense of exploring these 'basic' skills in multidimensional tasks – particularly by using number work (or other areas of mathematics) in, for example, problem-solving cross-curricular work.

This discussion does not rule out using ICT to present existing parts of the environment in new ways. Indeed, this can be a very effective use of ICT. For instance, Hughes, Desforges and Mitchell (1999) outline a scenario in Key Stage 1 where a teacher gave two pupils a series of pieces of card with either a sign or a number on them, for example 2, 5, 7, +, – and =. They were asked to explore how they could be arranged 'to make them work together'. The outcomes included 7 – 5 = 2 and 5 + 2 = 7. The outcomes were then discussed between teacher and pupils. It is not difficult to see how this activity could easily become a 'drag and drop' activity on the IWB, but the fundamental difference would be the speed at which resources could be retrieved and used – not to mention the saving of card! In the ICT scenario, the teacher could have a flipchart already prepared with an example on the first page to introduce the idea to the class, but this could be followed by a series of pages within the same file with differentiated sets of numbers for different groups of pupils to work on, finishing with a final page with a plenary activity. If the pupils use the IWB as a resource for the activity on a rotation (annotating the relevant page with their names using the pen tool), all outcomes can be discussed (reviewed) with the whole class or with other groups as required, before being saved as evidence for assessment. Extension activity can also be undertaken as the pupils are able easily to add their own numbers and signs to their page – or the teacher could have them already prepared on later pages. Similar principles apply to other number work, such sequencing, ordering and sorting activities.

ACTIVITY

Discuss how you could use the approach outlined above in sequencing, ordering and sorting activities. Either on your own, or with others, plan a lesson based on one of these and decide how and when ICT could be used effectively, exploiting its relevant features.

In the discussion above, an existing idea has been adapted effectively to use ICT in number work. We must now consider how *different* opportunities for thinking about and extending the teaching and learning of mathematical skills and processes can be achieved.

Shape, space and measure

As we have already seen above, there is a range of tools (such as rulers and protractors) built into most IWB software (free with boards), but these are likely to be tools for the teacher to model tasks. I would suggest that shape, space and measure are areas where practical activities are much better than using ICT. However, this does not mean that ICT has no role, but this role needs to be selective. For instance, Serow and Callingham (2011, p170) suggest that a mixture of group work involving 'constructions with concrete materials, electronic geoboard constructions, and written recording of known properties and relationships of shapes seemed effective in focussing students on the mathematics'. The ability to manipulate shapes and angles in 2D is a strength of the IWB and of other software packages on laptops or computers, so this may be a good use of ICT, whereas for 3D shapes, real shapes may be best.

When recording the results of investigations, however, ICT becomes a very good option, particularly if pupils have access to mobile devices and can therefore begin not only to record but also to analyse results both inside and outside school. In addition, digital photographs of the objects being measured may be useful in reporting back to the class about what a particular group did.

Handling data

One of the strengths of ICT is in handling data, and, in one sense, computers represent a manipulative for this area of study. In planning work in this area, it is necessary to remember that, although explicit direct teaching may be needed in the early stages of learning skills, wherever possible the English National Curriculum requires that 'pupils should make rich connections across mathematical ideas' and '[t]hey should also apply their mathematical knowledge to science and other subjects' (DfE, 2013, p3). To achieve this, it is likely that data will be considered in the context of cross-curricular activities, both in maths and in other areas of the curriculum, where data is encountered in authentic contexts (or at least as authentic as possible within the framework of the activities), so that the results of handling data have a meaning or application. The main advantages of ICT in handling data are speed and the ability to explore ideas (provisionality and automation). For instance, it is quite possible, and indeed necessary at times, for pupils to construct their own graphs with paper and pencil, but ICT can do it much quicker. In addition, having constructed a graph, ICT also allows variables to be changed with instant and observable changes in the graph. Even the type of graph can be changed instantly to see which is best suited to the purpose of the activity.

Calculators

Although calculators are a form of ICT, this is not really the place to discuss their role in any detail except to note that the features of ICT that apply are speed and provisionality.

SUMMARY

Overall, academic research in the area of mathematics and ICT is much less common in primary schools than in secondary schools. In 1999, Higgins and Muijs (1999) suggested that the emphasis on research in mathematics to date had been on CAI (computer-assisted instruction) and CAL (computer-aided learning), with most work concentrating on secondary schools or post-secondary education. More recently, there has been research on the influence of the IWB in mathematics, but this has again focused largely on secondary schools (e.g. Miller and Glover, 2007). We have seen that ICT, particularly the IWB, can play an important role in developing the teaching of mathematics in the primary school from an early age. As in earlier chapters, the most important concern is to use ICT only when it offers something that no other resources can, or does it quicker or more efficiently. As such, digital technologies should be used as interconnected environments for learning, rather than unrelated tools. Way and Beardon (2003) suggest that, in mathematics teaching (and perhaps more generally), there is a major difference between these two perspectives, which requires teachers to fundamentally change the way they teach. It is hoped that, if you have read this far, you will not need to change too much!

References

Cockburn, A. and Littler, G. (eds) (2008) *Mathematical Misconceptions*, London: Sage.

DfE (2013) *Mathematics Programmes of Study: Key Stages 1 and 2 National Curriculum in England*, London: Department for Education (DfE).

Hansen, A., Drews, D., Dudgeon, J., Lawton, F. and Surtees, L. (2014) *Children's Errors in Mathematics*, 3rd edition, London: Sage.

Higgins, S. and Muijs, D. (1999) 'ICT and numeracy in primary schools', in Thompson, I. (ed.) *Issues in Teaching Numeracy in Primary Schools*, Buckingham: Open University Press, pp103–16.

Hollins, M. and Whitby, V. (2001) *Progression in Primary Science: A Guide to the Nature and Practice of Science in Key Stages 1 and 2*, 2nd edition, London: David Fulton.

Hughes, M., Desforges, C. and Mitchell, C. (1999) 'Using and applying mathematics at Key Stage 1', in Thompson, I. (ed.) *Issues in Teaching Numeracy in Primary Schools*, Buckingham: Open University Press.

Manches, A. (2006) 'What can the digital add to physical learning materials in early years numeracy classrooms?', in Eagle, S., Manches, A., O'Malley, C., Plowman, L. and Sutherland, R. (2006) *From Research to*

Design: Perspectives on Early Years and Digital Technologies, Bristol: Futurelab, pp18–32.

Miller, D. and Glover, D. (2007) 'Into the unknown: the professional development induction experience of secondary mathematics teachers using interactive whiteboard technology', *Learning, Media and Technology*, 32(3), pp319–31.

Murphy, C. (2006) '"Why do we have to do this?" Primary trainee teachers' views of a subject knowledge audit in mathematics', *British Educational Research Journal*, 32(2), pp227–50.

Nunes, T. (2001) 'British research on the development of numeracy concepts', in Askew, M. and Brown, M. (eds) *Teaching and Learning Primary Numeracy: Policy, Practice and Effectiveness: A Review of British Research for the British Educational Research Association in Conjunction with the British Society for Research in the Learning of Mathematics*, London: British Educational Research Association, pp1–14.

Ofsted (2009) *Mathematics: Understanding the Score: Improving Practice in Mathematics Teaching at Primary Level*, London: Ofsted.

Samara, J. and Clements, D.H. (2009) '"Concrete" computer manipulatives in mathematics education', *Child Development Perspectives*, 3(3), pp145–50.

Serow, P. and Callingham, R. (2011) 'Levels of use of interactive whiteboard technology in the primary mathematics classroom', *Technology, Pedagogy and Education*, 20(2), pp161–73.

Turner, S. and McCullouch, J. (2004) *Making Connections in Primary Mathematics: A Practical Guide*, London: David Fulton.

Way, J. and Beardon, T. (eds) (2003) *ICT and Primary Maths*, Maidenhead: Open University Press.

Yelland, N. and Kilderry, A. (2010) 'Becoming numerate with information and communications technologies in the twenty-first century', *International Journal of Early Years Education*, 18(2), pp91–106.

Further reading

Ofsted (2009) *Mathematics: Understanding the Score: Improving Practice in Mathematics Teaching at Primary Level*, London: Ofsted.

O'Malley, C. and Stanton Fraser, D. (2000) *Literature Review in Learning with Tangible Technologies*, Bristol: Futurelab.

Useful websites

Ofsted: https://www.gov.uk/government/collections/ofsted-examples-of-good-practice-in-mathematics-teaching Examples of good practice in mathematics teaching.

10 ICT in cross-curricular teaching at Key Stages 1 and 2

In this chapter we will consider how teachers can use the range and the features of technology outlined in earlier chapters in powerful and empowering ways in the classroom for learners aged 5–11. We will consider the distinction between ICT's use within and across subjects and explore how viewing learning objectives through a variety of subject 'lenses' can help to provide new ways of planning lessons for teachers and new ways of using ICT for pupils.

As we have already seen, although pupils may have freedom to explore ICT uses in a heuristic manner, there is also an expectation that the teacher provides the structure and potential for such actions, as well as ensuring that they have the necessary technical skills. At the same time, teachers also need to ensure that they are encouraging a critical perspective about ICT use on the part of pupils. The same applies to ICT use on the part of the teacher, and there is evidence that teachers do make these distinctions across the curriculum (Beauchamp, 2011).

Categories of interaction in the primary school

It is particularly important in cross-curricular teaching that pupils are given a range of experiences, in a variety of places. To help with seeing how ICT may fit into this range of experiences, I have suggested elsewhere (Beauchamp, 2011) that a possible framework for planning in the primary school is provided by the categories listed below:

- physical dialogic interaction – learners with resources;
- located interaction – learners with classroom setting, place or physical community;
- community interaction – learners with peers, teachers and other adults;
- technology-mediated interaction – learners with ICT.

Each of these categories can be used individually, but also in combination: for example, different groups doing different activities for one lesson or moving between categories within a lesson. From the above you will notice that ICT-mediated interaction is only one possible approach, thus encouraging the selective use of ICT as advocated in earlier chapters. To help make some sense of these categories, and their possible use, we will examine each one briefly before moving on to consider their context in cross-curricular teaching.

Physical dialogic interaction: learners with resources

Using resources, both ICT and non-ICT, is something all primary teachers do. In this category, however, 'the specific intention [is] to use them to stimulate dialogue and debate rather than being an end in itself; a situation where learning is the result of the dialogue, as much as the use of the resource' (Beauchamp, 2011, p181). In other words, the pupils may not even need to use or manipulate the resource (although they could), as long as it stimulates dialogue based on the dialogic principles we have examined elsewhere (see Chapter 2). Physical dialogic interaction would include the use of manipulatives in mathematics (for instance, money in a Key Stage 1 shop), as well as anything from a mini wipe-clean whiteboard to a fossil or dressing-up box – in short, anything that can provoke meaningful discussion that can lead to learning.

Located interaction: learners with classroom setting and place or physical community

In this category there are two distinct but related settings (learners with classroom setting and learners with place or physical community). We will discuss each below.

Learners with classroom setting

Primary classrooms come in many shapes and sizes, and this is bound to have an impact on how pupils and teachers interact. A central feature of this category is the view that the classroom itself is considered a teaching resource and parts of it are the subject of planned interactions. Although perhaps more obvious in Key Stage 1 and early years classrooms, located interactions can take place across the primary school with class-room displays, on both wall-mounted boards and surfaces, or 'zones'. Evidence from a research project suggests that

> some classrooms provide small discrete areas for discussion in groups, others provide large open spaces with easy access for pupils (and teachers) to move around and interact or hold whole-class discussions, whilst others still (such as an L-shaped classroom in one school) make interactions much more challenging. This architecture-shaped discourse is a factor that teachers need to consider when planning lessons, but is not always a negative feature.
>
> (Beauchamp, 2011, p182)

These more unusual classroom, or school, layouts can be helpful in providing a variety of working areas for groups or individuals not possible in more open-plan settings. The interactions in this category can be between pupils and features of the setting, such as a mathematics table, but can also include the interactive whiteboard (IWB) or displays with QR codes or augmented reality images. In this context, the IWB is considered a feature of the setting (chosen for use as such, for instance for a group to record their thoughts on a problem on an ad hoc basis because it was to hand), not a mediating ICT resource.

Learners with place or physical community

Having made the decision to move outside the classroom setting, teachers make explicit choices about what the location can supply in terms of personal, physical or even emotional stimuli. This is particularly true when the size or context of the setting (for example a church or historical site, such as a prehistoric cave) adds something unique to the learning experience: something that could not be created using ICT. Some areas of the curriculum, such as religious education or history, may present more obvious choices for place or community interactions, but opportunities in other areas of the curriculum should not be neglected. One of the most important aspects of this category is the opportunity to work in a cross-curricular way, and ICT has a role in facilitating and recording such events. Indeed, it may be that once in the setting the interactions change to technology-mediated interactions – see below.

CASE STUDY

A class of Year 3 children are working with an educator from the local museum. He takes them on a trip to a prehistoric cave situated in the countryside some miles from their school. Prior to the trip the pupils have worked on musical compositions and are confident in working collaboratively with the educator. On the trip the class is split into groups, with some visiting other historical sites close by and one group visiting the prehistoric cave. The groups are rotated throughout the day. In common with the concept of 'strangely familiar' discussed later, one of the aims of the visit was to encourage pupils to listen with fresh ears (Shafer, 1994) by removing them from the classroom and putting them in an environment that added something unique. As one of the pupils reported in interviews after the visit, it was

different because 'cavemen lived in that actual cave you just feel that their spirits are still there . . . and you like come to life!' (Adams, 2011). Once in the cave, the pupils improvised some compositions reflecting the mood invoked by the cave and its history. This was recorded by a digital recorder for later appraisal in the classroom (a component of the national curriculum where the study was undertaken – the discussion of music using musical 'language' and terms).

Another important feature to note from this case study is that, as well as an emotional response, the setting was also able to invoke other responses based on its particular features, such as size, sound qualities or quality of light. In this case, Adams (2011) reports that it was the sound qualities of the cave that the children noted, and these offered a

(continued)

(continued)

unique level and type of feedback that they had not experienced in the school setting. They reported the following:

- 'When we were sitting down you could actually feel the vibration of the music on the floor of the cave. You could feel the beat of the music!'
- 'They were good vibrations . . . because I haven't ever felt my music before!'

- 'It felt like a herd of elephants jumping on the floor! The vibration made you want to move and to dance!'

In this example, we see that although technology was used – and provided a convenient, accurate and quick way of capturing the moment (which would otherwise have been ephemeral) – the main focus was on the interaction between the learners and the particular features and nature of the place.

Community interaction: learners with peers, teachers and other adults

In this category, teachers make a distinction between the physical setting that a community (class) works in (as above) and the setting as a community of practice (Wenger, 1998). The role of the teacher is to make interactions possible in a 'community of enquiry', which includes Wenger's (ibid., p72) 'three dimensions of the relationship by which practice is the source of coherence of a community': mutual engagement, a joint enterprise and a shared repertoire. In the primary school, with mainly one teacher for each class, this type of community is much easier to establish than in secondary schools, for instance. This type of community is exemplified by the language that teachers use in describing their classroom and how it works. One example from a recent research project (cited in Beauchamp, 2011) will serve to demonstrate how this works in a cross-curricular context:

> *each area of the classroom obviously is themed, you've got your doing table, your writing area, your sand table, you know the different areas and we try and contextualise it all, so this week we're doing spiders. On the gluing table we are making spiders, cutting out little bits of paper and different materials and they're sticking bits on spiders. On the art table we are going to do weaving in and out on card with spiders. Painting will be spider webs, our literacy time this week is on rhymes about spiders like Little Miss Muffet, Incy Wincy. The Science table has got books on spiders in the reading corner and we've got a bug house in the role play corner.*

In this quote, the consistent use of the word 'we' represents a level of mutual engagement and joint enterprise that, allied to effective classroom organisation, will lead to a shared repertoire of language, activities and routines. It could be argued that this approach pervades primary teaching, and it is hoped that, when combined with an interactive dialogic pedagogy, this community interaction facilitates a high level of engagement from pupils and teachers. It is also suggested that, with shared understanding of routines and language, pupils will be in a better position to become active co-constructors of their own knowledge. In this context, it is necessary to ensure that the 'shared repertoire' includes ICT skills on the part of both pupil and teacher.

Having examined three categories of interaction that are not reliant on the features of ICT, we will now consider what ICT can add.

Technology-mediated interaction: learners with ICT

In this category, technology (mainly ICT) is a 'mediating artifact' (Engeström, 2001) in the learning process. Sometimes the interactions are planned and instigated by the teacher, but they can also be where the technology is used 'to mediate interactions between learners in a manner not predicted by the teacher' (Beauchamp, 2011, p184). In this category the IWB would be chosen not just because it was there, but specifically for its ability to offer a way of communicating or exploring (mediating) ideas in a variety of ways that exploit the features of ICT; in this it is distinct from the use of the IWB as a feature of the setting discussed above. An important feature of this category is the sheer variety of interactions that ICT can facilitate. If the IWB, classroom PCs or mobile devices have an internet connection, we have already seen that this can mediate interactions between pupils not only within the school, but also anywhere in the world with the requisite facilities. In addition, as we have seen in earlier chapters, with mobile devices (such as iPads), pupils can also record and share thoughts in a variety of modes and media.

It is important to reiterate that the categories above are used by teachers in combination or in sequence and are not necessarily the basis for whole lessons.

ICT across the curriculum

This potential for ICT across the curriculum was outlined some years ago by Becta (2002, p2), and, although some devices may be slightly dated now, the breadth of activities available is shown when they suggest that

> *ICT gives pupils immediate access to richer source materials. Multimedia can present problems from real life which draw on the previous learning and experience of pupils and link it to their current learning. Using e-mail, pupils can engage in 'authentic' communications. In modern foreign languages for example, CD-ROM and interactive video allow pupils to interact with original source materials and on-line experts in new ways that can lead to more reflective work and deeper understanding. Data-logging equipment can be used in and outside of the classroom in conjunction with portables. Pupils can then input this data into spreadsheets and databases and represent it in a number of ways. Digital and video cameras can also be used to record field trips. This gives pupils experience of 'hands on' data collection and helps identify the practical application of ICT in the real world. Computer simulations also allow children to experience a variety of realistic experiences without risk.*

This list of possibilities only hints at the full range of ICT use across the curriculum. In an integrated approach, ICT is seen not just as a tool for a particular subject, but as a means of integrating subjects in a cross-curricular approach to teaching. This is important if we agree with Barnes (2007, p1) that 'our experience of the world is cross-curricular. Everything which surrounds us in the physical world can be seen and understood from multiple perspectives.' One of these perspectives may be that of a scientist, geographer or historian, and here the challenges begin in framing learning experiences for children in the primary school. I have written elsewhere that 'each subject gives a child a unique way of understanding the world and that viewing teaching ideas through, for example, a "scientific lens" can offer new insights into how to develop effective learning opportunities' (Beauchamp, 2010, pp169–70). In this situation, the particular 'lens', or combination of 'lenses', adopted would be decided predominantly by the teacher in the first instance, but this may well change as children develop their own ideas. Bennett, Hamill and Pickford (2007, p12) suggest that 'children finding out about their environment do not consciously signal changes in their thinking as they ask "geographical" questions about their locality or "scientific" questions about their environment, or use "mathematical" or "ICT" skills to measure and record'. Perhaps this is true of the very early years in primary school, but as children progress they are aware that, for example, mathematicians need to work carefully and accurately and that scientists need to observe carefully. It is within this context that the idea of subject lenses is proposed. It may well be that this operates at two levels (one for the teacher thinking of possible approaches to planning, the other for children thinking of ways to approach a problem), but the key idea is that you consider the possible benefits of approaching teaching and learning as, say, a musician or a historian.

The does not mean teaching a 'subject', but adopting a methodology appropriate to that subject to view the task through its lens. This allows something to become what Barnes and Shirley (2007) call 'strangely familiar'. They suggest that 'even familiar aspects of life could be looked upon as unfamiliar and that the new could be seen as unthreatening' (ibid., p164). By looking at familiar topics through a different subject 'lens', as well as through its own, it is suggested that new approaches and dimensions of the problem can be seen, which might provoke novel teaching approaches and solutions by both the teacher and the pupils.

To explore this approach further, let us consider history as an example. We are not interested in teaching just historical subject knowledge (for example, historical 'facts', such as the year of a particular battle – although 'drill' exercises or games on a computer could do this or reinforce this), but rather in looking at the problems as a historian – even if the subject is not history. Turner-Bisset (2005) suggests that the following processes of enquiry are appropriate for primary school 'historians':

- searching for evidence;
- examining the evidence;
- recording of accounts;
- summarising historical narrative or argument.

From what we have seen in earlier chapters, it should be apparent that ICT can have a role in each of these processes. Examples of using this in science are shown in Table 10.1, where a Year 5 class searches the school grounds for plants. The class works in groups looking for different plants and then reports back at the end.

Table 10.1	Using historical processes of enquiry in another subject			
Subject or area of learning	Searching for evidence	Examining the evidence	Recording of accounts	Summarising (historical) narrative or argument
Science	• Using the internet to research a plant – where it might be found . . .	• Taking pictures of the habitat were it was found. • Looking at leaves with a digital microscope and magnifying glasses.	• Taking pictures of the actual plant from a variety of angles and using zoom with the digital camera. • Using the digital recorder (or mobile device) to interview other members of the group about where the plant was found, what it looked like in situ and any other relevant factors. • Writing notes on a laptop or tablet and saving the interview sound files.	• Preparing and delivering a short presentation for the class using internet research, pictures, words and sound files of the interviews in a PowerPoint presentation using the IWB.

ACTIVITY

Using the headings below, make a list of how ICT can help in each process for your chosen age phase or range in a variety of subjects across the curriculum.

Subject or area	Searching for evidence	Examining the evidence	Recording of accounts	Summarising (historical) narrative or argument

In undertaking the activity above, you may have noticed that some of these processes are also used in other subjects. For example, with a slight rewording of the final process, all of these items are part of the process skills in science. Harlen and Qualter (2014) suggest that, in primary school science (the science lens), children begin to develop the skills and attitudes listed below.

Process (enquiry) skills

These include:

- questioning, predicting and planning;
- gathering evidence by observing and using information sources;
- interpreting evidence and drawing conclusions;
- communicating and reflecting.

ACTIVITY

Using the headings in the bullet points above, make a list of how ICT can help in each process for your chosen age phase or range. Then compare and contrast your list with the previous activity. What conclusions can you draw about the use of ICT?

In addition, Harlen and Qualter (2014) outline scientific attitudes that may also apply to other areas of the curriculum:

- willingness to consider evidence and change ideas;
- sensitivity to living things and the environment.

Another feature of using a scientific lens is the way in which scientists assess and address misconceptions. Much work was done on this area in science by the SPACE (Science Processes and Concept Exploration Project, 1991) and CLISP (Children's Learning in Science Project, 1984–91), but other studies exist in areas such as mathematics – see Chapter 9. In previous chapters, we have seen that ICT can present ideas in a wide variety of forms. As such, it may be that ICT can be very useful in presenting challenges to current concepts, in a variety of areas of the curriculum, that may provoke a fundamental rethink – hopefully towards a more 'correct' conception! It is perhaps easiest to consider this in a three-stage process:

1. assessing and recording current conceptions and/or misconceptions;
2. presenting alternative perspectives;
3. assessing and recording new conceptions (and new misconceptions!).

As this is a cycle, we will consider the first two below, with the assumption that the principles of the first will also apply to the third (see also 'Assessment with mobile technology' in Chapter 5).

> ## Assessment with ICT

Assessing and recording current conceptions and/or misconceptions

McDougall (2001) makes the important distinction between 'assessing *learning with ICT*' (assessing ICT use as part of learning) and '*assessing learning* with ICT' (using ICT to assess learning). As there are many books already that cover different modes of assessment (such as diagnostic, formative, summative, norm-referenced, criterion-referenced, ipsative and so on) in detail, we will assume that decisions about which mode of assessment to be used have already been made and we will deal with generic principles of how they work with ICT. In other words, what unique strategies of assessment can ICT offer in addition to more established methods?

When making assessments, we need to consider two broad categories, which in research terms might be called pre- and post-activity assessments: in other words, what the pupils know before the teaching and what they know afterwards.

Assessing existing understanding

This apparently simple concept, however, is not as straightforward as it may seem, as pupils rarely have complete understanding but a series of connected ideas, some of which are 'right' and some 'wrong'. Some form of broad, but nuanced, criteria are needed. Summers, Kruger and Mant (1998, p157) provide a useful framework for pre-teaching assessments in science, but this could equally be applied to other areas of the curriculum. They suggest that teachers could look for:

- *preconceptions* – either a misconception (that is, a scientifically incorrect idea) or a partially understood scientific idea;
- *missing* – a scientific idea for which there was no evidence of any knowledge or understanding;
- *knows* – a scientific idea of which the child demonstrated knowledge and understanding.

In making such judgements you could use a range of practical activities with no ICT, and it may well be possible to identify the level of the pupil's understanding using questioning, written tests or practical tasks. In addition, assessments can sometimes be made in unexpected situations, such as in a class discussion.

ACTIVITY

You are talking to your class, in this case Key Stage 2, about what they did over the weekend and it becomes obvious that one child in your chosen age range thinks that the moon is a source of light. The pupil has heard it in stories and their mum took

(continued)

(continued)

them for a 'walk in the moonlight' last weekend as it was a full moon – which the child tells you means that there was 'more light as the moon was bigger'. The child has dyslexia and is not keen on writing. How could you use ICT to support this child in explaining why they think that: 1) the moon makes light; and 2) the moon is bigger?

What we need to consider is what the features of ICT can add to this. In this context, the IWB can be a useful tool. When used in an interactive way, as discussed earlier, it helps to make explicit things that may have been internalised without ICT, as pupils share ideas or articulate their thinking. As Beauchamp and Kennewell (2008, p311) propose, 'the communal nature of the IWB, combined with the culture of valuing mistakes for their learning potential, may have facilitated the exposure of pupils' misconceptions. Many pupils were encouraged to articulate their thinking about key ideas and evaluate the viability of alternative perspectives.' Such an approach is very useful for helping teachers to assess (in real time and afterwards) and record (by saving) pupils' current ideas. This is not to say that the same thing cannot be done using more traditional resources, but as Beauchamp and Kennewell (ibid., p312) continue to report, teachers feel that the IWB is able to give 'better support for reflection than manual tools – particularly through sharing ideas with the whole class . . . displaying pupils' work and reviewing what was done on the board earlier in the lesson'.

Assessing understanding after teaching

Having undertaken teaching activities, it is also necessary to check the level of understanding. Summers, Kruger and Mant (1998, p157) provide the following post-teaching classifications for this process, which they suggest can be matched to the pre-teaching ideas:

- successfully acquired ideas;
- partially acquired ideas;
- incorrectly acquired ideas;
- ideas not acquired;
- unchanged ideas.

In making such judgements, the same features of working with the IWB will apply. Depending on the pupil's level of understanding, the teacher will then decide on the next course of action and on how to present alternative perspectives and what form these perspectives need to take.

Presenting alternative perspectives

Having established *what* pupils think, and *why* they think it, you then need consider how this can be addressed and how big or small the next steps will be. At the same time, you need to decide if ICT can contribute in any way, or is not needed at all – the guiding principle being 'Does ICT do it better than anything else?'

The example of moonlight above was deliberately chosen as something that is apparently simple but in reality is very complex, with many related challenging concepts (such as planetary motion) that need to be understood to address the original concept or idea. It may even be that you cannot address the main issue at all (at least in the short term), as there are so many underlying misconceptions that need to be dealt with first, or, perhaps more cynically, because it is not in the curriculum, or in the school scheme of work for your year group, so need not be addressed. (How do you feel about this latter argument?) A full understanding of what pupils think of all related concepts is important (if time consuming) and tracking back through underlying conceptions to see where the misconception begins is a vital part of understanding why children think as they do and how this can be changed. To do this, however, your own understanding of relevant concepts needs to be as complete as possible in all subject areas (which is the role of subject knowledge in primary teaching) and ICT can help with this as well.

Having established an area where you wish to represent ideas, and having made the decision that ICT is the best way to do it (because it can do something better than anything else), you are faced with a number of options based on one or more of the features of ICT explored in earlier chapters. In each case, however, you need to decide why ICT is better. To help frame this we will look at an example from science, based on Summers, Kruger and Mant (1998), which may be useful to set you thinking. Two scenarios are outlined below that focus on understanding the flow of electricity in a circuit. Both use an analogy to help teach the following key ideas:

- The battery is a 'pusher' of electrons.
- The electrons (already in the wire) all start moving at the same time.
- The electrons move in the same direction all around the circuit and are not produced by the battery.
- The strength of the battery is a measure of its 'push'.

In this analogy, the pedals represent the battery and the links in the chain are the electrons. The class has done some work on circuits already (to make a bulb light up) but in this task it became clear that they did not really understand the flow of electricity. The teacher decides to address this specifically and decides to use an analogy to help.

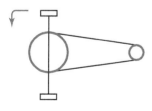

Scenario A: The teacher uses the IWB to show the class a video of an upturned bike (with the chain clearly visible). At the start of the video the pedals are still. Through open questioning, the teacher establishes that the children understand what this represents (e.g. pedals/battery; chain links/electrons; wheel hub/bulb) and the relative state of each (e.g. no current; electrons are present but not moving around the circuit). The teacher then plays the video and the pedals are turned. The teacher pauses the video and asks the children to look carefully at the chain and pedals – to focus attention on important features to avoid possible misconceptions. Again, the teacher plays the video and uses open questions to ask what is happening now (the battery is 'pushing' electrons in one direction around the circuit). The teacher minimises the video and uses the IWB flipchart software to ask a child to show the picture (left) and discusses what it represents. The teacher asks for a volunteer to label the picture and draw arrows around the 'circuit' to show the direction in which the electrons are travelling. The teacher then resumes the video in which the pedals are now turned faster. After pausing the video, the teacher resumes open questions to see if pupils understand that the strength of the battery is a measure of its 'push'. The teacher then minimises the video and returns to the IWB software and goes to the next page in the flipchart, which shows the following picture. This is then discussed and the teacher asks for a volunteer to label and draw the direction of flow of the electrons. The class then discusses what makes the current flow and the teacher introduces the notion of the person pedalling acting as a switch. Having addressed the aims of the analogy, the teacher then returns to practical work and the next areas of learning in this area.

Scenario B: In this scenario, the teacher brings a real bike into the classroom and turns it upside down on the table. The teacher moves the class around the bike and, through open questioning, establishes that the children understand what this represents (e.g. pedals/battery; chain links/electrons; wheel hub/bulb) and the relative state of each (e.g. no current; electrons are present but not moving around the circuit). The teacher then asks for a volunteer to turn the pedals and the lesson progresses as above, but the teacher has to draw the pictures on a whiteboard as there is no IWB. A second volunteer is used to turn the pedals faster.

ACTIVITY

Even if the teacher in Scenario B had an IWB, what are the benefits of each of the above? Which approach would you use and why?

Challenge 1: In the discussion, one pupil points out that the 'electrons' (chain) are going around the 'bulb' (wheel hub) and therefore asks how they can light it? How do you respond? *Key idea: this is only an analogy – refer to diagram.*

Challenge 2: Another pupil points out that when you stop pedalling (battery), the wheel will keep moving. They compare this to the bulb and ask will it stay alight? *Key idea: although the wheel is moving, the electrons (chain) are not – the wheel is not the bulb.*

It is likely, however, that teachers will use a mixture of ICT and non-ICT resources in the classroom, as demonstrated in the case study below.

CASE STUDY

A Year 5 class is studying 'Forces' in science. The class teacher decided that she wants the class to have practical experience with tangible objects. The practical activity involves running a toy car down a ramp and changing the angle of the ramp to see the effect on the distance travelled – the only variable changed was the angle of the ramp to ensure a fair test. There was only one ramp so the teacher made the pragmatic decision to use this with a group and rotate the groups so that all pupils undertake the practical activity during the lesson. The teacher decided that the other groups could do a mixture of revision and research activities related to the topic 'Forces', some aspects of which they had already covered in earlier years. One group did research on laptops using a science CD-ROM (as they had no wireless internet connection) to answer questions on a worksheet. Another group used the IWB to play a game of 'Who Wants to Be a Millionaire?' about forces, which the teacher had prepared using a PowerPoint template. In this group, one person asked the questions and used the IWB pen to advance the slides while the rest of the group were put into pairs to answer the questions – the teacher had told the pupils their partner in advance to ensure mixed-ability groupings. They recorded the scores on a paper flipchart next to the IWB. One group worked with a classroom assistant on unrelated reading activities, which were scheduled throughout the week. The final group worked with the class teacher on the practical science activity with the ramp and toy car. The teacher wanted to ensure that the correct conceptions were developed and that appropriate science language was used correctly. When the teacher was satisfied that they understood, the pupils in this group had to record their findings in their science books together with details of the investigation using a writing frame they were familiar with. The class teacher rotated the groups so that all had covered all the activities during the course of the lesson.

At the end of the lesson, the teacher gave the whole class individual voting devices connected to the IWB. A series of questions were asked relating to the work that had been covered and, after everyone had voted, the teacher discussed the answers based on the percentage of correct or incorrect answers. The software relating to the voting devices also gave the teacher an individual record of responses for their records. This voting was very quick and the pupils, who had used the devices on previous occasions, were very engaged in the questions.

ACTIVITY

In the final whole-class voting session in the case study above, we come across two issues that can apply to all use of ICT:

- It is possible to guess the correct answer?
- Sometimes pupils try to be the first to answer so they forsake accuracy for speed.

How could you avoid this in your lessons?

Other subject lenses

Having seen some examples from science, let us also look at how ICT and subject lenses may work in other areas, beginning with a study of a location using a variety of geography lenses.

Location

In examining a location, it is necessary to recognise that pupils 'are citizens of their localities, making contributions to their communities whether playing sport, interacting with others or simply "hanging out" with friends . . . [and they] have views about the past, present and future of their localities' (Pike, 2011, p17). These may be different from adult views, and it is necessary, as outlined above, to assess and use these views. One of the ways of doing this, and creating novel learning opportunities, is to explore locations both inside and outside the school using different subject lenses to provide alternative perspectives. Barnes and Shirley's (2007) 'strangely familiar' approach discussed above suggests that children first explore and then express the uniqueness of a place, integrating many areas of the curriculum, especially the arts, such as poetry, art and music. This involves using a variety of lenses, including those of the musician, the filmmaker, the poet, the artist or the dancer, but with control being passed to the pupils in selecting not only the perspective adopted but also the resources, including ICT, to be used. The activity begins with a journey, and the initial journey itself could be part of using ICT to make it 'strange' – this could be by showing them a video of the journey of a character that sets the scene or poses a challenge. Alternatively, and perhaps even better, try other non-ICT approaches such as 'characters' joining the bus to tell their stories – most schools have at least one teacher who could be persuaded to dress up as a pirate who could kidnap the bus and take it to his/her secret hiding place for buried treasure! Upon arrival, the pupils can consider which role(s) – musician, dancer, and so on (the subject lens, or combination of lenses) – they want to adopt in order to explore and report on their experience – although you will have to have the relevant equipment available (and charged!). Some possibilities are given in Table 10.2 below.

Graphicacy

Another geographical lens is provided by graphicacy, which 'can be thought of as the sub-set of visual-spatial thinking that applies particularly to geography. It refers to the essentially pictorial ways, from photographs to diagrams and maps, in which we

Table 10.2	Exploring a 'strangely familiar' location – lenses and ICT resources
Lens	**ICT resource**
The musician	• Sequencer • Keyboards • Digital recorders
The filmmaker	• Digital camera (still and movie) • Digital editing software – e.g. Movie Maker • IWB for showing the end product
The poet	• Word processor
The dancer	• Devise a dance for the setting – perhaps using digital recordings of music from the musicians above • CD player • Digital camera (still and movie) to record and appraise the performance
The artist	• Montage of digital pictures of odd or unique features of the local area – *everybody looks for the familiar and obvious things, why not collect images of the unexpected or strange features?*
The historian	• Podcasts or vodcasts using digital recordings (audio and/or video) of interviews with older members of the community who can provide first-hand experience and life stories of growing up in, or moving into, the area and different communities
The scientist	• Data loggers to measure the temperature and other features of the setting

communicate spatial information about places, spaces and environments' (Mackintosh, 2011, p7). At the end of Key Stage 2 this may involve using, for instance, Ordnance Survey (OS) maps and symbols, but preparation for this begins in the early years. ICT has an important role in this move from horizontal to vertical perspectives and from pictures to maps. For the first of these transitions, Figure 10.1 (ibid., p7) shows the contribution of digital images as the view changes from early Key Stage 1, with a horizontal child's-eye view of real objects from ground level in fieldwork, through to the end of Key Stage 2, with a symbolic representation of objects based on a vertical view.

In this transition, ICT devices such as digital cameras (comparing views of everyday objects from the side and above, viewed on the IWB or other devices), video cameras (panning from a side view in an arc to a view from above) and websites (such as Google Earth or Google Street View used with Google Maps) can offer a unique set of facilities not offered by other resources.

Model of place

Another geographical lens is offered by an adaptation of Goodey's (1973) model of place. Figure 10.2 shows a revised version to reflect the experience of primary schools

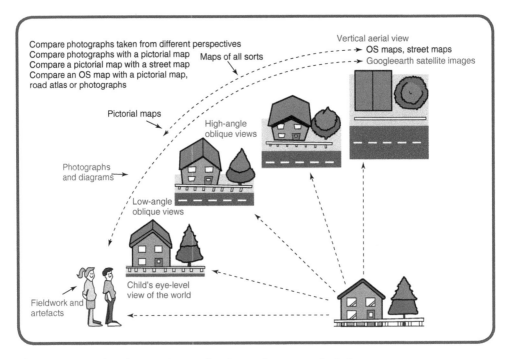

Figure 10.1   The change from a horizontal to a vertical view

pupils. This new model extends the original but also incorporates specifically the impact of ICT, which was not present in the original model developed more than 40 years ago. An integral part of the revised model reflects the fact that 'place' can now be a virtual concept. Pupils are very familiar with *real* places in other countries, but we are increasingly beginning to explore the educational potential of a range of *virtual* worlds – such as Second Life – particularly through gaming.

This model takes as its starting point the premise that young children begin (and return to at will) their explorations from their own 'personal space' – be it in the classroom, home or elsewhere. The concentric circles moving outwards from the centre show an increasingly distant range of places, from personal space to classroom places, near places and far places visited. The real places are in the bottom half of the circle, but the facility of ICT to 'visit' these places virtually, and at any time – even from within the child's personal space – is shown in the top half of the circle. This takes account of the ability of a very young child to be based in their personal space (at home or in the classroom) and yet able to 'visit' a very faraway place on a PC or through videos of a family holiday (on TV, a PC or a hosting service such as YouTube), or those of their friends, members of their community or anybody who posts a video! As well as these recorded visits, others can take place in real time using ICT, through live video feeds, such as those from zoo websites (for example, San Diego) or city centres around the world. Such real-time video feeds can also be useful in discussing time differences around the world as you can see some places are light and some dark (and they often display the local time), even if (at present) the images are sometimes not as high quality as you might hope. Indeed, the quality of these images will vary according

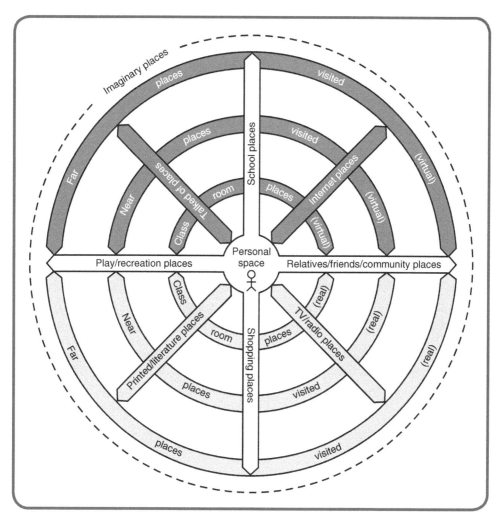

Figure 10.2   Model of place and ICT

to connection speed and other factors, but it might be worth the effort to use them in lessons – and remember that you can take screenshots at any time to keep a record or to use in other lessons.

ICT is included in 'play or recreation places', but this also takes account of real physical play inside and, more particularly, outside school or on holiday. All of these experiences can lead to 'imaginary places'. The final outer circle, representing these 'imaginary places', does not *need* ICT, as any early years classroom will evidence, but they can be created or recorded using ICT.

The model also acknowledges that more traditional resources, such as books or other printed materials, can help create a place (both real and imaginary) in the minds of young children. As well as printed stories, oral stories ('talked-of places') can also contribute to the understanding of a place; these can come from family members (who have lived elsewhere) or from within the local community.

The overall aim of the model is to help you realise that the concept of place, and how it is formed, is not always as simple as it may appear, particularly with recent advances in technology. Pupils are exposed to a wide range of experiences and their current conceptions of place may have been formed from many of the views in the model. When planning work on locations, it may be useful to use the geographical lens provided by the model above to consider how to present the location in a variety of formats (both with and without ICT) in order to ensure that pupils arrive at a secure and multidimensional understanding. What is not shown easily on the model is the role of the *people* in the various places, who pupils can meet and with whom they can discuss the location in real and virtual meetings. As always, the use of ICT should be because of its ability to do something faster, more efficiently or in a way that nothing else can.

ACTIVITY

In Chapter 8 we looked at a table showing how the features of ICT could be mapped against literacy activities. This table is repeated below but you need to add examples that demonstrate how ICT could be used in a topic-based approach – include as many areas of the curriculum as appropriate to use the technology to its best effect.

Possible actions for which ICT provides potential and structure

Action	Meaning	Example
Composing	Ideas can be recorded accurately as they arise	
Editing	The data stored and displayed can be changed easily with no trace of the original	
Selecting	Choice of pre-existing resource or procedure can be made (e.g. from a list)	
Comparing	Features of the same object from different views or different items displayed can be compared	
Retrieving	Stored resources can easily be retrieved for use	
Apprehending	The display (text, images, sound, diagrams) makes it easier for students to see or interpret	
Focusing	Attention can be drawn to particular aspects of a process or representation	
Transforming	The way that the data is displayed can be changed	
Role playing	Activities can be carried out in a way that is similar to activities in the 'real world'	

Collating	A variety of items from different sources can be brought together into a single resource
Sharing	It is easy to communicate and interchange resources and ideas with others
Annotating	Notes can be added to a process or representation at the time of use
Repeating	An automated or stored process can be repeated at will
Modelling	A process can be simulated by representing relationships between variables
Cumulating	Building up a representation of knowledge in a progressive manner
Revisiting	Repeating an activity or returning with a different focus
Undoing	Reversing an action
Questioning	A piece of dialogue requiring a response
Prompting	An action or piece of dialogue that suggests what someone should do
Responding	Action that is contingent on a previous question or prompt

Music

When using a musical lens, we need to examine the three fundamental processes of music in the curriculum: performing, composing and appraisal (using musical vocabulary to discuss performances). The position of technology is long established within music teaching in primary schools, but this has largely focused on equipment that helps organise or manipulate sounds, rather than using more generic ICT equipment in music. From the earliest use of records, and more particularly radio, technology took the place of teachers to give pupils 'opportunities for enjoyment and learning [in music] which ordinary teachers could not expect to muster' (Rainbow and Cox, 2006, p280). The influence of records and the radio was also significant in homes and wider society. This process was two-way in that technology used in society gradually took its place in schools. In more recent years, this has been reflected in technology that was developed primarily for the music industry, such as keyboards, audio recording and midi sequencers, but that has become an important part of primary school music. In short, 'the history of technology in the classroom has been inextricably bound up with the adoption of technological tools used in wider society'

(Gall and Breeze, 2007, p42). As I write this, I am sure that by the time you read it a new device will have arrived that will become common in society and will take its place in the classroom – and you will wonder why I did not mention it! It also seems likely that such changes are likely to happen more quickly. Nevertheless, it is easy to record (audio and video), notate, sequence, replay and share music without sophisticated recording devices or the associated technical skills that made this difficult in earlier times. As we have seen elsewhere, musical compositions can also form part of podcasts made by pupils. The use of mobile devices also means that activities are not restricted to the school classroom, or even the school itself. They also allow pupils to do these things with or without adult support, depending on their level of experience with ICT. In addition, recordings can be made in HD quality with devices such as flip cams and iPads (or iPods). These activities are, however, perhaps the most apparent use of ICT in music teaching, whereas a musical lens presents other, less obvious, opportunities.

ICT and all that jazz

The musical lens also suggests that musical compositional techniques can offer a useful framework for classroom organisation using ICT. The purpose of this framework is similar to that of the other examples noted above, in that as well as providing a tool for classroom analysis (in teaching and research), it also allows you to consider whether you are using all possible methods of classroom organisation within and between lessons. Although based on work with IWBs, the framework can also be applied to other ICT tools and resources. The analogies resulted from ideas discussed within a research team, and the following is a summary only – see Beauchamp et al. (2010) for full details. When observing lessons in a research project, we noticed that, although all lessons were planned in advance, there were occasions within lessons when teachers and learners moved outside the constraints of a predetermined lesson orchestration and began to improvise. These episodes varied in length, but 'the musical analogy is a powerful one in characterising the manipulation of features in the classroom setting in order to generate activity or "performance" which leads to learning' (ibid., p145). Zack (2000) suggested that the jazz metaphor could be used to examine and classify speech against musical genres and to see how these compared to Konitz's stages. Table 10.3 (from Beauchamp et al., 2010) shows how both could be related to ICT use in the classroom by mapping them against Beauchamp and Kennewell's (2010) categories of classroom interaction and interactions with ICT.

Some of the elements of this table will be familiar from earlier chapters, but the key distinction is that we are now labelling unplanned moments in a lesson, when serendipity provides the stimulus for a new direction. This stimulus can come from both teachers and pupils, or even from ICT – for instance, the discovery of a new feature of the IWB or iPad or a piece of software. Just because the resultant activity is not planned, it does not mean that the opportunity should be missed. In fact, having the confidence to see the potential of unplanned opportunities for learning, and to use them, is the sign of a good teacher.

Table 10.3 also provides an opportunity to think about the lessons you are planning. Are they all 'classical' or do you have some with more of a swing to them?

Table 10.3	**Musical genres and classroom interactions**			
Music genre	**Konitz's stages**	**Communication metaphor**	**Category of interaction**	**Interaction with ICT**
Classical – *minimal improvisation*	Interpretation	Formal, pre-defined, linear	Authoritative	Factual recall, following a standard procedure or browsing fixed hypertext
Traditional jazz/swing – *constrained improvisation within a well-structured context*	Embellishment	Predictable but flexible scripts; strict turn-taking and use of adjacency pairs – highly predictable statement and response pairs	Dialectic	Constructing product to a specified brief, involving the selection of options and sources
Bebop – *extensive modification of the tune using a wide range of notes and rhythms and some modification to harmonic structure*	Variation	Complex but structured conversation	Dialogic	Developing the product – requiring information seeking, hypothesis testing, comparison and the elaboration of material
Post-bop/free jazz – *maximal improvisation of the structure, content and rules of improvisation – 'functional anarchy'*	Improvisation	Emergent, spontaneous, interactive, mutually constructed conversation	Synergistic	Open problem-solving or creating the product – involving the identification of context or material, analysis and reflection

Video-stimulated reflective dialogue (VSRD)

It was noted above that it is possible to record 'performances' using audio and video as well as, for example, PE, dance and science investigations. This is particularly important in music, as the video recording allows you to look at the way in which instruments were played, or, for example, the way beaters were used to achieve a particular sound or effect, as well as to listen to the end result. The use of video to enable pupils to reflect on both their work and their learning has been used in research and is labelled video-stimulated reflective dialogue (VSRD), or variations of this. In this technique, which can be used in classroom assessment as well as research, video recordings are made of activities and then used to stimulate dialogue and discussion. The video helps children remember what actually took place (which is particularly important for younger children), but it also allows them (and teachers) to see what others were doing that they may have missed. Depending on the software, the features of ICT make it possible for pupils to view the movie immediately after the event (for instance, by plugging a flip cam into a laptop), to move backwards and forwards within the movie, and to replay either the whole movie or a small part of it as many times as necessary to clarify events or to focus attention on different things.

CASE STUDY

In a research project with Key Stage 2 pupils (Salisbury et al., 2011; Beauchamp et al., 2009), VSRD was used alongside a range of other visual elicitation methods to try to assess the understanding of science concepts with pupils for whom English was an additional language (EAL) – in this case children with Polish as the home language. The pupils were video recorded by researchers as they undertook a range of practical science activities that focused on 'Forces' as a topic. One of these was trying to drop a ball into a bucket as they ran past it, without throwing it in or exerting a downward force. Coloured cones were placed on the ground at intervals both before and after the bucket. The digital recordings were shown to the pupils in their groups as part of an interview process in which the video stimulated the dialogue.

At the beginning of the interview, the researcher used the mouse to control the video. It quickly became evident, however, that the Year 4/6 pupils involved were very keen to take control of the movie and one child spontaneously took the mouse and used it to move to a spot in the video to show the others an incident he had spotted. After this, other pupils also took the mouse and moved backwards and forwards through the movie by dragging the cursor, as well as pausing to look at specific instances. This was a particularly powerful tool as the HD quality of the video allowed a good still frame shot. It was in this way that the pupils discovered for themselves their relative positions in relation to the bucket when they dropped the ball. They soon realised that, although they thought they had dropped the ball over the top of the bucket when successfully getting it in, in reality they had dropped it slightly before, very near one of the cones.

Although the main purpose of the video had been to assess their understanding of the topic, by taking control of the video and using the provisionality and interactive features of the recording the pupils also co-constructed their own understanding of an important part of the topic.

Incidentally, the fact that they were looking at themselves in the video was a great source of motivation (and amusement at times!) for the pupils.

As with many aspects of ICT, there are some technical issues that need to be considered when making the video. For instance, you need to consider factors such as: where to place the camera so that all participants are seen (on a tall or short stand, or using none at all?); whether the battery will last long enough without a power supply; whether you need an additional microphone; and how to ensure that the camera view is not blocked. In reality, as this would probably focus on a small group (such as a group performance) rather than the whole class, most of these issues would not be a cause for concern. It should also be remembered that any recordings can be used as evidence of work or can be added to a digital record or e-portfolio.

SUMMARY

In this chapter we have considered how to approach cross-curricular teaching using a range of subject lenses to encourage unique approaches to learning and teaching. We have not covered all subject lenses, but I hope that the examples provided will encourage you to consider how the pedagogies of different subject areas can stimulate an alternative approach. This does not mean that proven pedagogies should be neglected, but rather that sometimes a fresh approach can reinvigorate both teacher and pupils. Within these approaches, the use of ICT remains selective and should exploit its unique potential.

References

Adams, D. (2011) 'Music-making at prehistoric sites', presented at Leading Music Education International Conference, Don Wright Faculty of Music, University of Western Ontario, 29 May–1 June.

Barnes, J. (2007) *Cross-curricular Learning 3–14*, London: Paul Chapman Publishing.

Barnes, J. and Shirley, I. (2007) 'Strangely familiar: cross-curricular and creative thinking in teacher education', *Improving Schools*, 10(2), pp162–79.

Beauchamp, G. (2010) 'Knowledge and understanding of the world', in Palaiologou, I. (ed.) *The Early Years Foundation Stage: Theory and Practice*, London: Sage, pp167–77.

Beauchamp, G. (2011) 'Interactivity and ICT in the primary school: categories of learner interactions with and without ICT', *Technology, Pedagogy and Education*, 20(2), pp175–90.

Beauchamp, G., Ellis, C., Haughton, C. and Salisbury, J. (2009) 'The use of ICT and video stimulated reflective dialogue (VSRD) in assessing conceptual understanding of science in primary school children with English as an additional language (EAL)', presented at BERA Conference, Manchester, 3–5 September.

Beauchamp, G. and Kennewell, S. (2008) 'The influence of ICT on the interactivity of teaching', special issue, *Education and Information Technologies*, 13(4), pp305–15.

Beauchamp, G. and Kennewell, S. (2010) 'Interactivity in the classroom and its impact on learning', *Computers and Education*, 54, pp759–66.

Beauchamp, G., Kennewell, S., Tanner, H. and Jones, S. (2010) 'Interactive whiteboards and all that jazz: the contribution of musical metaphors to the analysis of classroom activity with interactive technologies', *Technology, Pedagogy and Education*, 19(2), pp143–57.

Becta (2002) *ICT Supporting Teaching: Developing Effective Practice*, Coventry: Becta.

Bennett, R., Hamill, A. and Pickford, T. (2007) *Progression in Primary ICT*, Abingdon: David Fulton.

Engeström, Y. (2001) 'Expansive learning at work: toward an activity theoretical reconceptualization', *Journal of Education and Work*, 14, pp133–56.

Gall, M. and Breeze, N. (2007) 'The sub-culture of music and ICT in the classroom', *Technology, Pedagogy and Education*, 16(1), pp41–56.

Goodey, B. (1973) *Perception of the Environment: An Introduction to the Literature*, Occasional paper no. 17, Birmingham: University of Birmingham Centre for Urban and Regional Studies.

Harlen, W. and Qualter, A. (2014) *The Teaching of Science in Primary Schools*, 6th edition, London: Routledge.

Mackintosh, M. (2011) 'Graphicacy for life', *Primary Geographer*, June, pp6–8.

McDougall, A. (2001) 'Guest editorial: assessing learning with ICT', *Journal of Computer Assisted Learning*, 17(3), pp223–6.

Pike, S. (2011) 'Children, locality and the future', *Primary Geographer*, March, pp17–19.

Rainbow, B. and Cox, G. (2006) *Music in Educational Thought and Practice*, Woodbridge: Boydell.

Salisbury, J., Ellis, C., Beauchamp, G. and Haughton, C. (2011) 'What's occurring? The what, why, how and when of research capacity building in a modest pilot project with EAL learners and science', *Welsh Journal of Education*, 15(1), pp46–65.

Schafer, R.M. (1994) *Soundscape: Our Sonic Environment and the Tuning of the World*, New York: Knopf.

Summers, M., Kruger, C. and Mant, J. (1998) 'Teaching electricity effectively in the primary school: a case study', *International Journal of Science Education*, 20(2), pp153–72.

Turner-Bisset, R. (2005) *Creative Teaching: History in the Primary Classroom*, London: David Fulton.

Wenger, E. (1998) *Communities of Practice: Learning, Meaning, and Identity*, Cambridge: Cambridge University Press.

Zack, M. (2000) 'Jazz improvisation and organizing: once more from the top', *Organization Science*, 11, pp227–34.

Useful websites

10 Best Live UK Webcam Sites: http://gouk.about.com/od/picturegalleries/tp/UK_webcams.htm Links to live web cameras around the UK.

11 Teaching modern foreign languages (MFL) or a second language with technology in the primary school

In this chapter we will examine second language learning pedagogy and the role of ICT in providing authentic learning contexts. We will also discover how mobile technologies, the interactive whiteboard and sound and video technologies can support effective second language learning.

As we saw in the first chapter, the curricula of different countries in the UK are not consistent, and 'there has never been a UK-wide policy for primary modern foreign language provision' (Hunt et al., 2005, p371) – although there is some evidence that primary pupils are positive about learning languages (Tierney and Gallastegi, 2011). Nevertheless, at the time of writing, although modern foreign languages (MFL) are compulsory at Key Stage 2 in England, 'The situation relating to MFL teaching in the UK is complex and varied, as policy for the teaching of languages has not been consistent across the UK' (Pritchard, Hunt and Barnes, 2010, p209). One example is primary schools in other parts of the UK and beyond that have an autochthonous, or indigenous, language – even if this language may not be spoken by all or even the majority of the population. For instance, in Wales there are Welsh-medium primary schools (where Welsh is the first language, with English as a second language), in Scotland there are Gaelic-medium primary schools (with Gaelic as the first language) and in both Northern Ireland and the Republic of Ireland there are Irish-medium primary schools – although these schools are a minority overall in all these areas. Obviously, in these schools the teachers will all speak the relevant language, often as native speakers, as all activities in the school (both in lessons and at other times, like lunchtime) will be undertaken in that language – although parents do not always speak the language themselves. (There are also secondary schools that use the same language for children leaving these primary schools.)

Nevertheless, even where English is a majority language, the situation for primary teachers is complicated in schools in different parts of the UK. For instance, in English-medium primary schools in Wales (the vast majority of schools), like MFL in Key Stage 2 in England, *all* teachers are required to teach Welsh as a 'second language' regardless of whether or not they speak the language – but Welsh cannot be a MFL as it is the indigenous language. Unlike England, this happens from the time children enter compulsory education.

In trying to understand this complicated situation, Kirsch (2008) makes a helpful distinction, which we will use in the remainder of this chapter, between learning a *foreign* language – one 'generally not spoken by the main population of the country the learner lives in' (ibid., p33) – and a *second* language – 'when people learn a language subsequently to their mother tongue which is generally spoken in their home country' (ibid., p33). Using this definition, we can regard, for example, French being learned in an English primary school as a foreign language, and Welsh in an English-speaking primary school in Wales as a second language – which is how they are labelled in the relevant curricula. Unfortunately, not everyone makes this distinction clear, including academic literature, so in this chapter we will use the phrase second language (sometimes called L2) learning to represent both.

Unfortunately, there is not space in this book to explore the historical context of all of the above, but teaching a language you do not necessarily speak does present challenges and ICT can be vital in both providing support for teachers in learning a language themselves and then using it in the classroom. But, to fully understand how ICT can help support either MFL or second language teaching, we need first to consider the pedagogic thinking behind language teaching and learning.

Second language teaching pedagogy

Communicative language teaching (CLT)

Like many pedagogic approaches, language teaching pedagogy has changed over time and many primary teachers, even if they speak another language, are having to learn a new pedagogic approach from the one adopted when they learned a second language themselves. Whyte (2014, p2) asserts that:

> Language teachers and trainers are often faced with a great deal of contradictory and misleading information about how languages are learned and how they should be taught. Popular wisdom in books, on television and online has much to say about bringing up children bilingually, methods of accelerated language learning and how native speakers should teach their language. Methods or approaches to language teaching, some of which are tied to particular psychological theories of learning, also go in and out of fashion.

Whyte (2014) goes on to provide a useful and succinct summary of how language teaching has developed (see 'Useful resources'), reflecting different psychological theories of learning leading to the current use of communicative language teaching (CLT). She concludes that: 'The strong claim of CLT is that languages can be learned simply through exposure to comprehensible, preferably authentic samples of the language: the teacher's task is to help the learners to understand and create meaningful messages. This process will lead learners to become increasingly proficient without having to study grammar rules or memorize lists of vocabulary' (ibid., p4).

Not everyone agrees, however, that CLT is a straightforward concept. For instance, Çakir and Woods (2011, p382) label it 'a gesture towards an unspecified range of possible constructs and relationships that individuals dynamically construct and instantiate through experience', and conclude that 'we know little about what teachers really think, know and believe about CLT, and how these understandings develop' (ibid., p386). If this is true within the specialist language teaching profession, it is little wonder that the concept may be unfamiliar to primary teachers, most of whom (at least until recent times) will not have studied how to teach a language as part of their training.

In order to find a working definition, we need to identify the essence of CLT, which is 'the engagement of learners in communication in order to allow them to develop their communicative competence' (Savignon, 2007, p209). Or, as Ellis (2003, p27) puts it, 'CLT aims to develop the ability of learners to use language in real communication'. In this communicative process, Kirsch (2008, p58) adds that

> the emphasis lies on meaning and the focus is on spoken rather than written language . . . Teachers neither correct grammar not teach grammar formally. It is up to the learner to analyse the language and to acquire the grammatical rules inductively . . . The focus lies on meaning and authentic purposeful language use.

However, Kirsch (2008) does note that if the teacher leaves language learning entirely in the hands of the pupil, this limited guidance can lead to limited progress and frustration.

WHAT DO YOU THINK?

Reflect back on your own learning of a second or foreign language. Do you recognise a CLT approach? If so, how did you feel? If not, what form did your language teaching take? In both cases, how well prepared do you feel to undertake a CLT approach in your own teaching? Identify what skills and knowledge you need to develop to use this approach effectively.

As we have seen, a key part of CLT is the use of language in authentic, 'real-life' situations. These can be created by the use of specific tasks, such as role plays, discussions, debates and games, and we will briefly consider the use of task-based learning, or TBL, before examining the role of ICT.

Task-based language teaching (TBLT)

Calvert and Sheen (2015, pp226–7) note that: 'The growing prominence of tasks and the role they play in facilitating second language learning has been noted in recent task-based language teaching (TBLT) studies . . . [and] . . . The consensus based on the growing empirical literature is that tasks have positive effects on second language (L2) learning.' Ellis (2003) notes that definitions of 'task' vary, but essentially it is something that can only be achieved successfully by using language and hence involves communication. Whyte and Cutrim Schmid (2014, p51) further suggest that tasks 'have an emphasis on the use of the target language to complete purposeful activities with actual outcomes'.

While TBLT may be familiar within the language teaching community, it will be new for most primary teachers. Fortunately, as with many terms we have encountered in this book, TBLT is basically another label for something that primary teachers do in other areas of the curriculum. Many primary teachers are familiar with providing a context for an activity in which children have to undertake an activity (task) where they have to use and apply some existing knowledge, for instance using maths skills in a 'shop' set up in the classroom. In this scenario, pupils will not always be successful and will not always have all the requisite skills, but this does not stop it being a worthwhile learning activity. This type of task-based learning 'puts emphasis on an active, individualised learning process in a rich and complex learning environment. Task-based learning implies that students work on sizable assignments, real-life tasks, with a concrete result' (van Weert and Pilot, 2003, pp196–7). If we adapt this to task-based *language* learning, all the same principles apply but some different 'labels' are used.

The British Council suggests that: 'In a task-based lesson the teacher doesn't pre-determine what language will be studied, the lesson is based around the completion of a central task and the language studied is determined by what happens as the students complete it. The lesson follows certain stages' (http://www.teachingenglish.org.uk/article/a-task-based-approach). For the purposes of this chapter, we do not need to go into the details of the different phases, but the key idea is that the task is authentic, involves the need to communicate, and the 'pedagogic task involve[s] communicative language use in which the user's attention is focused on meaning rather than grammatical form' (Nunan, 2004, p4) – in other words, using language to communicate, rather than worrying about whether it is grammatically correct or not.

There is a role for ICT in planning, implementing, recording and evaluating such language tasks, and, indeed, developments in ICT can even affect the nature of the task itself. One interesting recent development is how ICT can provide 'authentic' tasks, at least for the pupils, in ways that teachers may not imagine. One specific example may be the growth of 'YouTubers', who make recordings of themselves talking about their life and interests – and often about subjects that may not engage the average teacher but might appeal to a primary school pupil! In other words, making a recording about your favourite make-up, or what you had for Christmas, changes from being an artificial task in the past to being one that is very authentic in the real life of pupils – and, at present, can lead to a very lucrative career! One lesson from this is that teachers need to consider tasks that are real and authentic to pupils, rather than as an adult. It may be that making a video in French suddenly becomes a much more appealing and meaningful task if considered in this context.

WHAT DO YOU THINK?

On your own or with others, consider if task-based language learning is really something new or just a variation of pedagogic tasks you would use in other areas of the curriculum. Identify common features and any differences.

Although TBLT has many advantages, and 'despite the increasingly well-documented theoretical and pedagogical value of tasks, the use of language learning tasks remains a challenge for many teachers because the realities of using tasks in the classroom are not always straightforward. Textbook-provided activities do not always meet the criteria of a task, and tasks that are readily available may not be appropriate to meet learners' goals and needs' (Calvert and Sheen, 2015, p227). Therefore, using ICT to develop tasks relevant to your class becomes even more important in making TBLT work.

Computer-assisted language learning (CALL)

These pedagogic approaches to language teaching have taken place alongside advances in technology. These have gradually been integrated into second language teaching, but the challenge remains of how to integrate new technologies as they develop. Much work in this area is still labelled computer-assisted language learning (CALL), although this perhaps does not adequately address the number of new technologies available and the different interactions that they facilitate. As Scarino and Liddicoat (2009, p56, cited in Hess, 2012) point out:

> Technologies provide enhanced opportunities to interact with speakers of the target language in a variety of ways – websites, emails, videoconferences, pod-casts, music and video streaming, etc. For language teaching, information technologies provide access to a vast range of contemporary material in the target language and about target language communities.

Dettori and Lupi (2010) highlight three phases of CALL that mirror the evolving psychological theories of learning noted by Whyte (2014) above (and also see Chapter 3 on theories of learning and ICT), and all three may perhaps still be found in language teaching in primary schools:

> behaviouristic CALL, where the computer is used as [a] tool to carry out drill-and-practice exercises; communicative CALL, in which the computer is viewed as [a] stimulus and as [a] tutor that can help develop communication skills; integrative CALL, which makes use of multimedia to propose learning environments [that are] close to real, where different language-related competences (reading, writing, listening) can be integrated; in this context, learners interact with each other with the mediation of technological tools, rather than with the computer, working individually.

Therefore, we need to adopt a wide-ranging interpretation of CALL for this chapter, which encompasses all technologies and the opportunities they afford. As such, when we use the term we are actually implying the use of *any* technology, rather than just the computer. Some sources also use the term technology-enhanced language learning (TELL), which Dooly and Masats (2015, p358) suggest is 'intended to cover a wider area, from the use of videos or cameras to the use of the internet or mobile phone'. Nevertheless, 'CALL remains the most popular acronym and nowadays serves as an umbrella term that incorporates a variety of equipment including flip cams, web 2.0 tools and mobile devices' (Pazio, 2015, p107).

With this in mind, we will now turn to examine how CALL, using the complete range of ICTs available in the primary school, can be used in MFL and second language teaching.

Second language teaching with technology

In deciding whether to use technology in language teaching, we should be clear about the pedagogic context. We will therefore use Nunan's (1989) 'definition of a pedagogic task as a piece of classroom work which involves learners in comprehending, manipulating, producing or interacting in the target language while their attention is principally focused on meaning rather than form'. We therefore need to consider how technology can help pupils to comprehend, manipulate, produce and interact with the language they are learning. As usual, the decision to use ICT is based on a consideration of whether it can do something better, quicker or more efficiently than other methods – or if you just cannot do it any other way!

This may often be the case, as Comfort and Tierney (2007, p2) remind us that 'ICT can help bring our language classes alive, make them visually interesting and stimulating. It can bring other countries, cultures and children into our classrooms. It can support you, linguistically, as well as developing both the children's linguistic and ICT skills.' This reminds us that it is important to consider how ICT can help you as a form of continuing professional development (CPD) – as we have seen with regard to social media elsewhere in this book – in addition to providing ideas and support in your teaching. In contrast, however, in common with all subjects, Gray et al. (2007, p424) note that for language teachers 'the fast pace of technological change might quickly render their hard-won teaching tool kit obsolete'.

Assuming, however, that you are willing to embrace advances in technology, there are many ways in which ICT can be used in second language lessons in the primary school by both pupils and teachers. In guidance for Australian primary teachers, Browett and Spencer (2006, p21) suggest that:

Languages students use a range of ICT to:

- practise language skills
- learn and experiment with new language
- access authentic information or texts
- create new texts in the target language
- plan and communicate their languages learning
- communicate with other language speakers locally and globally
- self-manage aspects of their learning.

Languages teachers use a variety of ICT to:

- create student interest and motivation
- personalise languages learning to suit the learning styles and interests of individuals or groups of students
- provide access to examples of authentic language use
- create networks of communication with target languages users for their own use and for the use of their students.

Nevertheless, whoever is using the technology, the key thing to remember in planning language teaching with technology is that 'the focus should be on the target language and learning' (Pazio, 2015, p117). In order to see how ICT can help, we will begin by focusing on communication, which, as we have already seen, is the key element of language learning. As we do this, we will also consider how ICT can help in this by providing 'real' and authentic opportunities and tasks for language acquisition and use.

Virtual exchange and twinning

Many primary schools will have experienced the benefits of undertaking exchange visits with schools in other countries, both personally, culturally and linguistically. Not every school can make the necessary links or easily access relevant funding, however. But, as Jones and Coffey (2013, p122) point out, 'technology has opened up several ways of corresponding with partner schools and has led to possibilities for redefining our relationship with the world'.

However, perhaps the greatest challenge is finding the right person or school to communicate with. If you have already visited a school in another country, you may well have good contacts; if not, a good starting point could be school websites, online communities or social media – see Chapter 6.

Videoconferencing

If you do find a virtual exchange partner or twinning school, you can begin to exploit real-time (synchronous) and recorded (asynchronous) communication using the various modes we have discussed elsewhere to facilitate whole-class, group or even individual interactions. Perhaps the most obvious is the use of real-time videoconferencing (VC), which can be used across the curriculum. Pritchard, Hunt and Barnes (2010, p211) suggest that the benefits of VC for teachers and learners are that it can:

- provide an authentic learning experience (experiencing the world outside the VC classroom);
- raise cultural awareness;
- provide access to experts (the ability to communicate with authors, artists, specialist teachers, etc.);
- improve social and communication skills (by developing listening and speaking skills);
- promote a measure of autonomy (break times are sometimes used to communicate with 'video pals').

Of course, another use of VC can be in sharing work or performances in other areas, such as music, with others in real time.

Specifically in terms of second language teaching, VC can also allow live communication, which is especially useful for developing oracy as 'participants can access the paralinguistic clues associated with face-to-face oral exchanges' (Phillips, 2010, p222). This can be done perhaps using the interactive whiteboard (IWB) – with a webcam attached – to allow live audio or video and screen sharing: that is, both partners can see each other and their screen content. Although there are many expensive ways of doing VC, it is also possible to use existing free technologies (such as Skype or Google Hangouts), as long as both parties have a good internet connection, a suitable camera and a microphone (often combined in one).

It is worth making the effort to explore VC, as Jones and Coffey (2013, p125) suggest that it

> *represents the ultimate interactional opportunity in terms of communication between children of different mother tongues. In fact, it could be what all the other ICT/MFL activities lead to and it dies such activities with meaning, since it results in children's concrete use of the foreign language in a real communicative context and in real time.*

Although this may be a little optimistic, VC certainly provides opportunities for language use with native speakers, and Whyte and Cutrim Schmid (2014) report that VC has been widely used in primary schools internationally in second language teaching. They do, however, balance the potential benefits when they highlight some challenges, including:

- the optimal positioning of the cameras and microphones;
- the quality of sound and video;
- establishing and maintaining partnerships with other schools.

It may well be that VC is one of the more technically demanding uses of ICT in the primary school, but it may also be one of the most beneficial in terms of developing communicative language teaching – although there are many other uses across the curriculum at all ages. The deciding factor is what can it add? Perhaps this is one of those things that you just could not do without ICT.

ACTIVITY

Consider how you would set up a videoconference with audio and video using a PC, laptop or even an iPad – on a stand – connected to the IWB. Also consider what speakers you would use, either through the IWB or separately. Then consider how you would organise the classroom space, the pupils and any associated resources so that your pupils could see the pupils from the other school and be seen by them. Finally, when the pragmatic set-up has been considered, decide on what learning tasks you could develop to encourage an authentic use of a second language with a class of learners from another country.

Twinning with secondary schools in the UK

Having managed to get the technology working with another country, it is also worth considering how you can use it more locally. As well as twinning with primary schools in other countries, you may want to consider building links with MFL teachers in local secondary schools – particularly if your pupils move on to that school. The importance of effective liaison between primary and secondary schools is stressed by Martin (2001), who regards it as one of the preconditions for successful MFL teaching, alongside mutual agreement on language choice, good record keeping, adequate ongoing funding and effective support and training for teachers.

The case study below shows a potential approach that could be adopted with a minimum of ICT hardware and software, and which would address all of these preconditions, particularly the provision on support and training for primary teachers of MFL.

CASE STUDY

Videoconferencing with a secondary school MFL teacher

A secondary MFL teacher visits the primary school and meets the Key Stage 2 class teachers and pupils who are going to learn French. The teachers plan a series of lessons using the secondary MFL teacher's specialist knowledge and the primary teacher's knowledge of the pupils and of links across the curriculum. The first lesson is taught face to face by the secondary MFL teacher with the primary teacher sitting in to help and support, but also to learn. Subsequent lessons are taught by the secondary MFL teacher from their own school using videoconferencing, with the primary teacher sitting in to support and learn.

In these lessons, the pupils rearrange the furniture facing the IWB so that the MFL teacher can see the whole class from the high-quality webcam pointed towards them from the top of the IWB. The pupils can communicate with the MFL teacher through a microphone built into this camera and the MFL teacher can be heard through the IWB speakers. The primary teacher is on hand to clarify any misunderstandings. The lesson is arranged after a break or lunchtime so that the teachers can test the equipment and stay online for the start of the lesson.

A short introduction is given by the primary teacher (who has not had any specific training to teach a MFL); this has been pre-planned with the MFL teacher, and either recaps on previous work or sets the scene for the new lesson. This forms part of the CPD for the teacher, and these introductions may grow longer as their confidence grows. The MFL teacher, who is visible to the class for the whole time, then takes over the lesson with the whole class on the IWB. The MFL teacher leads the lesson with the primary teacher monitoring and supporting the pupils. Specific pre-planned authentic tasks (see TBLT above) are undertaken in groups; for these, the primary teacher takes over with support from the online MFL teacher. This means that the primary teacher gradually becomes more confident in teaching French but also has the MFL teacher there to support any language needs. At the end of the lesson, the pupils come together again as a whole class and the MFL teacher recaps and concludes.

In between lessons, the teachers use phone, videoconferences and email to share ideas, plan, and answer any

(continued)

(continued)

queries. Occasional face-to-face lessons are used to allow the pupils to build a relationship with the secondary MFL teacher and for that teacher to get to know the primary pupils. These sessions grow more frequent in Year 6 as part of the transition to secondary school, but the pupils already know the MFL teacher well.

As the project proceeded, the secondary MFL teacher also realised that the GCSE and A level French students could benefit and helped

them to prepare group activities within some VC lessons. This provided a focus for their own work, but also helped the primary pupils to get to know the secondary pupils – which again helped with the transition process.

After periods of time working on specific language tasks, the primary pupils use their language skills in a videoconference with a primary school in their twinned town in France. These sessions are recorded as evidence of achievement.

Adapted from Pritchard (2007) and Dale (2009)

In this case, the teachers provide the lead in the videoconference, but it is also possible for pupils to be the focal point on the screen and in interactions. In addition, there is no reason why these contacts need to be restricted to the formal curriculum, as it is also possible to set up more informal virtual 'clubs' where pupils (supervised but with freedom to 'do their own thing') can socialise with pupils of the same age in another country. It could be argued that this open-ended communication, where pupils have to find a way to communicate, is one of the most 'authentic' experiences they can have. Certainly, if they were free to choose to use resources, such as iPads, many children will find a way to communicate with their peers in another country – even if it is not part of the formal curriculum.

However if VC works, it does not need to be restricted to whole-class sessions with the IWB, as many mobile devices offer the same facility to smaller groups or individuals. We will now briefly consider how this may work and why it might be worth trying.

Mobile technology and language teaching

It seems as though no area of learning is complete without a good acronym – and this is no exception! Kukulska-Hulme (2009, p162) highlights the 'developing field' of mobile-assisted language learning (MALL) and notes that:

MALL differs from computer-assisted language learning [CALL – see above] in its use of personal, portable devices that enable new ways of learning, emphasizing continuity or spontaneity of access and interaction across different contexts of use. Conceived in this way, mobile learning seems to belong more to learners than it does to teachers, although we know that most learners will struggle without a teacher's direction and guidance.

WHAT DO YOU THINK?

Heaney (2012, p164) suggests that the 'culture of the classroom is central to how children engage with their learning'. Do you agree that 'most learners will struggle without a teacher's direction and guidance'? What culture does this represent and do you think it will engage primary pupils? What are the implications for you and your pupils of adopting this mindset?

Regardless of whether you agree or disagree with the final part of this quotation, the idea of spontaneous use is important, alongside carefully planned use – whatever area of the curriculum you are looking at.

In Chapter 5 we considered in detail the affordances of mobile technologies, so it is not necessary to repeat these here, but we do need to consider how mobile technologies can encourage interaction and meaningful communication in another language. When learning a second language, pupils need to learn to read, write and speak the language, so many uses of mobile technology we have already seen can help – for example, e-books for reading, blogging for writing and podcasting for speaking. As with all technology use across the curriculum, you need to use your knowledge of the pupils and your pedagogic imagination to exploit the potential of mobile technology in language teaching.

Interactive whiteboard and second language teaching

We have examined the generic features of the IWB elsewhere in this book, so we need to consider here how it can be used specifically for second language teaching, both in its own right and in association with other technologies. This can range from a very basic use as a surface to project onto (Van Laer, Beauchamp and Colpaert, 2014) through to its use in games and digital storytelling. Colpaert (2014, pxiii) reminds us that the IWB is only one part of the whole classroom environment, but that it can have a 'unique, justifiable place in many language learning environments'. To exploit this uniqueness, you need to consider the distinctive capabilities of the IWB as a digital hub and how these can be applied to learners of all ages and abilities.

The iTILT European project, with seven partner countries, examined 'Interactive Technologies in Language Teaching', with a specific focus on the IWB (see http://www.itilt2.eu for videos of primary pupils using the IWB in Wales and France). Reflecting on the findings of this project, Whyte and Cutrim Schmid (2014) provide a detailed study of how the IWB can be used in second language education. We will briefly consider some of the activities and how they exploit the potential of the IWB.

Digital storytelling

All primary teachers will know how to use stories in the classroom. This ranges from teachers reading stories from books to their class to pupils creating multimedia stories on a mobile device. Kegenhof (2014) describes how the IWB was used with a class of

8–9-year-olds in a German primary school in three phases: pre-storytelling, storytelling and post-storytelling. The examples below come from these three phases but from different lessons.

In the pre-storytelling, for example, the IWB was used to introduce new vocabulary (for example, the names of countries) by using 'hide and reveal' (the name was covered at first and then the 'cover' dragged off to reveal it), the spotlight tool (dragging the spotlight over the word) or a 'hot spot' (a hidden word that appears when a certain part of the IWB is touched – e.g. a map). (See the iTILT training manual in 'Useful resources' if you are not familiar with these tools.) The IWB was also used to show videos of the countries to help develop understanding.

In the storytelling activities, for example, the pupils were shown a selection of items on the IWB. They also used the new and existing vocabulary to ask questions to identify what should not be there and used the pen tool to cross it out. They were also shown a piece of a story in the target language and they had to fill in some gaps using the pen or text tool. The pupils were also split into groups to play a vocabulary game created by the teacher. The pupils 'threw' the virtual dice in the IWB software (which comes with all boards) and had to pronounce the word associated with the number and gain points for their team. The words were later used in story-writing activities.

The post-storytelling activities included pupils taking turns to reconstruct a muddled storyline sequence (shown in 12 pictures) using 'drag and drop' and their language skills to state what they saw on each picture.

WHAT DO YOU THINK?

Would you have approached this type of activity in the same way? If not, how would you modify the activities?

Gamification as an aid to developing writing fluency

The term 'gamification' usually refers to using games design and thinking to enhance a non-game context. This has been little used in second language teaching, but a study undertaken in Spain (Stanley, 2014) with secondary-age pupils suggests that the use of points, badges, levels and leader boards can support the development of the writing process in a second language. Although this study looked at older children, it could easily be adapted to primary pupils.

The study was premised on the fact that learners disliked, and found it difficult to write, longer pieces of writing, and so the focus was changed to 'speed writing'. Pupils were allowed only five minutes to write as much as they could, but this could be adjusted to take account of the age and vocabulary of a younger person or any other form of differentiation. After the time was up, the pupils were encouraged to check and correct their work using any resources available. Pupils were awarded points on a leader board (displayed on the IWB) for their accuracy in using the language. The teacher also printed sticky badges to note specific achievements; these could be targeted to your own class. In the Spanish study, the pupils were very motivated by this approach, although not everybody liked the leader board being visible to others. During the course of the writing, the teacher could display vocabulary on the IWB (both planned and spontaneous, as the need arose) and could also use the pen and highlighter tool to discuss and correct examples of pupils' work. The teacher also used an online rewards system, which allowed the rewards to be personalised to the learning focus (in this case ClassDojo – https://www.classdojo.com), to reward the successful use of specific features of writing and/or vocabulary.

Although this approach makes limited use of the IWB, it does suggest a model that could be adapted to other forms of technology and that could form part of a wider approach to the teaching of writing in a second language, or indeed for any area of the curriculum.

WHAT DO YOU THINK?

On your own or with others, consider the positive and negative features of gamification, specifically in the context of language learning, but also in the broader context of the primary curriculum. Consider whether it might work better with different age groups, or if it is suitable for all ages. If you are not entirely convinced about it, are there any specific features of this approach that could be used effectively? If so, in what areas of the curriculum and with what technologies?

In learning a language, learners make use of a range of visual cues and other forms of non-verbal communication. If sound alone is used, these cues and signs will be missed – although it will focus pupils on the verbal communication. We will now consider how creating, editing and viewing sound and video recordings can be used in second language teaching.

Sound files and second language learning

In Chapter 8 we discussed how technology can be used to save, record and share talk. In this short section we will therefore consider how this can be applied specifically to second language teaching, rather than repeat ideas. One example is where generating a podcast to share with another school or on the school's website provides an authentic task for pupils at all ages within the primary school. The technology needed is very simple and is available on many mobile devices (see Chapter 8), or recordings can be created with free programs such as Audacity (http://www.audacityteam.org/) – although some of these may work better on a PC.

There are many examples of primary podcasts, but in second language teaching they could include podcast diaries of life in school (or at home) to be shared with another school, either near or far. They could also include songs in the second language or storytelling.

As well as podcasts, sound recordings can be used for pupils to listen to themselves speaking another language (another key skill); they can even edit the recording to remove any mistakes or hesitations to produce a 'perfect' version – which in turn can be shared or saved for evidence of achievement.

ACTIVITY

On your own or with others, do an internet search for 'primary school MFL podcasts'. Look at the examples and identify good practice. Decide how you could adapt what you have found to the age group you are currently teaching.

Video and second language learning

As we discussed above, adding video allows the viewer to gain visual clues and cues as to what is being said. A simple development from the podcast is a 'vodcast', which is basically recording with a video device rather than an audio device. Like all forms of video, this can be recorded and edited using a range of devices and software. When recording your videos, you may also want to remember our discussion of the use of green screening to apply a background to the video. In this case, it could be a place in another country or a background, such as a shop, that provides an authentic setting for the communication.

The vodcast is a very specific form of video, and you should not forget that just recording pupils communicating with each other, both in school and with others from outside the school, can be very valuable for them to view and reflect on their language use. In addition, these videos can be shared with others to show off the work that you are doing in language learning.

However, not every child will feel comfortable appearing on video, so one alternative is to use an avatar, or online character, which will appear to speak their words for them. One example of this is Voki (http://www.voki.com), which allows pupils to create their own character and background, before recording themselves speaking in the second language. This can be shared with others, but the normal considerations of e-safety must be observed. Although this site is currently free, it also offers specific extra features, such as the ability to manage students from more than one class. Like a lot of ICT, this is very hard to explain and it is much easier for you to go and 'play' with it yourself.

SUMMARY

In this chapter, we have examined a range of second language learning theories and how ICT can be used to develop effective communication in another language. We have noted that the features of ICT and mobile technologies can be exploited to provide authentic language learning tasks to support learners to acquire fluency in a second language.

References

Browett, J. with Spencer, A. (2006) *Teaching Languages in the Primary School: Examples from Current Practice*, Carlton: Curriculum Corporation.

Çakir, H. and Woods, D. (2011) 'Two dimensions of teacher knowledge: the case of communicative language teaching', *System: An International Journal of Educational Technology and Applied Linguistics*, 39(3), pp381–90.

Calvert, M. and Sheen, Y. (2015) 'Task-based language learning and teaching: an action-research study', *Language Teaching Research*, 19(2), pp226–44.

Colpaert, J. (2014) 'Foreword: interactive whiteboards – against the odds?', in Cutrim Schmid, E. and Whyte, S. (eds) *Teaching Languages with Technology: Communicative Approaches to Interactive Whiteboard Use*, London: Bloomsbury, ppxiii–xiii.

Comfort, T. and Tierney, D. (2007) *We Have the Technology: Using ICT to Enhance Primary Languages (Young Pathfinder)*, London: CiLT (The National Centre for Languages).

Dale, J. (2009) 'Integrating ICT into the MFL classroom', http://joedale.typepad.com/integrating_ict_into_the_/2009/04/esther-hardman-on-language-labs-videoconferencing-and-blogging.html (accessed 9 February 2016).

Dettori, G. and Lupi, V. (2010) 'ICT and new methodologies in language learning', *Procedia: Social and Behavioral Sciences*, 2(2), pp2712–16.

Dooly, M. and Masats, D. (2015) 'A critical appraisal of foreign language research in content and language integrated learning, young language learners, and technology-enhanced language learning published in Spain (2003–2012)', *Language Teaching*, 48(3), pp343–72.

Ellis, R. (2003) *Task-based Language Learning and Teaching*, 5th edition, Oxford: Oxford University Press.

Gray, C., Pilkington, R., Hagger-Vaughan, L. and Tomkins, S. (2007) 'Integrating ICT into classroom practice in modern foreign language teaching in England: making room for teachers' voices', *European Journal of Teacher Education*, 30(4), pp407–29.

Heaney, L.F. (2012) 'Promoting language learning in the primary classroom and beyond: a case study', *Gifted Education International*, 28(2), pp161–70.

Hess, C. (2012) 'Using technology in the languages classroom from the 20th to the 21st century: a literature review of classroom practices and fundamental second language learning theories', *Babel*, 46(2/3), pp4–11.

Hunt, M., Barnes, A., Powell, B., Lindsay, G. and Muijs, D. (2005) 'Primary modern foreign languages: an overview of recent research, key issues and challenges for educational policy and practice', *Research Papers in Education*, 20(4), pp371–90.

Jones, J. and Coffey, S. (2013) *Modern Foreign Languages, 5–11: A Guide for Teachers*, 2nd edition, New York: Taylor & Francis.

Kegenhof, A. (2014) 'Digital storytelling in the primary EFL classroom', in Cutrim Schmid, E. and Whyte, S. (eds) *Teaching Languages with Technology: Communicative Approaches to Interactive Whiteboard Use*, London: Bloomsbury, pp86–122.

Kirsch, C. (2008) *Teaching Foreign Languages in the Primary School*, New York: Continuum International Publishing Group.

Kukulska-Hulme, A. (2009) 'Will mobile learning change language learning?', *ReCALL* 21(2), pp157–65.

Martin, C. (2001) 'Early MFL learning for the millennium', *Education 3–13*, 29(2), pp43–8.

Nunan, D. (1989) *Designing Tasks for the Communicative Classroom*, Cambridge: Cambridge University Press.

Nunan, D. (2004) *Task-based Language Learning*, Cambridge: Cambridge University Press.

Pazio, M. (2015) 'ICT in modern foreign language teaching', in Younie, S., Leask, M. and Burden, K. (eds) *Teaching and Learning* with ICT in the Primary School, 2nd edition, London: Routledge, pp106–19.

Phillips, M. (2010) 'The perceived value of videoconferencing with primary pupils learning to speak a modern language', Language Learning Journal, 38(2), pp221–38.

Pritchard, A. (2007) Effective Teaching with Internet Technologies: Pedagogy and Practice, London: Sage.

Pritchard, A., Hunt, M. and Barnes, A. (2010) 'Case study investigation of a videoconferencing experiment in primary schools, teaching modern foreign languages', Language Learning Journal, 38(2), pp209–20.

Savignon, S.J. (2007) 'Beyond communicative language teaching: what's ahead?', Journal of Pragmatics, 39(1), pp207–20.

Scarino, A. and Liddicoat, A.J. (2009) Teaching and Learning Languages: A Guide, Melbourne: Curriculum Corporation.

Stanley, G. (2014) 'Using the IWB to support game education in order to enhance writing fluency in the secondary language classroom', in Cutrim Schmid, E. and Whyte, S. (eds) Teaching Languages with Technology: Communicative Approaches to Interactive Whiteboard Use, London: Bloomsbury, pp152–87.

Tierney, D. and Gallastegi, L. (2011) 'The attitudes of the pupils towards modern languages in the primary school (MLPS) in Scotland', Education 3–13, 39(5), pp483–98.

Van Laer, S., Beauchamp, G. and Colpaert, J. (2014) 'Teacher use of the interactive whiteboards in Flemish secondary education: mapping against a transition framework', Education and Information Technologies, 19(2), pp409–23.

van Weert, T.J. and Pilot, A. (2003) 'Task based team learning with ICT, design and development of new learning', Education and Information Technologies, 8(2), pp195–214.

Whyte, S. (2014) 'Introduction: theory and practice in second language teaching with interactive technologies', in Cutrim Schmid, E. and Whyte, S. (eds) Teaching Languages with Technology: Communicative Approaches to Interactive Whiteboard Use, London: Bloomsbury, pp1–22.

Whyte, S. and Cutrim Schmid, E. (2014) 'A task-based approach to video communication with the IWB: a French-German primary EFL class exchange', in Cutrim Schmid, E. and Whyte, S. (eds) Teaching Languages with Technology: Communicative Approaches to Interactive Whiteboard Use, London: Bloomsbury, pp50–85.

Further reading

Beauchamp, G. (2015) 'ICT and assessment', in Younie, S., Leask, M., and Burden, K. (eds) Teaching and Learning with ICT in the Primary School, 2nd edition, pp210–24.

Cutrim Schmid, E. and Whyte, S. (eds) (2014) Teaching Languages with Technology: Communicative Approaches to Interactive Whiteboard Use, London: Bloomsbury.

Hunt, M., Neill, S. and Barnes, A. (2007) 'The use of ICT in the assessment of modern languages: the English context and European viewpoints', Educational Review, 59(2) pp195–213.

Lynch, J. and Redpath, T. (2014) '"Smart" technologies in early years literacy education: a meta-narrative of paradigmatic tensions in iPad use in an Australian preparatory classroom', Journal of Early Childhood Literacy, 14(2), pp147–74.

Martin, C. (2000) 'Modern foreign languages at primary school: a three-pronged approach?', Language Learning Journal, 22(1), pp5–10.

Praag, B.V. and Sanchez, H.S. (2015) 'Mobile technology in second language classrooms: insights into its uses, pedagogical implications, and teacher beliefs', ReCALL, 27(3), p288.

Useful websites

Worsbrough primary school – French with Madame Bruff: http://french2014.worsbroughcblogs. net/ This site shows many ways in which ICT can be used in MFL teaching.

E-twinning – the community for schools in Europe: https://www.etwinning.net/en/pub/index.htm Erasmus+ site for teachers to connect and develop partnerships across Europe.

Technology in Modern Foreign Languages – A Practitioners Perspective: http://www.slideshare. net/boxoftricks/technology-in-modern-foreign-languages-a-practitioners-perspective This multi-authored slideshow provides many ideas you could use or adapt.

Interactive Technologies in Language Teaching (iTILT): http://www.itilt2.eu iTILT is a European project on 'Interactive Technologies in Language Teaching' that focuses on the use of IWBs in the communicative second language classroom. View over 200 examples of classroom practice, including videos of class activities, lesson plans and files, and commentary from the teachers and learners involved. The site also includes interactive teaching with technology for different languages, proficiency levels and age groups from seven European countries, helping teachers gain confidence with technology in communicative language teaching. It is now part of the website of the new iTILT2 project, with six countries exploring how other interactive technologies can be used in second language teaching.

Useful resources

Interactive Technologies in Language Teaching: Training Manual, http://www.itilt.eu/sites/default/ files/u3/itilt-manual/iTILT_Handout_ENGLISH.pdf (accessed 9 February 2016). This handbook gives detailed guidance and ideas about how to use the IWB in second language teaching.

12 Postscript: the future?

One thing we know about technology is that it will continue to change over time – sometimes with new hardware (such as the iPad) or software being developed that can potentially revolutionise learning and teaching. There is a danger that teaching and learning can be driven by developments in technology (technological determinism), rather than being driven by effective pedagogy. Facer and Sandford (2010, p76) propose that 'researching the future cannot simply be a case of producing a set of predictions of what "will happen" as though this were beyond the intervention of individuals or societies. Nor can it simply be a case of discussing what we "want" or "will make" happen, as though there were no prior contexts to shape our actions.' They continue to cite Bell's (1997, p73) options of 'possible, probable, and preferable' futures: 'what can or could be (the possible), what is likely to be (the probable), and what ought to be (the preferable)'. We saw at the start of this book that the English government used the needs of industry or the economy as arguments for introducing computing into the primary school curriculum. This type of argument has also been used by other governments and it is 'probable' that this will continue. This does not mean, however, that ICT developments driven by industry are a bad thing. Many devices, particularly the interactive whiteboard (IWB), have their roots in industrial settings and have been successfully adopted in education. For the remainder of this chapter, however, we will consider what might be *possible* or even *preferable*.

It is *possible* that new technologies will transform pedagogy in the primary school. This has been debated in the past in the research literate (for example, Somekh and Davies, 1991), but, even if there is such a thing as an ICT pedagogy, there has been little consistent evidence that new pedagogies have emerged – although there is some evidence that the iPad may be an exception. Indeed, the whole concept of one ICT pedagogy may prove a distraction. I have suggested previously (Beauchamp, 2006) that, in the primary school, there may actually be many ICT pedagogies that emerge as teachers view learning and teaching through a variety of subject lenses. What I hope has emerged in the preceding chapters, and what may be *preferable*, is that the role of the teacher will remain central to the effective use of technology, but with increased agency (input) for pupils. I would suggest, therefore, that it is *preferable* that ICT is used only if it does something better, quicker or more effectively than other resources, or if it can reinforce ideas by offering a unique range of different perspectives using different modes and media. There may also be other occasions when using ICT is the only way to achieve what you want – 'I could not do it any other way.'

There remain other *possible* futures. It may be that advances in artificial intelligence mean that eventually computers can not only interpret human emotions, but also use their intuition to formulate a range of responses based on knowledge of the child – but, until that time, ICT can never be a substitute for a good teacher. But, part of being a good teacher is knowing when your pupils are capable of being in control of their own learning. Throughout this book I have tried to convey the primary classroom as a partnership, where pupils take an active role in co-constructing knowledge and understanding, using a range of tools (including ICT) as appropriate. Providing access to these tools and equipping pupils to use them may remain the role of the teacher (or the school) in the first instance, but this should pass to the pupils as they move through the primary school. It is thus important that pupils understand how they themselves learn – otherwise known as metacognition. There are many definitions of this term, but it 'is usually related to learners' knowledge, awareness and control of the processes by which they learn' (Georghiades, 2004, p365). As well as self-awareness, de Jager, Jansen and Reezigt (2005, p180) suggest that 'metacognitive knowledge refers to the knowledge of learners about their own cognition, cognitive functioning, and possibly that of others'. In any definition, however, we are faced with the idea that, as well as having a generic understanding of how they learn in general terms, pupils also need to learn how to learn specifically with ICT (and perhaps in other subjects in the primary school).

In the current climate of accountability, such an approach may seem an ideal, but if we are to take personalised learning seriously – and ICT is an important enabler in this regard – we need to be prepared to make radical changes to the primary school culture. In this context, the roles of school leadership and management are central in facilitating the vision. A simple delineation between the two roles is that leadership is doing the right job and management is doing the job right (Beauchamp and Harvey, 2006). This distinction between strategic and operational tasks or skills could actually be shared with pupils, who are, after all, hopefully the main beneficiaries of changes, but who should also have some views in these matters. It may be that pupils assume some of this responsibility through school councils or other outlets for pupil voice. This may be especially important if we acknowledge the high levels of ICT skills in many forms that many primary pupils possess. Not only are primary pupils likely to be familiar with new technologies as they emerge, but they also may see the potential for learning with them – 'But you can do that quicker/easier with the . . . I have at home.' In other words, they may be in a good position to advise not only on the right job but also on how to do it right!

However, it may be that none of the above really matters if we take a more radical step and consider whether we need ICT at all. Effective learning and teaching took place before ICT and we need to be sure that we (pupils and teachers) are using ICT for a good reason and not just because it is there. I hope that this book has helped to convince you that we *do* need ICT and has helped you to consider why, when and how it can work best in the primary school with *all* pupils. In Chapter 1 I suggested that ICT can offer a range of unique features to teachers and learners that are not available using other means. Whether or not pupils experience these unique features remains in your hands, as teachers are the gatekeepers to the technology. I hope that this book has helped to convince you not only to open the gate to everybody, but also to open it in many different ways!

References

Beauchamp, G. (2006) 'New technologies and "new teaching": a process of evolution?', in Webb, R. (ed.) *Changing Teaching and Learning in the Primary School*, Maidenhead: Open University Press, pp81–91.

Beauchamp, G. and Harvey, J. (2006) '"It's one of those scary areas": leadership and management of music in primary schools', *British Journal of Music Education* 23(1), pp5–22.

Bell, W. (1997) *Foundations of Futures Studies*, London: Transaction Publishers.

de Jager, B., Jansen, M. and Reezigt, G. (2005) 'The development of metacognition in primary school learning environments', *School Effectiveness and School Improvement*, 16(2), pp179–96.

Facer. K. and Sandford, R. (2010) 'The next 25 years? Future scenarios and future directions for education and technology', *Journal of Computer Assisted Learning*, 26, pp74–93.

Georghiades, P. (2004) 'From the general to the situated: three decades of metacognition', *International Journal of Science Education*, 26(3), pp365–83.

Somekh, B. and Davies, R. (1991) 'Towards a pedagogy for information technology', *The Curriculum Journal*, 2, pp153–70.

Index